Good Morning Nantwich

Phill Jupitus

Good Morning Nantwich

Phill Jupitus

adventures in breakfast radio

For Charlie Gillett

HARPER

An imprint of HarperCollins*Publishers*
77–85 Fulham Palace Road,
Hammersmith, London W6 8JB

www.harpercollins.co.uk

First published by HarperCollins*Publishers* 2010
This edition 2011

1 3 5 7 9 10 8 6 4 2

ISBN 978-0-00-731386-0

Printed and bound in Great Britain by
Clays Ltd, St Ives plc

Contents

by Lauren Laverne

I first met Phill Jupitus when I was nineteen and a guest on *Never Mind the Buzzcocks*. I was in a band he liked at the time and, in exchange for a promotional badge for the defunct kids' show *No 73* (of which I had fond, childhood memories, and which he had visited during a stint as The Housmartins' tour manager), I gave him a C90 of our unreleased demos. I probably would have given him the tape anyway, since he was the only person on the show who (a) liked my band and (b) had not laughed at the fact that I was wearing chopsticks in my hair and makeup purchased from an actual clown shop. But the badge sealed the deal – we became firm friends. That Jupes was happy to part with this small but significant artefact in pursuit of new music is also, I think, testament to his enthusiastic and eclectic attitude to the stuff. I can't say I've come across that many people who can appreciate Vitalic's electro face-melter *La Rock 01*, hit the stage with The Specials *and* belt out a show tune in full drag with equal ease.

A few years after our initial meeting I had started presenting, which seemed (as it still does) like ludicrously well-paid fun. I didn't know that Phill had recommended me to his boss, Lesley Douglas, for the show after his on BBC 6 Music. Clearly I didn't get it. But I did get a gig covering Glastonbury festival with him, John Peel and Jo Wiley, and our first trip to Pilton was my introduction to the station. I agreed to pop in as a guest on Phill's Monday morning show, to round off the festival before catching a lift back to London with him and his producer. I arrived at the small hotel function room, from which the outside broadcast was taking place, to find my friend and colleague minimally rested and maximally refreshed after a belter of a weekend. And so it was that the very same day I was introduced to 6 Music, I was re-introduced to driving after letting my licence lapse for some five years. Specifically, driving Phill's automatic, left-hand-drive, tank-sized Jeep down the insanely busy M4 back to London while its owner slumbered in an ursine fashion on the back seat.

Not long after that, I deputised when Phill took a few weeks' holiday from his Breakfast Show slot. I was 23 at the time and had the kind of life where 5.00 a.m. is a time you're *still* up, not a time you *get* up. It was a huge shock to the system, and after my stint was up my then-boyfriend-now-husband made me swear I would never take another breakfast job because I'd been such a nightmare to live with. Suffice to say, I did. It was supposed to be a holiday romance with Dame Radio, but she had seduced me with her silky intimacy, immediacy, ability to communicate directly and her stellar taste in music. Within a couple of years I was hosting the XFM breakfast show, some of the best broadcasting fun I've ever had, even though I started so early the audience for the first hour consisted exclusively of milkmen and adulterers.

You see, TV is great – like being invited to a glitzy, ridiculous, gossipy party, packed to the rafters with fabulous people (OK, maybe not *Countryfile*, but you know what I mean …). Who wouldn't want to get involved? Radio is the opposite. It is not for the popular. It is not pretty. There is an infamous story about a much-lauded TV presenter who arrived at the country's biggest commercial station to start her new show and asked her producer, 'Where's my script?' When she was informed that there was no script, this was radio and she was required to *think of something to say,* she turned on her Louboutined heel and ran like the wind, never to bother a popshield again. In essence, the job is sitting in a windowless room, clutching a foul-tasting beverage from an inevitably malfunctioning coffee machine, talking to yourself and occasionally putting a record on. Yet for some reason, for some of us, it's bliss. And we know we aren't talking to ourselves, not really. We're talking to people like us. Radio is an industry largely run by oddballs and misfits, and specialist radio – like 6 Music – is the thick end of the nerd-wedge. To paraphrase *Spinal Tap*: There is none more geek. If you were ostracised, flushed, ridiculed and/or obsessed with music everybody else thought made you gay or a Satanist at any point during your school career, well … welcome home.

It's almost a decade since Phill introduced me to radio, and I haven't been without a show of my own since. In fact, I currently occupy the 10–1 slot on BBC 6 Music that he suggested that Lesley Douglas give me all those years ago. It's the most fun I've ever been paid to have. And the 6 Music audience are some of the cleverest, most interesting and hilarious people I have ever met. They also have impeccable taste. At the time of printing the first edition, the station's future was uncertain, which seemed unjust. Happily, it has since been saved. There should be a place like 6 on the dial – somewhere idiosyncratic and surprising where you can hear Jarvis Cocker present a Valentine's Day show dedicated to the Chaucerian idea of love, or get your favourite Zombies record played out at 10.00 a.m. A place where imagination, creativity and music are held so dear *must* be of value. I hope that the station Phill helped launch is allowed to carry on and – if not – that it will be remembered fondly by the people who loved it. I also hope that this book gives you an insight into the mind behind the mic, some tales that make you laugh and an insight into the way a man's love of broadcasting might drive him to madness and beyond. Possibly to Nantwich.

The Life Pursuit

By the spring of 2002 I had spent over a decade as a successful stand-up comedian in the UK. This job not only gave me a creative outlet, it provided immediate feedback from my audience and, above all, complete autonomy. So why exactly would I chuck in such freedoms for a job, which would give me a good deal *less* control? Where I would be answerable to a lengthy chain of management and feedback would be minimal at best and the audience reaction was something we would not discover for eighteen months? As I look back at things now, this is a question that I wish I had asked myself a lot sooner in life. But even if I'd had the prescience to ask it back then, the answer would have been the same then as it would be now. I love radio and I was reminded of that fact a week before Christmas in 2009.

18 December was quite a busy day one way and another. I woke up weary and a bit achy as I'd been singing and dancing while dressed as a lady in the musical *Hairspray* the night before. I had a day off scheduled in order to go up to the NEC to do a gig with The Blockheads and on the way there I was going to do all my Christmas shopping.

It was also the day that Terry Wogan would broadcast his last-ever breakfast show, *Wake Up to Wogan*.

In September of that year Terry finally announced the day that his be-cardiganned legions of fans had been dreading. He would be pulling down the final fader on his breakfast show just before Christmas after twenty-seven years. The outcry was almost immediate at his replacement, the titian-haired host of Radio 2's drivetime show Chris Evans. Listeners had been irate enough when he was brought in to replace Johnny Walker, but replacing Sir Terry? Yet to be honest, whenever anybody stops doing anything there is an immediate outcry from somebody who's not happy about it. The British as a race are resistant to change. We felt it more so in Wogan's case because there were a few million of them.

When I first heard that Terry was going, I thought back to our rare snatched conversations on the pavement outside Western House or in the lift to the studios. Occasionally I would work up the courage to ask him the question. 'How long are you going to give it?' He'd always briefly ponder before saying: 'I don't know. Maybe next year. But I'm still enjoying it …' Then after a beat: 'You don't want to overstay your welcome …'

We shared a knowing glance. Sir Jimmy Young had overegged his Radio 2 pudding by at least a decade, finally departing his lunchtime show with about as much ill humour and as little grace as anybody could possibly muster. Then in his *Sunday Express* column he proceeded to retrospectively bite the hand that fed him – quite nicely, thank you – for over thirty-five years. I frankly think if he'd kept doing the recipes and left the politics to the professionals, he'd have been alright. But one gets the sense that he genuinely thought he was the new Robin Day. As I listened open-mouthed to his grumpy and bilious final show in December 2002, I do remember thinking, 'Make sure to jump before you are pushed ...'

With the loss of Terry, people were going to have to make a huge adjustment. Indeed the effect on many would not be unlike a bereavement. Terry had been a huge part of their lives for decades. They'd had almost thirty years where they would get up, stretch, reach out and turn on their radios and hear the very same voice from Monday to Friday. Without really meaning to, he subtly wove himself into the fabric of the lives of millions. His easy-going manner, ready wit and soothing voice had been heard in the bedrooms, bathrooms, kitchens and cars of the nation for decades. This wasn't going to be some bloke quitting a job. This was like losing a member of the family.

But surely the comings and goings of who presents what at which radio station are insignificant in the grand scheme of things? Indeed so, yet it's worth bearing in mind that avid radio listeners somehow take it more personally. They develop a kind of symbiotic relationship with favoured presenters. And when that relationship, as is customary, ends abruptly, they have no control over it. They feel powerless against such sudden unwanted change. Conversely, those who manage radio stations *do* have power, but think about their networks as a whole. They strive to find the right chemistry between their many diverse presenters who fill the schedules. Usually this involves tinkering around until they get just the right mix. Unfortunately they often forget that their tinkering affects the listening routines of thousands, and as a listener this can be frustrating. It's not like football, when the manager takes off your favourite player and you get to scream and shout at him for ninety minutes. If your favourite deejay gets bounced, your only recourse is to fire off a surly email or phone *Feedback*.

When I heard the news about Terry, I thought back to my own somewhat smaller-scale departure from the breakfast show for BBC 6 Music at the end of March 2007. I pondered our respective statistics. Wogan had a commanding twenty-seven years behind the mic to his name, while I had only managed a paltry five years and three weeks. His audience was a stunning 8 million while at my final peak I'd hit just under 500,000 with a following wind. Terry was a national institution while I remained the big bloke who was always rude about Van Morrison on that pop quiz thing.

With each passing record that Terry played on that last morning, I found myself getting quite misty. Even though it was a rare occasion when I'd turn over from *Today* on Radio 4 to tune in to him, I simply felt better just knowing he was there just a few kilohertz down the dial. I knew my mother would be listening to him, just as she had done ever since the 1970s. Oddly enough she listened to his last show on the DAB radio I had bought her so she could listen to me on 6 Music. To the best of my knowledge she only ever listened to my show a few times, if that, but like my relationship with Wogan I assume she felt better just knowing I was on air, so didn't feel the need to actually tune in.

On that final Friday, Terry was obviously only playing songs from his own collection, but each one seemed just that bit more mournful that the last. Even though he was mostly cheerful and upbeat during his links, you could feel the audience were in tears from the moment he went on air. When he played Peter Gabriel and the Black Dyke Mills Band's haunting 'That'll Do' even I found myself welling up. As he launched into his final link on the show, a tear rolled down my cheek …

'This is it, then. This is the day I have been dreading – the inevitable morning when you and I come to the parting of the ways, the last *Wake Up to Wogan*. It wasn't always thus. For the first twelve years it was the plain old Terry Wogan Show and you were all Twits, the Terry Wogan Is Tops Society. When I returned to the bosom of our family, it became *Wake Up to Wogan* and you all became TOGs, Terry's Old Geezers and Gals. It's always been a source of enormous pride to me that you have come together in my name, that you are proud to call yourself my listeners, that you think of me as a friend, someone that you are close enough to laugh with, to poke fun at and occasionally, when the world seemed just a little too cruel, to shed a tear with.'

Halfway through this poignant final moment I pulled into a lay-by as I felt sure that my constant eye wiping might pose a hazard to other drivers. It was the perfect goodbye from a perfect gentleman. It's difficult to explain to someone unless they've grown up with Wogan as part of the cultural landscape how important he was, but I'll give it a go. Imagine that you have a favourite uncle. (Perhaps you don't have to imagine.) He's the slightly wild one who would take you shark fishing, or out in his sports car with the top down in the rain, or let you have a go on the aerial runway over that bonfire, or insist you stay up late on a school night, and he was always hilarious at weddings so you desperately wanted to sit next to him, and he was kind and polite and only ever swore by leaning towards you in that conspiratorial way so auntie couldn't hear. That is how I saw Terry Wogan, and now he was gone.

As the Jeep churned through the December morning slush, I realised that this was truly the end of a radio era. With Wogan gone the way was left clear for the ragtag assortment of 'popular' deejays hoping to profit from the chaos that would ensue in the wake of his departure. The Harriets and Jamies and Evanses and Moyleses and Neil Foxes of this world – loud, hugely successful, un-challenging, award-winning, lowest-common-denomina-tor, ratings-busting radio, which I have always found, in a word, unlistenable.

* * *

As the tracks of my tears dried on my cheeks I remem-bered that the very show I had left nearly three years ago was currently in the hands of a fine broadcaster in the shape of Shaun Keaveney. A former alumnus of XFM, Keaveney was a laconic Northerner with a soothing voice and a snappy line in banter. Not for him the early morning histrionics of his peers. No, Keaveney had, if anything, an even more laid-back style than I did. I have to admit that when I was told he would be taking over the show I hadn't heard him. But when I did tune in from time to time, he was funny, he knew his music, and was a cracking listen. As a member of the audience, my breakfast radio future would be kept safe in the bosom of the station I had launched, BBC 6 Music!

Then, just two months later, my inbox pinged with the arrival of an email from my mate Celine who worked at

Guardian Online. 'Hey, wanna do something for us on 6 Music? Gimme a bell ...'

To be honest I wasn't all that keen. I'd left and the station had taken a new direction. An ambitious young man called George Lamb had been given the mid-morning show. He was dead set on a television career but for some reason was approaching it via niche radio. He was an absurdly handsome West London hipster, whose interest in music seemed secondary. Despite this he picked up a whole new chunk of listeners whilst simultaneously drawing the extremely vocal ire of old regulars with his shouty shenanigans. He rapidly became 6 Music's first Marmite deejay and was even regularly lampooned in the pages of *Viz*. You have to wonder at the logic of following the breakfast show with what was ostensibly *another breakfast show*, but to be fair if I knew how to run a radio station then I'd be doing that instead of writing this book.

In the wake of 'Sachsgate' and Lesley Douglas's controversial departure from radio and 6 Music, Lamb's employer and principal advocate was gone. He was quietly moved to a weekend show and the sassy and bright Lauren Laverne was given his slot. This went down very well with the majority of the audience as she was not only someone with a broad musical knowledge, but had been in a band, was a regular on BBC2's Culture Show and the main host of the corporation's annual Glastonbury coverage. The high points of her show were always when she strayed away from the playlist and introduced us to new sounds. Her obvious enthusiasm for the job is infectious. When I heard Lauren was joining 6 Music I couldn't help but laugh as I had suggested her to Lesley Douglas as a presenter back at my very first meeting in 2001.

But I didn't really understand why the *Guardian* wanted me to write about 6 Music, so I called Celine. After two rings she picked up.

'Alright, girl, it's Jupitus.'

'Hey you, how are you? Missing frocking up for *Hairspray*?'

I reverted to my standard response to mates on the phone when I was doing fuck all.

'Only the eyeliner really. Other than that I'm not bad. Trying to get going with that radio book I told you about ...'

'Well, it's funny you should say that, we were wondering if you wanted to do a piece about 6 Music closing down?'

'What?'

'Oh no, haven't you heard? Yeah, apparently Mark Thompson's got some budget review they've been working on and they're losing a load of online stuff. Asian Network's going and so is 6 ... They're announcing it officially next week.'

A mix of emotions welled up inside me. Even though I had nothing to do with the network any more, I had mates still working there. And it was a really really good radio station catering for an audience of licence-paying outsiders who had *never* had any kind of representation during the daytime radio schedules. At least, not since the original XFM sold out to GCAP. My head fell into my free hand and I ran a hand down my face and shouted in my kitchen, 'Oh, for *fuck's* sake ...'

The dog looked up, somewhat startled.

'I know,' Celine continued, 'just as they got rid of George bloody Lamb and started to turn things round ...'

First Wogan, and now this. I always knew radio was due for some radical changes but assumed they'd come from the competition posed by podcasts and internet radio. When 6 Music was launched I was hugely optimistic about its chances of success as there was no radio station like it. And now after spending over £40 million on running the station and building up an audience, and a year before the digital switchover, they were cutting them loose. Genius.

Radio was something that I had grown up with, and through a combination of sheer luck and the odd bit of conniving I had managed to do it for a living for five years. Now it appeared to be all changing for the worse. Wogan was doing weekends, 6 Music was on notice and I wasn't on air any more.

* * *

I had been a Radio 1 listener since its launch in 1967. Broadcasters like Tony Blackburn, Dave Lee Travis and Jimmy Saville were known to millions through their daily shows as well as countless television appearances on *Top of the Pops*. So as I walked into a building that represented everything that I knew about radio, it is fair to say that I was a little overwhelmed. It was on a Saturday afternoon in the autumn of 1985 when, as a fresh-faced twenty-two-year-old, I wandered hesitantly into the reception of Egton House, the then headquarters of the nation's favourite radio station.

The interview had been organised by the promoters of a gig I would be taking part in the following day called The Ranters Cup Final. East London's legendary performance space, the Theatre Royal Stratford East, would be playing host to the aforementioned 'Ranters'. Ranting Poetry was a briefly popular movement of poets, most of whom were absolutely terrible. This ragtag bunch of new 'young' performers would spew justifiably terrible things about the government of the day while simultaneously attempting to be funny about their personal lives. This might not have been quite so bad if they'd had the decency of sticking to iambic pentameter. At the time I was known as Porky the Poet, a name combining my habit of self-deprecation along with the self-delusion that I was any kind of poet.

Myself and another performer at the event, Bradford's excellent Little Brother, had been selected to go on national radio in order to give the people a flavour of what they could expect from the gig, and hopefully in the process sell a few tickets. In the mid-1980s performance poetry was in the ascendancy. In the late seventies John Cooper Clark and Linton Kwesi Johnson had opened the doors for a whole new raft of performers in the post-punk years. The music papers gave glowing reviews of some of these new acts, which I can only assume is the reason that Radio 1 were interested. If it's good enough for the *NME* then it's good enough for us, seemed to be their *modus operandi*.

It was only when I had worked in radio myself that I began to understand the constant demand for content to fill the hours of airtime. Combine this with the fact that the promoters weren't about to knock back some free national exposure and we were dispatched to the West End and a short walk north from Oxford Circus tube. Egton House was tucked away in a tiny mews off Portland Place to the side of Broadcasting House just behind All Souls Church. As we walked up to the very ordinary-looking doors, I was somewhat underwhelmed at what I saw.

In my imagination, the premises of the country's top pop radio station had always been a vast, beautifully designed concrete, steel and glass affair, dense with exotic palms and ferns. As you wandered through the silently welcoming automatic doors, a bird of paradise would streak past you and perch on a nearby stone plinth. You would look away from its dazzling plumage and notice with delight that set upon that very same plinth was a shining bronze bust of Simon Bates, smiling beatifically. As you cast your gaze around the regally appointed lobby you would see a number of similar likenesses of the Radio 1 greats of the day: Gary Davies, Noel Edmonds, Bruno Brookes, DLT – The Hirsute Cornflake – the completely hilarious Adrian Juste ... every few yards you would spy yet another broadcasting legend. The base of each of these monuments would be surrounded by the offerings of their loyal legions of fans: soft toys, underwear both unwashed and brand new, flowers, cakes and home-made cards all declaring neverending devotion.

Oh it wasn't like that at all ...

A large and lightly perspiring man sat on the opposite side of the counter in the standard security guard uniform of white shirt with epaulettes and dark blue tie. We nervously gave our names and our reason for being there, just in case the names alone weren't enough. He jotted them down in a book and handed us each a yellow sticker stamped with the day's date and the familiar BBC logo. He barely looked at us while picking up a telephone and mumbling into it before pointing in the direction of a nearby cheap sofa. 'They'll be down for you in a minute. Take a seat please ...'

The reception area could best be described as 'utilitarian'. I felt like a character marooned in some backwater of the Eastern Bloc in a Cold War spy novel. This thought had me muttering 'Yes we have no bananas' under my breath in Russian. You couldn't fault my tradecraft. Presenters of the day grinned forlornly from framed photos on walls, which clearly looked embarrassed about having to display them, and by the doors a rack groaned with cheesy postcards of the same faces and a few others. I wandered over and took out a John Peel postcard for myself, simply because he looked so deliciously uncomfortable at having his picture taken. Dave Lee Travis, on the other hand, appeared to be over the moon. He had opted for 'wacky' from his extensive catalogue of looks.

Once we were introduced and on air the time whizzed by. As I glanced around our surroundings I was delighted to note that studios really did have a red light up on the wall that said 'on air' when the microphones were faded up. I had always thought that was just a Hollywood conceit. Little Brother performed his excellent parody of Stanley Holloway's monologue about Sam the soldier, which he had re-imagined for the recent Falklands War. We both chatted with the presenter for a bit and then I read out my poem 'They've All Grown Up in the Beano'. I can remember that as I spoke I experienced the dizzying sensation of my heart hammering in my chest combined with a simultaneous delight in what I was doing. It was a feeling I'd only ever experienced before when kissing girls.

Our segment was soon finished and we were politely ushered out just as quickly as we had arrived. And before we knew it, we were stood out on the windy pavement of Portland Place like nothing had happened. This being the age prior to mobiles, there was no instant debriefing phone call like one might expect these days. David and I looked at each other and wandered off to a nearby pub to drink the remainder of the afternoon away. I was fizzing with excitement. I had just made my first broadcast on the radio. And it was *so cool*, they had microphones and soundproofing, and a control booth through the glass; and everybody who wasn't on air still had a role to play.

While the experience was a bit of a let-down in one sense, the actual working environment was oddly inspiring. These people were being paid to do what I had done for pretty much every day of my life since I was thirteen, which was to play records and chat. This could very well be a future career! When I really thought about it, radio was the only thing that I was in any way qualified to do. So why not do it? It was one of the first times I experienced any kind of aspiration. I wanted to get myself a job in radio.

Even though this was the first time in my life I'd felt such a powerful surge of ambition, it took another ten years of poorly attended benefits and ropey gigs in the back rooms of pubs, plus the rise and fall of Red Wedge, my debut at the Edinburgh Fringe, a tour with Paul Weller, a few ill-advised television shows and the birth of two daughters, before I was to walk into a radio studio again ...

Chapter 1

Workers' Playtime

Corner office. Those were the two words that were going through my head as I walked into the bright, airy room. I had never before understood the significance of a 'corner office' or why one should be so desirable. Now I was actually stood in one, I understood. It's all about having more square feet of windows than your subordinates. Simple really. While your many underlings crawl around in cubicles and subterranean studios, their pale waxy skin craving just the odd shaft of natural sunlight to bring them some much-needed vitamin D, you can bask in your greenhouse, knowing that when the sun goes just that bit too far west you can simply lower the blinds on the acres of windows adorning your west-facing wall. Presumably those fortunate souls who had risen to the higher echelons of management at the BBC required such rarefied conditions because, in addition to their corporate abilities, if push came to shove, they could also photosynthesise.

Addison Cresswell is my agent. He is very loud, very talented and on occasion almost unintelligible. And he was on the line.

'Hello Ad ...' I said nervously.

It was autumn 2001, two years after I had walked out of GLR. As soon as I saw Ad's name flash up on the screen of my mobile phone, I inhaled sharply and braced myself.

Whenever Ad called personally it was either really good or really bad news. It seemed that nothing between these two extremes was reason enough for him to pick up the phone, so I always experienced a frisson whenever there was a call from him.

'PHILL!ADDISON!LISTENMATEI'VEHADACALL FROMMYMATELESLEYDOUGLASHERAND JIMMOIRWANTSTOSEEYOUSOWE'REGOING TOGOINANDSEETHEMBOTHNEXTWEEK ALRIGHTMATE.'

'Ummm …'

'BRILLIANTTHEYWANTUSTOGOINNEXT WEDNESDAYATELEVENO'CLOCKATJIM'SOFFI CEI'LLCOMEINWITHYOUANDWE'LLSEEWHAT THISISALLABOUT … LOTSALOVEMATE!'

Much like you have just had to very slowly re-read and pick apart the words in the above barrage of capital letters, any listener also has to slowly deconstruct a phone call from Addison. But mercifully, this one was both brief and to the point. We had been called in to see Jim Moir at Radio 2.

Jim Moir was a broadcasting legend, who had more than earned the corner office in which I was now standing. But Jim Moir didn't need to photosynthesise because the sun shone out of *him*.

When you meet Jim Moir, he is one of those characters for whom the phrase 'larger than life' seems tailor-made. A huge, red-faced, charismatic and incredibly funny man, I always thought that he is exactly what

Santa would look like if he'd chucked in the whole toy thing, lost the beard and gone into middle management. As a bit of a fanboy I was slightly in awe of him as he had produced *The Generation Game* with Bruce Forsyth, as well as undergoing a stint as the BBC's Head of Variety and Light Entertainment. His career at the Corporation spanned decades. Admittedly today you can't throw a doughnut off a double-decker bus in London without hitting a TV producer, but Moir was producing ratings-busting television programmes back when there were only three channels … I know – *three*. We were all like the fucking Amish in the seventies.

Big Jim had been handed the stewardship of Radio 2 in 1996, and in no time at all had deftly changed its image from that slightly starchy station where they played show tunes that your mum listened to into a hip, fun, sparky and forward-thinking network which swiftly became the highest-rated radio station in the country. Addison already had clients Mark Lamarr and Jonathan Ross with weekly shows on 2 and in the light of his manic phone call to me it was reasonable to assume that I might well be joining them on the airwaves.

I started to mentally flick through the schedule to try and work out what slots might soon be coming available. None of the heavy hitters like Wogan, Ken Bruce or Steve Wright would be going anywhere as they were all doing very nicely thank you. The recently rehabilitated Johnny Walker was going great guns on drivetime, and as for Sir Jimmy Young, he just seemed to be permanently locked in his lunchtime studio like it was a high-tech sarcophagus. The only place that man would be moving to, if he was lucky, was the Egyptology wing of the British Museum.

So it might be a weekend slot. Jonathan Ross owned Saturday mornings with his slick blend of great music and hilarious interviews, apart from one memorable encounter with a surly Dannii Minogue who had apparently undergone a sense-of-humour bypass. Maybe they'd be asking me to do something on Sunday mornings. Might Steve Wright's 'Sunday Love Songs' be getting the old 'Spanish Archer'?

I spent odd moments pondering over what the gig might be as the day of the meeting approached, but couldn't work it out with any degree of certainty. It did cross my mind that this sort of thing can often turn out to be nothing more than a cursory meet and greet. 'Let us know if you have any ideas for a show, we'd really love to work with you!' was quite often the end result of two hours on the trains and tube and sitting with a big grin slapped on your face in front of somebody who occasionally nodded. These speculative encounters mean that they get to put a tick in their managerial 'job done' box, but it feels like a colossal waste of time.

* * *

I met up with Addison in reception at Western House in Great Portland Street, just north of Oxford Circus in London's glitzy West End, and we were whisked up to the first floor and Jim's office.

I looked wide-eyed around the walls. There were photos of Jim arm in arm with various dignitaries and celebs. Awards for shows jostled for position with Ken Pyne cartoons from *Private Eye*, archly mocking Moir. There was a large coffee table in the centre of the room and a couple of standard-issue big managerial sofas and a vast desk behind which sat the commanding figure of Jim Moir himself. As I looked down at the coffee table I wondered how many people had been fired over its dark, forbidding surface. Had Jim ever had to arm-wrestle Wogan on it during contract negotiations? Also in on the meeting was Moir's second-in-command at Radio 2, Lesley Douglas. A no-nonsense Geordie, throughout the time I knew her Douglas was passionate about just two things, radio and Bruce Springsteen.

While Ad sparred around with the two of them I sat and smiled to myself, and mentally prepared for the vague promises of the 'We'd love to work with you sometime!' chat. I couldn't have been wider of the mark. After Ad had finished verbally knocking our hosts about, we took our seats and got down to business. Moir looked round at me.

'Now then, we will be launching a brand new music radio station in the March of next year, and we would like you to be the host of the breakfast show.'

I took a slightly firmer grip of my coffee and cocked my head towards him in an inquisitive fashion, not unlike a puzzled Labrador.

'The BBC are going to be starting a number of new digital radio services in partnership with existing stations,' Jim thundered on. 'Radio 4 will be launching one, as will Radio 1, and we will have one as well.'

I looked at the beaming face of Moir and mustered up all my intellectual reserves to come up with a trenchant response to his very kind offer.

'Oh … right!' were the only words I could muster.

'Ah, the new digital services,' I thought to myself. With the advances in technology, the BBC, like all broadcasters, would be slowly transferring all of its radio and television services to digital platforms. The digital switch-over meant that everybody in the UK would be listening to radio and watching television on digital receivers by 2012. I really should have been more aware that this was happening as the BBC had used me to front a television campaign to promote this rapidly approaching techno-logical wonder. I spent two days in a van and on location with Andy Parsons and Henry Naylor who played my hapless film crew. We were supposedly making a 'fly on the wall' documentary about this exciting new techno-logy. The loose gag of the thing was that as we went from place to place we kept being caught by our unwitting subjects. The first day was spent shooting with Leslie Grantham, Sanjeev Baskar, Kulvinder Ghir and a couple of puppets. I had a fairly energetic time of it, jumping through hedges, falling off a ladder and getting wedged in a serving hatch.

On day two I was lucky enough to spend a few hours on a studio set with John Peel. Peely's role involved him listening to a digital radio while he was taking a bath, while I, naturally enough, had to stick my head through a cat-flap in order to see what he was up to. As the army of technicians fussed around the set, I sat with John in the hospitality area, me in a rather nice Tonik Blue two-piece and John in a dressing gown and swimming trunks ready for his bath scene. As we sat there I did my level best to hide the obvious joy at finally meeting him. I thought a nice neutral opener would be to say how much my wife and I enjoyed listening to *Home Truths*. He sipped his red wine and sighed. I had the feeling I might have inadver-tently touched a nerve.

'Yes, it's a good show, but I don't know …' He paused before going on. 'They do too many of them. That's the thing with the BBC, as soon as they find something that does well they always want more of it. I hardly get any time off because I'm always recording bloody *Home Truths*.'

John had been with the BBC since the late 1960s and had become one of the leading lights of change in music with the arrival of the punk scene in 1976. But one of the problems with staying loyal to the Corporation is that you can end up being completely taken for granted by management. Each new controller of Radio 1 didn't seem to know what to do with him. At the same time, none of them had the balls to fire him because they knew just how much outcry there would be. The time slots of his show were shuffled around with little regard for the man who had championed so many bands throughout his career. So as time went on Peel's shows became more and more marginalised. He was a kind of broadcasting equivalent of the ravens at the Tower of London. *Home Truths*, which aired from 1998 on Radio 4, was a programme driven solely by contributions from the listeners, and was presented by John. Within the course of one show the subject matter often veered from the side-splittingly hilarious to the tear-jerkingly tragic. But at the centre of it all was the avuncular Peel, who handled both, deftly. Having finally met him, it was somehow sad to think that he didn't enjoy the show as much as we enjoyed listening to it.

In the van home later that night Andy Parsons pointed out that John was on air, so we got the driver to tune in to Radio 1. As the record finished Peel began to speak.

'As you might imagine I am on occasion asked to do some quite unusual things in the name of "promoting" the

BBC but I can reveal that I spent most of today sat in a bath of lukewarm water while Phill Jupitus stuck his head through a cat-flap.'

My first mention on Peel's show, while only in passing, remains a favourite memory. Had I never listened to his shows as a child, I might not be sat in a prominent BBC executive's office being offered a job as a deejay.

When you are presented with a deal of that stature, your thought processes start to accelerate and, somewhat unwisely, you do find your mind wandering out of the room. While Moir and Douglas enthusiastically explained the ambitions and workings of what they were currently calling 'Network Y', I did not hear a word of it. In my head I was furiously working out the day-to-day logistics of being a breakfast-time broadcaster and how it would affect my current working life. In the late nineties I had done four weeks deputising for Johnny Vaughan on Channel 4's *The Big Breakfast* and was acutely aware of how much that impacted on my existence.

My mind was racing. 'Right, so I can still do *Buzzcocks*, but I'd probably have to stop doing stand-up, but I can still do the *News Quiz*, but I couldn't really go to see music gigs any more … and I'd have to get up at like half four every day and drive into town five days a week … and if I do happen to get offered any big telly gigs I'd have to turn those down … and I can't do the Edinburgh Fringe …'

I was frantically working out how being a breakfast deejay would fuck up my life, while the people in the room were conversely explaining just what a good idea it would be.

Lesley began to explain that this exciting new station would be more music-focused, aimed at those who read music magazines every month and regularly go to gigs and festivals, but who don't really care for the usual chart fare. To reflect this, there would be a more 'alternative' playlist, specialist shows, a varied selection of classic pop and rock as well as extensive use of the BBC's own archive of session recordings. This was the point at which I began to sit up and take notice.

When it first started, XFM was just such a bold and innovative station, run by a small core of people who truly loved music. But as soon as it started performing well commercially it was sold to the Capital group, and almost overnight all of the fire and originality were slung out of the window and it was turned into a playlist-based, high-rotation, revenue-gathering machine. But here was a chance to be part of a new kind of radio station, one which would pay respect to the huge legacy that new music owed to its past. In my head I started thinking of all the old Peel sessions I might get the chance to air again. The first Fall session, Bethnal, The Members, Siouxsie and The Banshees, Three Mustaphas Three ... My mind started reeling at the mere thought of not only hearing these gems once more but playing them on the radio. At fucking breakfast time!

Meanwhile, back in the real world, Lesley and Jim patiently told us about some of the other people who they would be approaching with a view to presenting shows. Janice Long, Tom Robinson, Bruce Dickinson and Billy Bragg were all mentioned. But back in my troublesome brain I was still far too preoccupied, mentally indexing even more John Peel sessions ... The Specials, Altered Images, Madness, Elastica, Wire, Sham 69, Buzzcocks, Pulp ... By this point in the proceedings it was fair to say that I had sustained an erection.

My agent could see that my mind wasn't really what you could call focused, so he manfully filled the breach and duly explained that we'd have to go away and think about it. Moir nodded, but at the same time he was having none of it.

'You're our man, Phill!' he boomed in my direction. 'You are the man we want to launch this station!'

I nodded weakly and crossed my legs with a slight sense of disappointment as I recalled that The Clash never recorded any Peel sessions. Then I smiled weakly and thanked them for their interest and it was all hearty hand-shakes, backslaps and goodbyes. As he grasped my fragile hand within his meaty paw Moir stared deep into my eyes. My attention was drawn to the glorious mane of silver hair atop the powerful head that filled my field of vision.

'You're going to do this ...' he growled into my face. My nascent erection was immediately lulled into submission.

As we stepped out into the brisk bright London after-noon Addison looked round at me.

'THATALLSOUNDSALRIGHTTHENDON'T ITWHATI'LLDOISHAVEATALKWITH LESLEYLATERTHISWEEKANDBEATTHEM UPOVERTHEMONEYANDSEEWHATWECAN GETOUTOFTHEMSEEYOULATERTROOPER.'

And with that he was gone. I was left there on my own, reeling. I'd just been offered a proper high-profile BBC gig for the first time. But I was left with a bit of a conundrum. On the cusp of my forties and with a good career as a stand-up, did I really want to be a full-time breakfast deejay?

For someone who loved radio as much as I did, surely such a question was a no-brainer. I was being offered a daily alternative music show on a plate. This was something I had always wanted, wasn't it? Not to mention there was also the opportunity to launch a brand new network and a dazzling array of new media technology to go along with it.

And yet my contrary 'glass-half-empty' outlook was already undermining this thought. Of all the various jobs I had done since leaving the civil service, surely 'disc jockey' was the easiest. It was a doss. A blag at best! You do nothing more than sit in a room, prattle and press buttons. In a reductive sense, you are performing the kind of task that a well-trained chimp could manage without much bother. You are nothing more than a jukebox with mood swings. Playing music and chatting is something I had happily done throughout my entire adolescence without feeling I should be drawing a wage for the privilege. But maybe the time was right for me to think about a change in my life.

In one sense, the BBC would now ostensibly be paying me to regress back to my teenage years. My job description was playing good music and shooting the breeze between seven and ten in the morning, five days a week for around forty-six weeks of the year. The majority of the various shows I had made for GLR were weekly, which gave you the luxury of six full days to think about what music to play and what subjects to talk about. You didn't exactly sit down and plan the show as such, but you were mindful of it for a whole week, so it just sort of percolated forwards to the front of your brain over the six days. This suited my pace of thought nicely. But a three-hour show five times a week early in the morning would be a different prospect altogether. This would be high-turnover stuff. As I ambled slowly towards Oxford Street, I began to formulate a rough plan. I'd do it for a couple of years and then get out. That was assuming that they hadn't already sacked me at some point in the first year. And so the state of mind with which I decided to take on one of the biggest jobs of my life was one where I had already started to work out when I could quit.

Despite the apparent luxury of knowing when I would finish a job I hadn't even started yet, I still needed to give some serious thought to what sort of breakfast show I wanted to do. Right away I knew I would be on a very sticky wicket. Not only would I be launching a new radio station, but it was one that was only available via new media. Indeed it was so new that when we started broadcasting in March 2002 the only people who could listen were those who subscribed to a digital TV service that also carried BBC radio, people with computers and a broadband connection, and the eight geeks in the UK at that point who actually owned DAB radios. In those early days a lot was made of the phrase 'potential listeners'. Indeed, if you added up everybody in the country who had cable or satellite, broadband and the eight dateless wonders with the DAB radios, our total potential listenership was around several million. And eight.

However, people are simply not in the habit of listening to radio on their televisions. It just feels weird! Booting up their computer first thing in the morning presented its own problems. Once you'd forgotten the system password for the third time, the machine would be hurtling out of an upstairs window. And the DAB radios we had heard so much about were about as easy to come by as rocking-horse shit. Admittedly at the time of writing DABs are now available in all good electrical retailers.

Not to mention the several radio applications for the iPhone, which allow you to stream live radio from almost anywhere in the world. But back in those almost feudal days of early 2002, such flights of fancy would be considered the insane ramblings of a deranged madman, or Steve Jobs, the CEO of Apple to give him his full title. To my mind, the only way to pull in the punters to something that required such a Herculean effort to listen would be to do a show that no one else would do. In order to accomplish this I would have to be mindful of what the competition was putting out.

Breakfast radio is an area of extremes. At the quiet end of the spectrum you have the kind of non-threatening programming which lulls you into your day. These would be programmes like *Today* on Radio 4 or Terry Wogan on 2, Radio 3, Classic FM, BBC local radio and the gentler, more easy-listening-based commercial stations. Then in the middle there's not very much choice before you suddenly hit those shouty people at the opposite end of the spectrum who think that just because they are up at seven o'clock in the morning then you should be as well. I have never fully understood the ethos behind the 'perky' breakfast deejay. I am more than aware that millions of people truly appreciate the breezy banter and lively tone of the majority of breakfast broadcasting. However, I had always wondered why you never heard anybody on the radio who woke up at the same variable pace as you.

I admit that on occasion I have been known to wake up in a good mood, and do feel quite chirpy. For me this is maybe one day a year, and my entire family are similarly disposed. I have two teenage daughters who as a matter of course do not use verbs until gone nine o'clock. I consider the coarse wakey-wakey style of broadcasting an insult to the injury of perfectly good sleep interrupted. Instead of a raucous 'GOOD MORNING!' how about a more considered and laid back ... 'Alright?' The 'shouty' breakfast shows all appear to be predicated on deceit. Nobody really likes getting up in the morning, but let's *pretend* that we do! Not only do these shows lie to you, the listener, but they then have the audacity to invite you to participate in the deception. This is not entertainment. It is mass hypnosis. To have some jumpy idiot telling you what a great day it is before going on to assault your ears with the accumulated wisdom of Robbie Williams in 4/4 time and C major just seems rude. And turning the dial of my radio I have found legions of these shrill, mindless early-morning liars.

Perhaps that is a bit harsh, you know ... 'liars'. But in my defence we can all tell when somebody on the radio is using fake diction, and if you listen to radio stations all over the world I would estimate that at least half of the people on air are not using the natural voice they grew up with. How did this happen? Who decided that people who played records on the radio should evolve such an absurd style of speech? How can the people who do it even begin to think that it is a normal way to behave? I have been in rooms with radio interviewers who have spoken to me quite normally when I arrive before experiencing a sudden and terrifying transformation:

'So anyway Phill, this is being recorded for tomorrow's breakfast show and we'll be putting it out just after eight thirty ... so here we go and ... HEEEEEEYEEE! GOOOOOO-OD MORNING EVERYBODY YOU'RE

LISTENING TO THEEEE BREEZE NINETY SEVEN
POINT SEVEN AAAAAAAND IT'S TIME TO WELCOME
A BIG BIG BIG BIG FRIEND OF THE SHOW, APPEARING
AT THE QUEENS THEATRE ON WEDNESDAY NIGHT
IIIIIIIIIIIT'S MISTER PHI-I-ILL JEEE-YOOOW-PIDDUSS!
HEY PHILL HOW'S IT GOING?'

How I have never physically beaten one of these fakes
about the face and neck with the shitty radio station coffee
mug that was in front of me, I'll never know.

Do you think that there's any psychological damage
that you can do yourself by repeatedly using an artificial
voice as part of your day-to-day work? I imagine not, or
they'd have banged up Rory Bremner years ago. But
these apparently troubled individuals are affecting an
entirely constructed personality. They are pretending
to be something they're not, and in order to somehow
facilitate this further they have decided that it would be
a great idea to use the voice of a complete mental defec-
tive. Mindful of this fact, I decided that in my own case
it might be an idea just to be myself and talk to people
in calm and measured tones. After all, I wouldn't want to
have to quit suddenly due to the onset of schizophrenia
or a bruised larynx.

To be brutally honest it felt like I was on a fool's
errand in even taking the job on. My own regular breakfast radio listening was restricted to just two stations out
of dozens of contenders. I was either tuned to the steady
procession of grim news coming out of Westminster and
the Middle East on the *Today* programme on Radio 4,
or in the event that I fancied something a little easier
on the ears I would slide over to the wonderful Terry
Wogan on Radio 2. These two shows for me represented

the zenith of early-morning radio. And the reason they did so was that they were consistently good at what they did, and had both built up a reputation for excellence over decades of broadcasting. Mind you, the only reason I didn't listen to anything else at breakfast time was that the kind of music radio I would want to listen to simply did not exist. What I wanted to listen to was a kind of Frankenstein's monster of a show with the intelligent chat of *Today*, shackled to the humour and irreverence of Wogan, all bolted to the best bits of John Peel's playlist. Christian O'Connell came very close to this, but the playlist at XFM was leaden, not to mention that the second I heard an advert I'd want to hurl the radio into a lit furnace.

As a music fan I had a collection which encompassed just about everything except heavy metal and progressive rock (and within the year even that would change). I loved the chaotic slalom of John Peel's musical selections. I would giggle with glee when he'd dovetail techno with old rhythm & blues, or grindcore with country & western. My shorthand for this was the Peggy Lee/Ruts theory. I saw no reason at all why you shouldn't play 'I Enjoy Being a Girl' and immediately follow it up with 'Staring at the Rude Boys'. Surely any halfway decent radio show should thrive on just this kind of wilful eclecticism? Just because you play contrasting musical styles from decades apart is no reason people should tune out, and if they do, then bollocks to them. A good radio show should be for those with open ears as well as open minds. If somebody actually wants to hear the latest inane stadium-filling toss from bloody Coldplay and fucking Razorlight, then by all means they could listen to Radio 1. It's a free country.

I began to get quite inspired by the notion of offering up some kind of alternative for listeners in the morning. At the same time I was seemingly unaware of the inherent contradiction of offering them 'choice' while at the same time denying them whatever I judged to be rubbish. Like so many before me, I envisioned myself as a revolutionary liberator but in the end turned out to be more of a benign dictator with a big CD box. My inner template was the driven farmer played by Kevin Costner in *Field of Dreams*, and the words he heard in his head, 'If you build it, they will come.' I naively thought that if a radio programme like the one I imagined existed, then people would just eventually get to hear about it and in no time at all we'd be a massive hit. Oh yeah, I thought lots of crazy shit back then.

My personal vision for the show was simply to make a morning programme that me and my mates would listen to. I had a large group of friends who covered a wide age range so if I aimed the show at them then it should cover a potentially interesting audience. When I imagined the potential listeners for this new network, they seemed to be quite a disenfranchised bunch. They cared naught for the charts, but were keen on hearing new artists. They were also music enthusiasts, which would discount age as a specific demographic marker.

This was something that marketing people would have a dickens of a time dealing with, since their formulas tend to use age groupings or comparative income as defining factors. It was a very non-specific bunch whose radio listening habits I was hoping to change. And not just their radio habits: with them being music fans, the majority would already have a large and diverse mix of sounds

filling their personal MP3 players. So in addition to dragging them screaming from their radio station of choice, I
would have to tear them away from their very own music
collections as well. I was about to become broadcasting's
answer to the Child Catcher in *Chitty Chitty Bang Bang*.
'Sweeeeets ... Lollipops ... Gang of Four session tracks ...
Futureheads B-Sides ... new Johnny Cash!'

Another of the initial misgivings I had about taking the
job was the level of commitment in terms of time. I wasn't
sure that I wanted to be working a five-day week all over
again. The principal reason that I had got into performing in the first place was that office work really wasn't my
bag. And it's not like I didn't give it a fair shot – I was a
clerical officer in the Manpower Services Commission for
five years. And those five years were enough to make me
realise that it wasn't really the right environment for me
to flourish in, unless judging performance on the huge
improvement in my doodling skills.

So I called home and spoke to my wife Shelley and
told her all about the job I'd just been offered. She quite
rightly pointed out that we had always talked about me
doing regular radio a bit later in life, the dream gig being
a weekly show of some kind on Radio 2. But in the light
of the new offer we didn't take long to decide. The regularity of work and a steady income would be a refreshing
change after the seasonal vagaries of life as a stand-up
and TV performer. The fact that I would no longer be able
to tour or do gigs was actually a bit of a bonus family-
wise. I also told her about my idea to just do the show for
two years, which also met with a resounding thumbs up.
After agreeing with her that it would be nice to have some
stability for a couple of years, I then somewhat foolishly

added that I'd now have a perfect excuse to buy limitless CDs! On hearing this Mrs Jupitus started swearing profusely, and I pretended we were going into a tunnel and hung up.

Workers' Playlist

'Fear Is a Man's Best Friend' – John Cale

'Theme from *The Godfather*/Al Capone' – Jazz Jamaica

'Get a Job' – The Chordettes

'Start' – The Jam

'Good Morning' – The Beatles

'Hitsville UK' – The Clash

'Rez' – Underworld

'Train Song' – Holly Cole

'What Do I Do Now?' – Elvis Costello

'A13, Trunk Road to the Sea' – Billy Bragg

2

The Boy in the Corner

As long as I can remember I have loved radio. A love which has become all the more bittersweet since I got the opportunity in the second half of my life to actually work in the medium. The actual time when the idea of radio was hard-wired into my consciousness was the 1960s. Commentators are wont to wax lyrical about this brisk little decade, perhaps best summed up in an episode of *The Simpsons* where Homer's view on it was a concise and brilliant 'Mmm … turbulent …' Memories of it are sketchy as I was born in June 1962. I was a sixties 'love child' born to my mother Dorothy at Newport on the Isle of Wight. Having fallen pregnant with me, Mum was keen to avoid any trouble with her father, so with her savings and my grandmother's knowledge, she relocated to a caravan park on the Isle of Wight to await my birth.

My original birth certificate from Newport Hospital has an anonymous handwritten dash in the box marked 'father' which has bothered me over my life a good deal more than any piece of punctuation ever bothered Lynne Truss. Before long, Dot and I were moving on to Aldgate, Barking, Ryde on the island again, back to Barking,

Horndon on the Hill, back to Barking yet again before eventually settling in the quiet dormitory town of Stanford Le Hope in 1970, pausing only for her to reconnect with her college boyfriend Bob Jupitus who, much to my joy, manfully took on the job of being my stepfather in 1968, after which, as far as we were all concerned, he became Dad. Apart from our brief sojourn back on the Isle of Wight, it did seem that for some reason Mum always liked to stay close to the A13. I'm not sure why she felt the need to do this, unless her freewheeling gypsy spirit dictated that she should never live more than a mile from a main arterial road. On reflection that's one of the many ways that Mum differed from George W. Bush, in that she has always maintained a well-thought-out exit strategy.

The first home that I clearly remember was the Brewery Tap, a huge pub located on Ripple Road in Barking, Essex. For the development of interpersonal family relationships, living in a busy working pub is something of a double-edged sword. The environment is absurdly hectic. Every day, dozens of staff would come and go, huge brewery lorries would arrive, groaning with crates and barrels of fizzy Ind Coope keg beer, then between noon and midnight hundreds of strangers would come into what I considered my home to drink, bicker, laugh, chat, cry, flirt, dance, vomit and fight with each other, mercifully not in their own homes. Despite the fact that I considered such behaviour not a little rude, it took place without interruption and regular as clockwork seven nights a week, fifty-two weeks a year.

The king and queen of this boozy monarchy were my maternal grandparents Sid and Edie Swann. Sid was a tall, broad, prepossessing man with bad feet and a spectacular line in malapropisms (he once memorably described Mum's Mini Metro as a 'hunchback'). The family feared him, the punters adored him, and the brewery revered him. He was a publican with the golden touch, able to turn dodgy pubs round over the space of a few months. Wherever he found himself, he always managed to remain onside with the local constabulary and villains alike. He was never so crass as to try and play them off against each other, he was simply savvy enough to make sure the two groups were never in on the same night. The peace was maintained, and by keeping a foot in both camps he had two places to turn if there was ever any trouble.

Regardless of who he was talking to at the bar, he had the knack of making them feel like they were his sole confidant. He would mutter things whilst pulling pints and they would gently smile and nod, thinking that only they had been vouchsafed the most precious of landlordly secrets. Then he would take their money, share a conspiratorial wink with them, and the hapless drinker would wander off, laden with light ales but now feeling part of Sid's select inner circle. As soon as they were out of earshot, he'd tell the next bloke exactly the same stuff in the same way and another acolyte would be born. He was hardly Machiavelli, but he knew the kind of simple things that made people feel good.

My grandmother Edie was a very different kettle of fish, a chain-smoking, chain-knitting, passive-aggressive Essex matriarch, controlling the comings and goings of the family with almost military precision. One of her shrewdest moves was to only tell Sid what he absolutely needed to know about what was going on with the family outside of the pub. A great example of this spectacular ability to control the flow of family information was the first time he heard about my mother's pregnancy. Mum had returned to Barking carrying a new addition to the Swann clan. She marched into the lounge without a word, then I was matter of factly thrust into my grandfather's arms by Mum with the words, 'This is your new grandson.' Then she went downstairs for a drink. Nothing dissipates a sense of anger quite as quickly as a two-week-old baby.

Generally Nan had a quick temper, but when she was out from under Granddad's shadow she became more breezy and outgoing. To the general public during opening hours they were a sparkling double act like George Burns and Gracie Allen, each working their own areas of the bar with a slick grace and minimum of effort. Jokes and lively banter would fill the air. But once the doors were bolted shut, the bar had been wiped clean and they trudged upstairs, the knowing smiles and conspiratorial winks were turned off and the day-to-day business of making other people's lives pleasurable was somewhat perversely put on hold for the members of their own family.

One of the afternoon golden rules for us at the Brewery Tap was never to wake Sid up when he was having his nap. It made for an unusual upbringing. I saw two extreme sides of my family members, a lively public façade and a sullen private one. Even as a small child I realised that the public faces were a lot more fun to be around, which is why I hung around downstairs as often as I could get away with it …

To have the run of a large pub outside of opening hours is not unlike having a wardrobe with Narnia in the back of it. Your home is located over the top of a big, scary place where you weren't really supposed to go. Behind the bars themselves was a dense tangle of pipes, wires, pumps and bottles, which I was only allowed near when I was helping the head barman, Jock, with the daily rigmarole of bottling up. After seeing off a bowl of porridge, I'd leg it downstairs and Jock would take me down into the huge dank cellar. To this day occasionally when I'm in a pub, I'll catch a whiff of that combination of the odour of stale beer and damp mortar and I'm back down that old staircase. Jock would consult his pencilled list, then point me towards various crates and ask me to fetch 'baby' bottles of tonic or bitter lemon, as he humped the weighty crates of light and brown ale up the stairs. I've often counted myself lucky that I was able to enjoy the early knockings of my childhood at a time before Saturday morning children's television started the profitable business of distracting young people from the world around them.

Mum and I shared a bedroom on the first floor that was directly above the cavernous saloon bar at the front of the building. The bedroom windows looked out over the street with Barking Broadway just to the left. I can dimly recall being awoken by screams, shouting and the smashing of glass on a fairly regular basis, which would usually be followed by a short lull in proceedings before the familiar blare of the approaching police sirens. Then I would stare up at the ceiling bathed in the contrasting orange glow of street illumination and the blue strobe of the police lights. Being short, I mercifully couldn't get high enough to see down on to the pavement immediately below the window. What I could see was the staggering participants being held up against the street railings for their own good. The real victims of these incidents remained mercifully out of view.

I never found such violent events frightening or disturbing; the most they brought out in me was idle curiosity. The noises were completely foreign to me, so my innocent young mind couldn't fill in the ghastly images they represented. Conversely I found domestic arguments completely terrifying. My family were unashamed screamers when it came to their own petty rows, which they didn't seem to mind tearing through with a wide-eyed four-year-old in the room. The legacy of this family quirk is that to this day I find it impossible to handle confrontation directly and tend to react either with glib responses or with incandescent rage. You've gotta love genetics.

We shared our room with an impressive wooden radiogram. Ninety per cent of the time I used it to listen to Sterling Holloway retelling the story of *The Jungle Book* on the Disney LP that we bought after seeing the film. As it was the only album in the bedroom for two years, it got a fair hammering. But eventually even I'd had enough of 'I'm the King of the Swingers'. And this is how my inquisitive little hands eventually found their way to the tuner.

There are fewer sounds more seductive than the multifarious looping swooshes, crackles, squeaks, hisses and whistles of a radio being tuned in. It's like a form of music in and of itself. I soon realised that the slower I turned the ridged ivory and gold plastic dial the more stuff I could hear. This was the first place I ever listened to the sound of a foreign voice. Without leaving my bedroom, I opened a door on another world. Overlapping stations would phase in and out with each other depending on their signal strength. You'd slide past a German bloke talking about who knows what, which would slowly give way to the sound of Doris Day or BBC news or the Russian weather forecast. Having no idea what all these strange sounds signified was part of the joy of listening. I would spend ages wandering through this sprawling audio desert up the dial and all the way back down again. None of it had any particular meaning to me, nor did it need to. The simple combination of my own curiosity and funny noises was apparently enough. It's not a thousand miles from what I call 'the-box-it-came-in principle': you buy your child a vast and financially crippling toy and they end up playing with the box it came in. I wasn't listening to the radio as was intended. I was playing the radio …

Eventually I started occasionally listening to programmes, the news being the most regular daily fare. As a child it seemed to me that the radio carried news, while our telly in the living room seemed to be mainly for wrestling, *Thunderbirds*, *Pogle's Wood* and NASA space missions. So naturally enough I felt myself privy to information that the rest of the family were sadly denied by TV. One broadcast was to provide some much-needed grist to my eager young conversational mill. In March 1967 a supertanker called the *Torrey Canyon* hit rocks between the Isles of Scilly and Cornwall, spilling over 30 million gallons of crude oil into the sea. It was one of the first real headline-grabbing environmental disasters, and was widely reported on the radio. The coastline of southern England and even the Brittany Coast was devastated.

My young mind was obviously keen to impart this urgent nugget to anyone who would listen. Mum was entertaining one of her friends with tea, biscuits and 'grown-up talk' and I was being frozen out of proceedings.

Eventually, when I could contain myself no more I blurted to her friend, 'Have you heard about the *Torrey Canyon* disaster? It's very bad.'

The two adults stared at me in silence for the briefest moment before bursting into fits of laughter. I consider this the sole reason I never moved into current affairs as a career.

At the age of six, we lived in a shack in the scrubby Essex woodland just north of Horndon on the Hill with Bob. It was here where I crystallised the notion that the radio was something that could be listened to for the pure enjoyment of its actual content rather than just the daft noises you could get out of it. This discovery was facilitated by the shack not having any mains electricity, which precluded telly. I listened to the radio because there was little else to do in the morning, or at night. The only outside entertainment coming into the shack was weekly copies of *The Beano*, *Dandy* and *Victor* and the various broadcasts on what Bob delightfully referred to as 'the wireless'.

It was in this rural idyll that he would sit me down to listen to *The Goon Show*. These absurd tales with their endless parade of silly voices and effects punctuated by the elegant swing of Ray Ellington and the band or the incredible harmonica of Max Geldray were the soundtrack to my woodland years. No child could fail to be entertained by such madness; even if the majority of the jokes did go soaring over my head, the joy was implicit in the sound. Bob explained to me that he had listened to it as a boy and the shows were actually over ten years old! That seemed incredible to me, that I was listening to something made before I was born.

Despite being born in the television age, 1968 for me was my radio year. In the evening we'd all sit around the radio and just listen. I'm quite glad that I had the chance to experience family evenings in the same way my parents had. On one occasion listening to *The Goons*, I leaned against one of the supporting beams in the middle of the room in my pyjamas and slid down it to sit on the floor. As I did so, a one-inch splinter of wood buried itself in my back. I remember Bob doing his Eccles voice in an attempt to distract me from my howling as Mum dug the splinter out with the aid of Dettol, hot water and the business end of a safety pin.

During the day the radio was always on, just burbling away in the background. So one of my first solid memories is of Jimmy Young doing his recipes, with the assistance of 'Raymondo'. There was something almost hypnotic about the timbre of his voice and the repetition of the instructions.

'Take eight ounces of self-raising flour …' Then he'd say it again but slower. '… That's eight … ounces … of self-raising flour.' After he'd told you the ingredients, Raymondo would pipe up with his Pinky and Perky high-pitched voice, 'And this is what you do …' I thought Raymondo was hilarious when I was five.

* * *

All the while the music of the day was burying itself in my mind, only to surface again decades later when I listened to Brian Matthew's *Sounds of the Sixties* on Radio 2. It's a really odd feeling to hear something that you haven't heard in forty years. You feel an uneasy wave of familiarity even though the name of the song and the artist doesn't ring a bell. The fact that radio was operating on me in this subliminal way, at a time when none of us knew what subliminal meant, has always made me aware of its power as a medium.

We moved back to Barking briefly in 1969. The only reason I am sure of this is that I remember watching Neil Armstrong take his first steps on the Moon from the vantage point of Granddad's Parker Knoll reclining chair. I was blithely unaware of the significance of the events fuzzily unfolding on the screen in front of me. This was what most people nowadays cite as the single most important television moment, but I just thought the picture was rubbish.

Also in the mix was my Aunt Josie. She was a vital conduit to the teenage culture of the day. She and her mates Lynn and Helen would spin Motown and Trojan records and ensure that the kitchen wireless was tuned to the new Radio 1 whenever they were around. The sounds of Detroit and Jamaica were now a fundamental part of my childhood in suburban Essex. The turbulent sixties ended in just that fashion, with Sid running off with Peggy the barmaid. Nan's seemingly unassailable rule had been broken along with her heart and her spirit, and she was never the same again. Those of us left in the wake of this disaster left the Tap and Barking behind us and carried on. Nan and Josie went to live with Auntie Pat in Suffolk. Uncle Gerald went to work overseas as a diving engineer, and we went back to Bob who had left the shack for a new home.

We moved to Stanford Le Hope in summer 1969 and, as I was growing older, so music and radio were becoming more and more a part of my life. Our house was a former manse and conveniently situated next door to Stanford Junior School where I would be a pupil for the next four years. It was here that I met up with people who had older brothers. And older brothers had record collections. Children are slavishly populist by nature so it takes an outsider to show you what kind of alternatives might be available to mainstream culture.

Mark Tindale's brother David was a guitar-playing hipster deep into his Lou Reed and David Bowie. The record player in his room was on a plywood board suspended from the ceiling on wires. I remember going round to his house and picking up the guitar and swinging the neck round and accidentally hitting the record player, sending the stylus skidding noisily across the surface of his brand new copy of *Transformer*. I was never allowed into his room again. Brian Gooden's brother John worked for a record label in London so we had all kinds of unknown white label treats available to listen to at Brian's. Every Thursday I watched *Top of the Pops* religiously. It came on immediately after *Tomorrow's World*. Now I could see those bands who were playing the great songs I was listening to on the radio: Slade, Marc Bolan, David Bowie and my own favourites, The Sweet.

For Christmas one year I got my own small transistor radio. It was a black plastic model with a volume dial, a tuning dial and a socket for an earpiece. My nights were often spent cruising the ether looking for more strange sounds. Every Sunday I would listen to the chart count-down show for what new entries had arrived and how the bands had fared since last week. Some of my friends were so clued in that they recorded their favourite tracks with the condenser microphones that came with their cassette decks. Listening to Radio 1 on medium wave on a Sunday night, however, meant that your enjoyment of the show was usually marred by the repetitive call signal of Radio Prague, a sonorous brass and woodwind jingle that would play for five seconds, then a ten second pause, then it would play again. This would annoyingly go on for the entire hour of the chart countdown no matter how much you tried to fine-tune your receiver.

Mum always had the radio on during the day, so whenever I came home at lunchtime I'd hear what was on. She can't have been listening to Radio 1 because I often heard comedy shows like *I'm Sorry I Haven't a Clue, Hello Cheeky* and *I'm Sorry I'll Read That Again*. Years later I appeared as a panellist on *Clue* alongside Tim Brooke-Taylor, who didn't seem that happy as I told him that I used to listen to him when I was at junior school.

Radio started to fall out of favour with me when I got my first record player, a beige boxy Ferguson model with a lid and four speed settings. Now I could pick exactly what I listened to, who needed radio? I had access to music or comedy on my own now and whenever it suited me. Mates would come round with boxes of 7" singles or comedy albums and we would sit around and listen. The Goons and Peter Sellers were the frontrunners in the comedy stakes. Judge Dredd was a popular musical choice because his songs were all so filthy.

* * *

In 1973 I was taken out of Hassenbrook School because I was bombing academically, and sent to a place called

Woolverstone Hall. Renowned at the time as 'the poor man's Eton', it was a former manor house located on the Shotley Peninsula just east of Ipswich. The school came under the control of the Inner London Education Authority, so its diverse intake ranged from the sons of the military to those of well-to-do green-grocers and scholarship cases, which was where I came in. Although my cousins were there, I never liked it from the moment I arrived. The second my parents drove away on my first day, I knew I'd made a colossal mistake. I was terrifically homesick and basically spent two years crying myself to sleep. Eventually, though, you get used to anything and more through boredom than resilience the tears diminished, and the only way I could show my displeasure at being sent there was by sucking at all of my subjects.

I was at Woolverstone from September 1974 until June 1978, a time when British pop music was going through one of its most radical upheavals. On my arrival, the sixth form dorms were forbidden to us juniors. But I did occasionally get a pass to go and visit cousin Stuart. There were few ways to denote one's coolness and sophistica-tion in a boys' boarding school. Smokers had a certain bad boy cachet, but were ludicrously easy to expose as their blazers would always reek of the stuff when they came back from their hiding places. Cheesecloth shirts were the garment of choice for the sixth form Lotharios whose beautifully parted and feathered hair and icy stares concealed the fact that the constant chafing of their nipples must have been agonising. Then there were of course the mad bastards. These boys would be avoided by staff and pupils alike, and had a propensity for sudden explosions of irrational behaviour. Going to lessons in dressing gowns, openly smoking pipes, joining the gun club and on occasion fighting teachers, the fact that these ordinary seventeen- and eighteen-year-old boys seemed like grown men to me only added to their cool mystique.

The greatest weapon most possessed, however, was their collection of long-playing albums. In 1974 progressive rock was the music of choice for your average hipster teen rebel about town, and the biggest band of the day was Pink Floyd. Nowhere was immune to the music of *Dark Side of the Moon*. Every single study boomed with the chords of 'Money' or 'Great Gig in the Sky'. As a fan of chart pop music, I was intrigued. I'd never heard *anything* like this stuff. Songs rambled on for over ten minutes, with lengthy instrumental passages and lyrics that were vague, elliptical and full of mystic imagery. Being twelve, rootless and emotionally frail, I was of course drawn to these strange new sounds and inexorably in the winter of 1974 I tragically entered my musical wilderness years.

It turned out that Pink Floyd were just a gateway band. Oh sure, the Floyd sound really cool, man, but if you like them then you'll bloody love Genesis! Or Greenslade, or King Crimson, or Curved Air, or Steve Hillage, or Van Der Graaf Generator! Rather than studying, my free time at school was spent in pursuit of ever more obscure bands. And with every new study that you were allowed into, there was yet another wild-eyed advocate of some new and unheard-of band. In order to ingratiate myself with these spotty, brushed-denim-clad arbiters of taste, I would always wax lyrical about how right they were and how brilliant the music was. But it was a false dawn. I was a teenager, and teenagers aren't supposed to sit around listening to music and nodding sagely. We're supposed to throw ourselves around like dervishes, uttering primal howls of delight, rage and lust. We should be drinking too much cheap cider and scrawling gory Quink ink tattoos into our arms with a compass. We should be completely frustrated and enraged by both everything and nothing all at the same time. In short we should be listening to The Sex Pistols.

Just before Christmas 1976 the nation was rent asunder when a slightly podgy guitarist from Shepherd's Bush called an even podgier local news television presenter a 'dirty fucking rotter'. The whole country was outraged, the media went crazy and punk rock was delivered mewling and bloody onto the dingy sheets of mid-seventies Britain. As the eye of punk rock's storm was in London where most of Woolverstone's pupils came from, so it made its way on to dormitory record players faster than the rest of the country. Chief among the proto punks were Lance and James Jowers. Hailing from West London, they came back to school after holidays with tales of the Roxy in Covent Garden and brilliant singles from bands like The Stranglers, The Clash, The Damned, Buzzcocks and The Jam and truly dodgy ones from Johnny Moped, Wayne County and Eater. The prog lads were being backed into a corner by the energetic new sounds of the punks. And having had all the fight smoothed out of them by listening to *The Lamb Lies Down on Broadway* and *Tales from Topographic Oceans* for the past three years they went belly up in less than a month.

The do-it-yourself ethos of the punks was taken up by two school bands. Lance Jowers was first with his combo Personal Problems, followed swiftly by Dan Gladwell with The Addicts. (Dan's Addicts were nothing to do with the later and more successful Clockwork Orange obsessives who bore the same name.) These were the first punk bands that I saw; in fact, they were the first live bands that I saw full stop. Lance was stupidly good looking and had a brief flurry of success in the 1980s when his band 5TA were signed to MCA. But in the confines of that school assembly hall with his dog lead chain round his throat and ripped sleeveless T-shirt he was nothing less than a god.

It was in this year of punk that I wanted a piece of the action, and so borrowed a bass guitar from A-level student and Queen fan Clive Roberts and started to teach myself how to play. From my point of view I never ever fitted in with the hip Woolverstone punk crowd because I never had my hair cut by anybody other than my mum. The same loopy pudding bowl style was worn by me, my brother and my sister for over sixteen years. If I'd been an early fan of The Ramones, I might have got away with it. But I was never really cut out for rebellion: a hesitant nature and desire not to upset anybody borne from those early days in Barking made me risk averse.

The overriding positive that I took from the punk and new wave years was that I started to listen to the John Peel Show on 'wonderful' Radio 1. Like the sixth formers at my school, Peel had been a prog rock advocate who could now see that the cultural wind was changing and wasn't about to get caught up in the storm. Over the space of a few months his show went from being a patchouli-scented bastion of all things delicate and ethereal to a one-stop shop for brash two-minute nuggets of teenage rebellion.

But Peel was much smarter than we were as kids. Whereas we saw punk as the new thing crushing all in its path, Peely understood that it was just the latest wave of youth culture breaking on our shores. He saw that characters like Johnny Rotten, Siouxsie Sioux and Joe Strummer stood shoulder to shoulder alongside the likes of Gene Vincent, Billie Holiday and Roy Orbison. So rather than giving his show over completely to the ill-mannered new youth phenomenon, he juxtaposed it with other musical forms to give it some context. Just as Don Letts, the deejay at the Roxy Club, was augmenting the fury of punk with the righteous indignation of dub reggae, so on our radios between ten and midnight John Peel was showing us a brave new world while reminding us of the debt it owed to earlier pioneers.

Listening to John Peel was like no other radio show I had ever heard. Gone was the artificial inflection of the voice and fake bonhomie. Gone were the constant trivial features and phone-in competitions and incessant time checks and jingles of the daytime output. Here was somebody who played music for one simple reason – because he actually liked the records. I genuinely thought that for some reason you weren't allowed to do that when broadcasting.

Every deejay I had ever heard up until that point had played the music completely on autopilot. Their attitude seemed to be that *everything* was great. All the records were fabulous, life is fantastic, and how about that weather out there? Their shows hurtled along with a minimum of fuss, and these wireless giants were every bit as famous as the artists they were playing. They had big, talented, exciting and let's not forget wacky personalities. They were on for their three-hour slot five days a week and *of course* you were going to listen to them because they were great! Then at the end of their show there would be a bit of the old cheeky banter with the guy doing the next great show, with all the same records you just heard only in a slightly different order, and wasn't everything great, and how *about* that weather outside! And so it went, over and over and over again …

Once I had heard someone normal on the radio I was forever changed. A bloke who at least twice a week would play records at the wrong speed, and instead of making a zany joke about it to cover the foul-up would just mumble about his own incompetence and apologetically put it on at the right speed. A man who would often talk in affectionate tones about his family, especially his beloved wife. I recall the giddy excitement in his voice after the birth of one of his sons, Tom (one of whose whose middle names, and indeed those of his other three children, was a tribute to Liverpool FC). Also the anguish and occasional petulance he would exhibit when his beloved Liverpool lost a game. You couldn't fail to be entranced by the genuine enthusiasm in his voice when he played a record fresh out of the envelope and, like us, was listening to it for the very first time. The moment when he described the single 'The Word Girl' by Scritti Politti as 'achingly beautiful' was the moment that I knew that being a deejay could be so much more than we were being given during the daytime.

John Peel is the reason that I said yes after I had sat in that office with my agent, Lesley Douglas and Jim Moir and they offered me my own breakfast radio show.

Corner Sounds

'I Wanna Be Like You' – Pookiesnackenburger
'Ying Tong Song' – The Goons
'Angelina' – Louis Prima
'Double Barrel' – Dave and Ansell Collins
'ABC' – The Jackson Five
'Take Me Over' – McKay
'Roll With It' – Star Turn
'Flowers in the Rain' – The Move
'Intro/Sweet Jane' – Lou Reed (from the *Rock n Roll Animal* LP)
'Phoenix City' – Perfect Thyroid

The Golden Age of Wireless

These days it's pretty much taken for granted that the breakfast show on any radio station is the most important show of the day. But why is that exactly, and how did it happen? Like anybody else facing such an all-encompassing question I googled it. Just typing in 'breakfast radio' yielded 32 million results. That might be a bit time-consuming. So I narrowed down my parameters a little and tried for 'history of breakfast radio'. Yes! 16,400,000. Let's narrow the field a little more: 'history of breakfast radio in the UK'. 4,100,000. This was all well and good but I had a few specific questions about the form, which I'm not sure even the mighty Google could handle.

One of the most fascinating developments in broadcasting over the last twenty years is how many universities and colleges have started to focus their attention on training people for jobs in media in general, but radio in particular. Most people who I have encountered in radio were pulled towards it by a desire to work in the field, but at the time there were no formal qualifications as a radio presenter or producer. People would generally start by volunteering and then if they were good at their job and got noticed they'd be offered the odd paid shift, and on it would go. Several high-ranking editors and producers I have worked with over the years started their careers in just such a fashion.

One of the country's leading facilities for learning about radio today is the Media School at Bournemouth University. Indeed the first time I visited there was to present one of the 6 Music breakfast show's regular outside broadcasts from the student radio station. The night before I went with my producer Phil Wilding (of whom, much more later) to present one of our regular outside broadcasts from the student radio station. The night before, we went to interview Swedish pop outfit The Concretes who were playing a student club in town called The Firestation. I remember walking up to the exterior just after we arrived in town and looking round at Wilding whilst uttering, 'Wow, it looks just like a fire station.' I have often been grateful for the restraint that Phil showed over the years, especially in the face of my colossal ignorance. Especially when it came to quite obviously repurposed municipal buildings.

We were due to be interviewing singer Victoria Bergsman and set up our microphones in some dim backstage nook and patiently waited for her to finish soundchecking. As various healthy, Nordic members of the band and the crew darted around us conversing with each other in Swedish, Phil and I could only sit there gurning like idiots every time a new face poked round the door. Each friendly Scandinavian face offered a friendly smile usually followed by, 'Can I help you?' Each time this happened one of us would blurt out something about being from the BBC and waiting for Victoria. 'Ah yes, she is soundchecking at this moment, but she will be with you soon, I think!' I couldn't be that polite in English, let alone a second language.

I wandered out into the auditorium to watch them running through the brilliant opening track from the *In Colour* album, 'On the Radio'. I always had a weakness for songs about radio. One of my favourite bands, The Members, had two belters in 'Radio' and 'Phone-in Show'. Joe Jackson had 'On the Radio', Costello sang 'Radio Radio', electro keyboard whiz Thomas Dolby had 'Radio Silence'. There was 'Rex Bob Lowenstein', 'Radio Sweetheart', 'The Spirit of Radio'. Possibly my favourite song about radio is 'This Is a Low' by Blur which uses the Radio 4 shipping forecast as inspiration. The list in my head was growing as I watched the band wander through another perfunctory rendition for the benefit of their sound man. As I dwelt on this, Wilding gave me an urgent wave: it seemed our interview was now on.

Now I can't speak a word of Swedish, and that as far as I'm concerned is my loss. But even without it I could sense that Victoria was not too happy to be doing an interview now. This would always throw me in an interview situation. I was always far too reliant on the good will of my subjects. I found it almost impossible to maintain a sheen of journalistic detachment. Whenever this happened, I'd try to find some common ground or some link with the band, which might open up the talk a little. Victoria's English was OK and possibly a little better than she was giving us at first, but I took a gamble on a compliment. 'Can I just say, Victoria, that having heard the new album, and seen you soundchecking briefly, you do remind me very much of another band ...'

She eyed me with curiosity. 'Really? Which band?'

'Fairport Convention.' She smiled and the rest of the chat was a breeze. It was a calculated gamble that paid off. I often wonder how things would have gone if I'd said Dollar.

The studio facilities at Bournemouth University were actually a little bit better than those we had at Broadcasting House. It was a much newer desk, and there were two fully functioning vinyl decks as well as the CD players. The room was full of students, all of whom were studying for a career in radio. In fact shortly after this Jo Tyler (who lectures in radio at Bournemouth) invited me to do a question-and-answer session with a group of students. After an over-long and quite sweary session, I thanked the students and made my way out of the room. As I did so a smiling, bearded man approached me.

'I think you know my son-in-law, Dylan Howe! I'm Zoe's dad, Sean.'

Professor Sean Street has been working in and around the world of broadcast radio for forty years. As he was now the Director for the Centre of Broadcasting History Research, I felt quietly confident that he could give me a good deal more background on breakfast radio than the internet. Well, perhaps not more, but certainly less than 32 million websites. I started out by asking him how breakfast radio came to be so important to the daily schedules rather than at night like prime-time television is.

'In the beginning both here and in the States it was the other way round. Before television, families would gather round the radio in the evening. In pre-1940s America the great desire was to lure people away from the evening radio where they knew they could sell advertising because everybody was listening. The trick was to try and get people to listen to pre-nine o'clock radio in the morning.'

So it was the pursuit of new revenue streams for radio which drove it to develop new programming for the morning audience. But surely this would require a completely different style to those big variety shows that families listened to in the evening?

'The first radio show I could find with the word "breakfast" mentioned in it was *Don McNeil's Breakfast Club* and that ran from 1933 until 1960 with the same presenter, Don McNeil. He totally built the show around his persona. It had music, inspirational readings, philosophy, a bit of poetry, all that kind of thing. It was a variety-based entertainment show, and it was completely unrehearsed, there was no script, they had a live band and the whole thing was done in front of a live audience. There was one famous incident where Bob missed his train, so they just had to soldier on without him. Then in the middle of an interview he arrives and it's all "Look who's here!" The whole thing was totally ad-libbed. Meanwhile in this country the BBC wouldn't allow anything on the wireless unless it was *very* tightly scripted.

'American broadcasters were also trying other shows at the time like the husband-and-wife hosted *Breakfast with Dorothy and Dick* with Dorothy Kilgallen and Richard Kollmar. This show actually came from their home, and they made breakfast and chatted and he'd say things like, "I've got a headache. I shouldn't have drunk that wine last night ..." and all that sort of thing. But the whole approach was very gentle.

'You always come back to America when talking about breakfast radio because the whole issue was being addressed far earlier than it was here. The first thing that could be called a breakfast radio show ran in the States from 1930 to 1943 and was presented by a man called Tony Wons. It was a fifteen-minute mixture of chat and poetry. He used material that he sourced, but he also used items from listeners, so people would think, "I've got a quote he might like to read," and they'd send it in. So he developed the idea of that relationship with the listeners where they contributed to the show.'

So while American commercial radio was defining the form, the BBC was operating along very different lines. In fact the BBC didn't start to develop breakfast radio properly until the 1960s. Sean recalls that period quite clearly:

'The switch came about in this country in the early 1960s with the arrival of the transistor radio. This is the first time that you have music that's truly portable. And kids who would want to listen to Radio Luxembourg or the pirates or later on Radio One have a means of getting away from their parents' space. My awakening to breakfast radio was with Radio Caroline and Radio London and that sense that when you were getting ready to go to school there was actually something cool to listen to on the radio and there never had been before. The Light Programme had Breakfast Special presented by John Dunne, but I had very little recollection of what had gone before. For a teenager in the early sixties, having Radio Caroline and listening to Johnny Walker playing really cool stuff was a revelation. I didn't think getting up in the morning could be fun.'

So the pirates were the first people to make mornings fun, but how long after that did it take the BBC to get on the early morning radio bandwagon?

'The thing is that the BBC is so often held up as the history of broadcasting in this country and yet when you look historically at it the BBC has more often than not responded to trends rather than creating them. It did it in the 1930s because commercial broadcasting hit a market that they weren't hitting, which was Sundays. This was because Reith believed that Sunday was the Lord's Day, and you only broadcast hymns and prayers. In comes Radio Normandy broadcasting from outside the country on a Sunday with a programme sponsored by a firm of bookmakers and blowing the audience completely out of the water. Then the war comes along and they get their act together, and out of the war comes the Forces Network which then becomes the Light Programme. But by the 1960s they've lost their way again and suddenly The Beatles are there, the whole Merseybeat thing has happened but on the BBC it's Bob Miller and the Miller Men playing versions of popular hits. You could only hear The Beatles on Luxembourg and occasionally on Saturday Club with Brian Matthew. Then the pirates come on stream around 1964 and Radio 1 arrives in the August of 1967.'

So, the tardiness of the BBC aside, breakfast radio has been around for years. And there are a number of different kinds, which have evolved from very simple beginnings. Had I known that a live band and a studio audience were an option I might have tried to revive the idea of those early broadcasts. Indeed as part of the preparation for the book I spent a week working at Nerve Radio, the student radio station of Bournemouth University Students' Union. Our Friday show was held in the cafeteria and students were invited to come and watch.

I have to say that there's a quite natural feeling to doing radio with a live audience in the morning. Everybody in the room is in a similarly fragile state and it's quite nice to share the whole waking up experience. Maybe Don McNeil was on to something.

But why were breakfast radio listeners so partisan? The wailing and gnashing of teeth surrounding Terry Wogan's departure seemed a little out of proportion for somebody simply not making a radio show any more. I asked Sean why he thought people got so upset about it.

'People get very tribal about what radio station they listen to because they understand how to listen to a show. They understand the code, they know the format, they never have to stop and think what's happening now because they've got the shorthand. Listeners want that security. If you have a regular spot on your show at five to eight and for some reason you miss it and play it at ten past eight, your audience is completely thrown. People are extremely sensitive at that time of the morning.'

Indeed they are, and that was one of the reasons why I was always very careful to have the inertia of 6 Music breakfast build slowly over the three hours of the show. The low-key opening to the show was no accident. There was no need for me to be chirpy if I was playing music because the music would do that part for me and I could wake up alongside the listeners. But it seemed that in the radio landscape I was on my own. The style of most breakfast shows, especially commercial ones, was much more in your face. Also, lots of stations have two presenters at breakfast time, a man and a woman. But not like the easy-going Dorothy and Bob back in the 1940s. The current style is lively, in your face and above all loud. How has this happened?

'You tend to think that it's just because you're old and it's not for you. But I do think that commercial radio has lost its way. I don't think the people who run commercial radio get out enough and just talk to the audience. You look around and see the mess that commercial radio has been in over the past few years and you think, "These are bright people, they're not stupid, so why are we still wallowing in this?" Why can't we plan a radio strategy that thinks beyond the next RAJAR, which they can't seem to be able to do? They would say we're aiming this at a particular audience, it's not for you so we don't expect you to like it. They think it doesn't matter if the speech is vacuous because it's having a laugh, isn't it? It's a lack of imagination. If the people who ran commercial radio bought Tesco's, they'd walk in and go, "Well, this is all great but it's full of shelves. If we got rid of all this *stuff*, then we could make some more space." It's like they've got it round the wrong way.'

So while broadcasters are striving to make a perfect breakfast show, are they missing the point that the show is actually defined by its listeners?

'It took thirty years for Wogan to build that programme, but it comes back to the fact that it was actually *the audience* that built it. He developed this persona of a presenter who's talking to people who are like himself, just a year away from a home for the bewildered and are constantly misunderstanding things. And he's not trying to be chirpy, he's just being like you are. And that strikes a chord in the audience, they get the joke and they play the joke, and that was the genius of it.

'It seems an obvious thing to say, but I think that these days we don't consider the audience enough. We do the brash young presenter thing because we think that's cool. But are we actually broadcasting to anybody or are we just talking to ourselves? Are we having fun and excluding everybody else? I used to listen to Chris Evans's earlier breakfast shows, especially the "zoo radio" stuff, and it was like watching somebody else's party, they were having a great time but I'm excluded. They don't really care, and I think there's a lot of that still goes on. Maybe it's the fact that a lot of the managers and controllers now grew up with the zoo format and they still think that's the way to do it.'

As technology advances, the amount of choice available to listeners seems almost limitless. With internet radio and features like the iPlayer, audiences are able to 'time shift' shows to a listening time that is convenient to them. If I'm in America in Boston, I get up and can listen again to that day's *Today* show on Radio 4 five hours after it was broadcast. At home in the mornings I quite often listen to the previous week's edition of *God's Jukebox* from Radio 2. Has breakfast radio as we have known it been served notice?

'My wife was a massive Wogan fan,' says Sean, 'but can't stand Chris Evans. So when she saw him coming over the horizon she discovered internet radio. She comes from Liverpool so now through the internet radio she listens to Radio Merseyside. You've got stations that were only ever meant to broadcast to a local area but which, thanks to the internet, can be heard anywhere in the world. That's the quantum change: breakfast radio is available to anybody anywhere.

'I listen to a lot of Canadian radio on the internet. I listen to a brilliant NPR jazz station from New Jersey. I can dip into other people's breakfast now, I'm listening to their reporting of the New York rush hour; it's not my rush hour but I'm vicariously feeding off it in a way. I find it fascinating because with somebody else's breakfast show you get a sense of the rhythm of the life of the place in a way that you would never get at any other time of the day. That's the exciting thing. Why would I want a DAB when I've got 2,500 stations on my internet radio?'

So is the appeal of a breakfast radio show that it defines more than just the radio station?

'In the morning we're raw, we're receptive, we are probably most ourselves at that time, and a good break-fast show understands that – maybe it doesn't know it understands that, but intuitively it does.'

It's interesting to note that even the earliest breakfast radio shows were partially informed by what was being done in the evening. That was pretty much my game plan for the 6 Music breakfast show: to take an evening radio specialist music format and tailor it for a breakfast audience.

If I had sat down with Sean Street before making my own breakfast show then I might have had a bit more consideration for the audience. A show of that kind, at that time of the day, was a difficult listen. The music was quite often 'challenging' to say the least at a time of the day when people might not want to be challenged. It's the start of their day and they've been asleep, so do they really want to be woken up by 'Ace of Spades'?

In retrospect I should have thought a little more about what I was doing and had a little more regard for the opinions of the audience as well as those of the BBC staffers guiding me. But in the isolated world of the stand-up comedian the only voice in your head that you trust is your own, and my time at 6 Music at least taught me that that voice can on occasion be extraordinarily unreliable.

But in 1978, on the brink of leaving boarding school and facing the time in my life when I would have to make some serious long-term decisions about my future, the idea of being a deejay was about as likely as me going on tour with Paul Weller or working on a hit comedy TV show for BBC2 or having a football column in *The Times*. It was time for me to knuckle down to grim reality, and lower those expectations.

Bournemouth Mix

'On the Radio' – The Concretes
'Stateside Centre' – Surfing Dave and The Absent Legends
'Reasons to Be Cheerful (Part 3)' – Ian Dury and The Blockheads
'Limbo Jazz' – Duke Ellington and Coleman Hawkins
'Poison Ivy League' – Elvis Presley
'Rat Race' – The Specials
'Lady of the Sea' – Seth Lakeman
'Seaside Shuffle' – Terry Dactyl and The Dinosaurs
'I Can See Clearly Now' – Jimmy Cliff
'Everybody's Free (To Wear Sunscreen)' – Baz Luhrmann

4

London Calling

Unlike all of those British post-war rose-tinted views of school as 'the happiest days of our lives' I have to say that it was the day that I actually left boarding school that was the happiest day of mine. After scraping a few O levels, I attended Palmers sixth-form college. It was at this point in my life when I discovered girls and Jamaican ska almost simultaneously but under unrelated circumstances. After royally screwing up any chance of A levels, I took my meagre qualifications and found a job working for the Manpower Services Commission at Gray's Jobcentre in Essex as a clerical officer on 1 July 1980, the paradox of this being that there weren't any jobs.

Partially as a reaction to my newly confined life as a desk jockey, I became an unstoppable doodler. I was already a fan of comics and graphic novels and had rudimentary drawing skills of my own. Indeed I was on one occasion officially reprimanded for the state of my desk blotter, covered as it was with cartoon pigs, tanks, stick figures, pretty ladies and band logos. What little income I had was spent on comics, maintaining girlfriends, buying records and going to gigs. It was at one of these where I saw a bunch of poets, some of whom were so unbelievably dire, I decided to add 'poetry' to my extracurricular portfolio alongside 'blotter cartoonist'. My rationale being, 'If those idiots can do it then so can I ...'

Under the name Porky the Poet, I started performing light-hearted political nonsense to partisan crowds in November 1983. Alongside such luminaries as Swift Nick and Kool Notes, I performed increasingly angry poems to increasingly angry audiences and even got a nice review in the *NME*. On 8 March 1984 I met Billy Bragg for the very first time and my life was changed forever. We had common ground in that we both came from Barking and shared a love of comics and West Ham. A year later, Billy invited me to be the opening act on his 1985 Jobs & Industry Tour, which allowed me to quit the civil service and start life properly. I will remain forever in his debt for that.

Between the winter of 1985 and the summer of 1990 I was employed by record label Go! Discs, who at the time were releasing Billy's records. When I started there, the job description stretched no further than answering the phones and hanging about a bit. But over the years this gradually expanded and I found myself writing press releases, doing mail-outs and babysitting bands before ascending to the dizzy heights of regional press and radio officer. I was living the dream, sending copies of The La's debut album to the *Bournemouth Echo* and Clyde FM.

But however cool this might sound, it's show*business* not show*friends*, and my jaundiced view of life backstage in the world of music eventually sucked the joy out of it for me. The constant bickering and contractual wrangling, the petulance of the artists, the tedious jargon of plug and marketing all eventually got to be too much.

When I left in the spring of 1990 to become a stand-up comedian I really couldn't care if I never saw another record again.

Life threw me a wonderful if unexpected curveball when I quit Go! Discs and discovered that my girlfriend Shelley was pregnant. This caused an initial panic about what our prospects might be with her a pregnant primary school teacher and me an unemployed poet/comedian/cartoonist. But we knuckled down and stuck to the game plan. I had nine months to try and crack the London comedy circuit, and crack it I did. Within a year I was a regular at clubs like the Comedy Store, Up the Creek, The T&C2, Ha Bloody Ha, the Banana, the Red Rose and the Meccano and I was making the same money I had been on at Go! The beauty part of being a comedian was that I only gigged at night, so when Shelley went back to teaching I had the luxury of five glorious years as a house husband raising my two daughters Emily and Molly.

By the mid-1990s, while by now earning my keep on the UK comedy circuit doing twenty-minute sets in pubs and clubs, my part-time personal crusade to become a radio deejay hit several brick walls – or, to be more accurate, speed bumps, not the least of which being that I was doing so much work as a stand-up comedian that I had no free time left to indulge in my wireless pursuit. It's a sad fact of the business that until the internet gets the right user-friendly hardware sorted out, television will remain popular media's alpha dog. You get paid more for network TV appearances, and in our post-Murdoch world there are many more outlets than on radio. While there is an undoubted cachet to appearing on a high-profile show like *The News Quiz* on Radio 4, you come home with just

£250 and the satisfaction of a job well done, whereas a guest slot on BBC1's *Have I Got News for You* will earn you a few grand and about 4 million viewers. For any pragmatic agent, the decision is quite cut and dried in terms of what to pitch your client for.

Occasionally I'd be invited to make guest appearances on radio shows where my job was to keep the presenter company with a bit of inoffensive chat and light banter. The quid pro quo of this arrangement was that they'd read out a list of the next few places I was gigging. Whenever I got one of these invites, I would always make sure I took a CD of whatever I was into at the time and then vainly try to get it played. More often than not they would politely refuse, citing the strictures of the playlist or timings on their script as the reason. In 1995 I was invited in to talk to presenter Simon Fanshawe on his Sunday morning show on the BBC local radio station for London, GLR. Simon had recently won the Perrier Award, and was a sassy and bright host. I'd bumped into him from time to time on the comedy circuit and as he seemed like a nice bloke I agreed to appear on his show.

At the time GLR was attracting a cult following with its bold, slightly off-kilter programming. This was mostly down to the jam-packed Filofax of its quixotic former controller Matthew Bannister, not to mention the ground-breaking style of his diverse team of presenters. Emma Freud, Chris Morris, Danny Baker and Chris Evans all had shows that just went slightly against the grain of what national radio was doing. Most regional radio had that unmistakable homespun local sound, but GLR at the time sounded fresher and more interesting than Radio 1 and 2. Magazines like *Q* and *Select* had identified an entire generation of music fans who were too old for Radio 1's pop fare and too young for the smooth sounds of Radio 2.

GLR's music policy squarely addressed the heart of this demographic. It had a more alternative and adult skewed playlist, and a bright staff of presenters who did other things aside from deejaying. Morris was a skilled comedy writer and producer who would spend hours in the basement studio in the run up to his show editing and assembling all the various components. Former NME scribe Danny Baker spoke to the inner hipster in all of us, and his hilarious reminiscences about his own youth helped to establish a loyal and creative fan base. Without Danny Baker's radio show, I doubt that Channel 4 would have ever thought about developing those endless *I Love the Seventies* shows. Danny, along with his loyal cadre of sparky, trivia-obsessed listeners, had been reminiscing about the self-same subject matter for nearly a decade before the first of those shows was produced for television.

GLR proved to be such a massive success that Bannister was rapidly propelled upwards by corporation management to revitalise the tired and emotional Radio 1, a move that ultimately proved to be a costly if timely mistake. The wholesale changes that Bannister brought in when he got to Radio 1 upset listeners and alienated the old guard. Dave Lee Travis's famous on-air resignation speech must have been seen by some, including the Hairy Cornflake himself, as a majestic and principled stand, a bit like Mel Gibson's 'Freedom' speech in *Braveheart*. Instead, it became the perfect example of exactly why all the old guard had to go. It was arrogant, self-regarding nonsense. The main problem was that the hitherto untouchable

Radio 1 deejays had laboured under a misapprehension that they were bigger stars than the artists whose records they played.

To a certain extent this wasn't their fault. Radio 1 had been pretty much unchallenged as the nation's favourite radio station for a good decade until commercial radio finally got its act together. It was in a climate of falling ratings and an ageing on-air staff that Bannister was charged with revitalising the flagging network. And of course he rehired his best people from GLR, half a mile West in Marylebone. You might expect such a body blow to have done damage to his old station. Instead, during the post-Bannister years GLR stayed very much on its feet. Specialist music shows from Gary Crowley and Bob Harris were backed up by superlative daytime output from Fi Glover and Gideon Coe, Peter Curran, Robert Elms and Johnny Walker. The weekends were given over to Charlie Gillett, Ranking Miss P, Norman Jay and Ross Allen as well as shows from comedians Bob Mills and Simon Fanshawe.

Fanshawe was a brash, ebullient host and remarkably well read, so he liked to keep the tempo of his show 'up'. My first appearance was alongside the editor of *Cosmopolitan*, Marcelle D'Argy Smith. We were there to do the round-up of the Sunday papers, a regular feature of many weekend broadcasts. This was the first time I'd been on the radio in a more casual way. I had no particular gigs to plug, and felt under no pressure to trot out my stand-up. Simon engendered a very free and easy vibe where, and without ever talking about it, we all slipped into our appointed roles. Marcelle was the media matriarch, Fanshawe was the educated devil's advocate and I was the gag monkey. For me it was liberating to be able to chat on air like you were three people just having a spot of breakfast together.

As I sat there, I realised that this was how I wanted to work in future, freed from the tyranny of punchlines, talking seriously about issues when it was warranted, and throwing in the odd gag if you felt like it. And as if all that wasn't delightful enough, we also got warm croissants and fancy schmancy coffee from Patisserie Valerie over the road so all in all I found it a tiptop way to spend a Sunday morning.

I appeared once more with Simon on a Sunday, and was on the verge of asking if there was any chance of him giving me a regular slot. Although we were very different personalities, we seemed to get on well. His south coast intellectual drawl and my Thames estuary squawk seemed to complement each other. Also from a purely selfish point of view, it was a great way to get some more airtime under my belt. In performance terms, live radio made a completely different set of demands on you from stand-up comedy. In front of an audience you had completely free rein. Profanity was rarely an issue, and if you did stray off script it was with a sense of complete and utter freedom. On stage we were wisecracking libertines. But on the radio you really had to be on your game as swearing was completely out of the question. I have always been somebody who uses the word 'fuck' or 'fucking' as a form of casual verbal punctuation. This may partially be an Essex thing. It simply buys you a little bit of thinking time. When I first appeared on GLR I was genuinely worried that I was getting so relaxed that I might swear and end up never working on the radio again, but this never happened. There seemed to be some kind of four-letter firewall installed in my frontal lobes. Ironically it was Simon who crossed the broadcasting line with an off-the-cuff remark about Prince Edward, which had him dismissed from the station immediately.

With Fanshawe now off the air, it seemed to me that the chances of blagging my way onto a radio show went up in smoke. My salvation came in the form of Mark Lamarr (nine words that if you ever happened to catch us on *Buzzcocks* you probably thought you would never read in your lives). Mark had risen to national prominence with his appearances on *The Big Breakfast* and *The Word*. His uncompromising style, sharp look and razor wit found a ready home on Channel 4 where he achieved near legendary status after accusing Shabba Ranks of homophobia during a live interview. Mark's first love, however, was music. It was a common frame of reference between us when we first met. Although it quickly became apparent that while music was something I regarded with love, Lamarr cherished it with an all-consuming passion. He would travel the world in search of music, always returning home loaded down with rare vinyl and CDs.

Around this time, Lamarr was also a regular guest on Mark Radcliffe's late-night Radio 1 show. As a result of this he was called in to deputise whenever Radcliffe was away on leave. This was how on a wet Thursday night I found myself taking a taxi from Manchester's Piccadilly Station to the BBC studios in Oxford Road to be a guest on a Radio 1 show for only the second time in my life.

One habit that Lamarr acquired at the time was to start the top of every hour with two records back to back. They may have a connection, they may have none at all, that wasn't the point. The idea was to always have a really striking start to every hour, to draw the listeners in. As I wasn't brought in to contribute to the show for thirty minutes or so, I was able to sit and watch the producer working the desk in the control booth. Although the sprawling panel looked quite complex, the operation seemed fairly straightforward. There were two CD decks, two vinyl decks for playing out music and a minidisc machine for playing trails and jingles, and four guest microphones. Each of these was assigned a particular fader. I was spellbound by the hands of the producer as he went from record to record, eventually bringing Mark back on air. It looked like he was playing some arcane musical instrument.

Immaculately turned out in classic period casuals, Lamarr didn't look unlike the jazz legend Chet Baker from the cover of a Blue Note album. The studio was in almost complete darkness aside from a few ceiling-mounted spotlights, and so the distraction-free atmosphere and soundproofed walls were conducive to the whole listening experience. I often forget the debt that I owe to Mark in terms of how he changed my appreciation of music. In any given two-hour show with him you would hear artists as diverse as The Four Tops, Howling Wilf and The Veejays, Stina Nordenstam, The Clash, Eddie Bo, Shirley Ellis, Pulp, Toots and The Maytals, Richard Thompson, The Pretty Things, The John Spencer Blues Explosion, Buzzcocks, Willie Nelson, The Small Faces, Link Wray, Misty In Roots, The Skatalites, The Who, James Brown … The list just went on and on. Just when you'd been completely blown away by one song, he'd then top it with the next. It was for any fan of music an utterly exhilarating experience.

In the mid-nineties Mark took over from Simon Fanshawe on the Sunday mid-morning shift at GLR. The overall effect of this was that there was less chat and more music, which was no bad thing in my book. Mark would invite friends from the comedy circuit, musicians, authors and actors to come and join him. Basically, anybody who didn't mind getting up on a Sunday morning and schlepping into the West End was welcome. I got the call to come on quite early in his time at GLR and was usually the first guest on. This meant I'd be in there for the whole three hours, which for me was something of a luxury.

At the beginning Mark sat to the side of the desk with his box of CDs which he would hand to whoever was operating. Then after the customary two records we'd have a quick chat, and at some point in the conversation we'd reach some kind of natural conclusion, Lamarr would point at whoever was operating and this was their sign to bring in the next record. It was here that I first realised that there was a certain logical grammar to this kind of radio. The records could be used as punctuation. If you had a freeform show, the trick was to keep the balance between the chat and the music.

On the show I was a guest alongside Jo Brand and Barry Cryer. Jo I had known since my time as Porky the Poet in the mid-eighties, when she first started doing gigs under the name The Sea Monster. Barry Cryer I had been a fan of since my childhood. His raucous laugh was familiar to me on shows such as *I'm Sorry I Haven't a Clue* and *Hello Cheeky*. Unlike many of his peers, Barry embraced the younger comedians, who would usually end up enthralled in his company as he told tales of life working with the Monty Python team, and playing the Windmill in the

1950s. The only clear memories I have of that morning are who was there and that we had a laugh for three hours. This is what GLR excelled in, effortless, accessible but above all entertaining radio without a rigid format.

If you had approached a network station and described such a show to them, they wouldn't have touched it with a bargepole. Station controllers like to know exactly what they are getting. What are the features, how many competitions, how many phone-ins, will you have guests? The busier a programme looks, then it's logical to assume that more work has gone into it. So a simple idea sounds like no thought has gone into it at all. But that doesn't mean that a simple show isn't a good one. When you think about it, the format for John Peel's show was 'a bloke walks into a room with a boxful of records he likes and plays them'. That for me has always been the best kind of radio. Somebody with a genuine passion who has the ability to communicate it to others …

I became a semi-regular on Mark's Sunday morning show, going in every couple of months just to sit and watch and listen and join in with the good-natured carnage. The collision of ideas between Mark, his contributors and the listeners who would phone in made for ramshackle but wonderful radio. By the time of my second visit Mark had been taught how to drive the desk himself, which made the show even slicker than it was before. This being nearly twenty years ago, Mark was what I would term an enthusiastic smoker. The image of him wreathed in cigarette smoke, casually segueing from one record to another by swiping the fader up with a quick flick of his wrist is one that I will always remember from these Sunday mornings. That and my burgeoning emphysema.

Eventually, it happened that Mark was away on holiday and I was asked to fill in for him. This was it. I spent more time putting together the records I was going to be playing than anything else that week. I went through my collection again and again and ended up with ten times as many CDs and albums as I would actually need for the three-hour slot. In the studio that day was Gavin Lawrence, who was operating the desk, and fellow Essex stand-up John Mann.

These early shows, while not exactly lucrative, were incredibly instructive. I found myself adopting a pastiche of Lamarr and Peel's anti-jock style. Subjects for phone-ins would emerge organically from the chats I had with John in the first half hour of the show. The listeners were a bright, friendly and funny bunch who would always make the most fleeting of ideas come alive. One morning we were chatting about the weird things your parents did when you were young, and one caller revealed that her mother was constantly threatening her with being taken into care. However, she exacerbated this by saying that her mum told her that they would come in a yellow van. So every time she saw an AA van coming down the road she thought it was social services.

The Sundays deputising for Lamarr went so well that GLR senior producer Jude Howells offered me a three-month run doing Fridays for Robert Elms while he finished writing a book. The slot would be from ten until one, and in the last half hour would include a live session band down in the basement studio. My producer would be Suzanne McManus, who had looked after me when I sat in for Lamarr. At the weekends it was mostly quiet, apart from the frenetic Saturday afternoons when Simon

Crosse presented the excellent GLR sport. But more often than not the only people you saw were the newsreader, the staff of the show before you and the staff of the show after you. But Robert's show was a lot different from Mark's as midweek GLR was a very different place.

Between Monday and Friday GLR was a bustling cauldron of activity. Located in Marylebone High Street, the offices were built around a large central open-plan space where the newsroom and sports department were based. There was no natural light in this thrumming inner sanctum, so ceilings hummed with flat white utilitarian neon. Heavy trolley-mounted reel-to-reel tape machines sat beside desks groaning under the weight of lumpy computers and stacks of newspapers. The usual personal knick-knacks adorned what limited free space there was. Toys, Polaroids, stained mugs, postcards, football scarves and promotional baseball caps were scattered everywhere. Walls were festooned with laminated health and safety notices, yellowed press cuttings, faded BBC memoranda and reams of densely scribbled duty rosters.

Producers, presenters, editors and broadcast assistants battled for desk space in the tiny offices that sprang off this central area. Every single horizontal surface was covered with CDs, records, books and magazines. Whenever you sat down to try and work, the first order of business was to clear yourself a big enough space to do so. This could only be achieved by putting piles on top of other piles. Nearly every office was just a casually misjudged elbow away from a potentially fatal compact disc and magazine avalanche. People jostled shoulder to shoulder for workspace and on occasion they also had to jockey for content in their programmes. There was fierce if cordial competition for guests as everybody's show featured them at some point in their running order. The daytime weekday programmes successfully coexisted in this atmosphere of gentle rivalry. Production teams often reached for the diary, only to discover that their young actor had already been booked for an appearance by Peter Curran. If two shows were both chasing the one guest, then it was generally agreed that first come first served was the order of the day, and next time they came to town the losing show would get first dibs.

Meanwhile, the news shows were a very different animal. When I would arrive just after nine it was the lunchtime news team who were running about the place, hastily gathering interviews, calling contributors and tweaking scripts. Drivetime, meanwhile, were just walking around at a regular pace; their agenda would be set by the news cycle later in the day. During my brief weekday tenure, GLR Breakfast was in the hands of the brilliant Gideon Coe and Fi Glover. This sparky duo had the ability to swerve effortlessly between hard news stories and entertainment features without it sounding in any way clumsy. It was the most grown-up entertainment and news radio show I ever heard. I was in awe of their skill and professionalism when it came to the transition between vastly different topics. The last hour of the breakfast show was reserved for specialist features, the best of which was the weekly food and drink slot with Nigel Barden.

Barden was a small, wiry food journalist, rugby enthusiast, part-time actor and quite coincidentally one of the funniest human beings I have ever met. Well educated and sailing just the right side of posh, he would burst into the studio usually laden with some insanely delicious foodstuffs for Fi and Gideon to sample. Nigel was a great contributor to any radio show. His wonderfully descriptive language, extensive knowledge and boundless enthusiasm for food and drink came over perfectly on air. As you listened, you could almost taste what they were eating, such was his brilliance at conveying the whole epicurean experience.

One fateful morning at Barden's suggestion, the breakfast show would be celebrating the release of that year's Beaujolais Nouveau, which of course meant that a judicious amount of wine tasting would be taking place. Barden set the item up in his usual style, talking about all the different vineyards, their history and the quality of their produce. In the background you could hear the familiar squeak and pop of corks being pulled from a number of bottles. The presenters were offered glass after glass of deep red wine from all over France. They 'ummed' and 'ooohed' with each rich fruity mouthful they swallowed. As soon as one was finished, Barden uncorked a new bottle and offered them another to comment on.

'Now this one is from a more southerly vineyard. See if you can taste the difference …'

Glover became a little giggly but maintained a steady hand on the tiller. Coe also kept his on-air cool but started to sound more and more 'comfortable', like the studio was slowly turning into his front room. And at the centre of it all, like a frisky Bacchus, was the irrepressible Nigel Barden, who knew *exactly* what he was doing. By the end of a truly memorable show the presenters certainly weren't what you would call roaring drunk but I can't imagine anybody was going to be driving home that day. For me the abiding memory was the parlous state of the entire breakfast show team half an hour after they had finished broadcasting. People were loosely sprawled on chairs and over desks, as they finished off the last of the wine. There was talk of seeing if the pub might be open. It was moments like this that made me love working with these people.

The charm of GLR to me was that it seemingly functioned without any hard-and-fast rules. Unlike its national counterparts, it eschewed the media gobbledegook of marketing consultants and focus groups. It stuck to a simple formula of mixing a solid team of professional broadcasters with a group of radio-friendly enthusiasts who they then turned into broadcasters. These people were in turn served by a brilliant backroom staff of producers, editors, broadcast assistants and interns. And underpinning everything was a communal sense of pride in what was being achieved. Trained broadcasters like Jeremy Nicholas and Peter Curran presented brisk and engaging magazine-style shows, peppered with great interviews. Robert Elms brought his journalistic background and abiding love of London to the fore in his show, which still runs to this day. His boundless enthusiasm for the city and his skill at harnessing the knowledge and curiosity of his listeners has helped to make the show a truly interactive experience. And cementing the whole thing together was an eclectic and fabulous selection of music.

Everybody who worked there understood that they were doing something unique in British radio. Being located in the centre of a capital city gave them access to a much greater range of material than their provincial counterparts. Internationally renowned bands would turn up every day to do live sessions for Robert Elms in his mid-morning show. Actors, authors, comedians, politicians …

Personalities from all over the world found their way into the studios of GLR. Shows were intelligent and funny and played the kind of music that few other stations would even think of playing during the day. It was kind of like Radio 4 interspersed with pop records, and people simply loved it.

My Friday mid-morning show ran for three months in 1996. Suzanne McManus, my producer, was a bubbly, enthusiastic Dubliner who loved her job. One day in the pub over the road before I started my short residency she turned to me and asked, 'What d'ye want to call the show?' This stopped me in my tracks. Now I had a radio show I should really give it a name, I suppose. I took a sip of bitter and mulled over the idea. It had guests and live music as well as the odd selection from my own CD box.

'How about Big Phill's Friday Mixed Grill?'

She smiled immediately. 'Fantastic. What are you drinking?'

Working in radio seemed to be what Suzanne was born to do. She would gee me up before every programme with a big old coffee and a stack of notes on the guests. She'd provide questions, if I needed them, but was always perfectly happy with me going off piste during an inter- view. Also helping Suzanne produce the show was Bernie Caffrey. She would bring guests in, settle them down, check I was OK and then toodle back out to the control room. She would also screen callers, nip down to the record library in the event of any unexpected requests, and basically mother me. Occasionally she'd switch on the talkback to pop a fact I was grappling for into my headphones.

On the music side, Jon Myer was GLR's taciturn and owlish record librarian. He or his second-in-command, the hip, urbane Laurence Arnold, would bring me a pile of CDs from that week's loosely assembled playlist. With it they would also bring four 'free needle time' compilation CDs. These were basically classic soul and pop tracks that you didn't have to pay any money to play. Laurence handed me the pile of ten playlist CDs.

'Try to play all of these,' he said before handing me the other discs, 'and try to play at least one track from any of these albums each hour.'

I looked up at him. He sensed my curiosity. 'The rest is yours,' he said, 'but just avoid any artists who are on the playlist.'

This seemed eminently reasonable and meant that I'd get to play a nice chunk of the music I'd brought from home. This laissez-faire approach to the music policy gave GLR a distinctive sound. Every other station had to adhere to rigid playlists while GLR gave its presenters room to air the kind of sounds they would listen to off duty.

Now I had a regular albeit temporary slot, Jude Howells thought it was about time I was taught how to drive the controls. So later that week I came in early and made my way down to the basement studio for my first lesson in deejaying. I was more excited and more nervous than I had ever been in my life about a job. My instructor was Gavin Lawrence, the man who had been the operator when I did the shows sitting in for Lamarr. Gavin was a large, bespectacled Kentishman who for me defined what I like to call 'The Geek Paradox'. This basically means that the more old-fashioned an engineer looks, the more up to date he is with his knowledge. Gavin was chunky corduroys; sensible pullovers and button-down oxfords with rolled-up sleeves all the way, and therefore I knew in my heart of hearts that he was a bloody high-tech genius. He was one of the first people I ever knew who sent emails and, that being the case, I had no reason to doubt that he didn't carry some sort of home-made death ray around with him.

On my first training day Gavin sat me down in front of what looked like an acre of knobs, dials, switches, faders and buttons. He slowly explained how each one was assigned to a different channel and then went on to outline how I should only send clean feed to the travel people, not the news studio. At this point he lost me really, but I knew that to 'send clean feed' I would have to adjust that knob he had showed me. To this day I don't know what 'sending clean feed' means, but I still drop it into conversations if I do ever meet engineers. It's a bit like somebody who knows nothing about engines knowing the word 'solenoid'. You don't know what it means, but you feel big and clever when you use it. Big Gav went on to explain how I could record jingles and music beds on to tape cartridges or 'carts' and then demonstrated how to choose between push button or fader start. I nodded keenly and smiled while still not really understanding a single word of what he was on about. But I was gripped by every one of these new and puzzling concepts and slowly began to get the hang of how to turn the running order in front of me into a real live radio show.

One of the more selfish responses on learning how to actually run a desk was that I could creep in late at night and make some really killer compilation tapes for my mates. Then the realisation that the next day I had to drive my first radio show on my own evaporated all thought of fun, larks and C90 cassettes. I put together a rough list of music I'd take along and jammed CDs and vinyl into a holdall. Having to negotiate the last knockings of London's rush hour was always a pleasure. But all thought of the clammy commuters around me was obscured by the adrenaline pumping through my veins. I was going to be presenting a proper daytime radio show – and not only that, I was going to be operating all the knobs myself! I felt unusually grown up at this point, completely disregarding the fact that it was only once a week for three months. But of all the varied jobs I had done since leaving the civil service in 1985, this felt to me like the best fit. I wondered if I had finally found my career.

The beaming faces of Bernie and Suzanne as I got to the office settled my nerves a little. They clucked around me and checked that I had everything I needed. Laurence brought me my music and a few extras. At about twenty to ten we made our way into Studio 2. As I sat down at the control desk I exhaled and began sorting my music into manageable piles. Bernie talked me through all the cartridges for jingles, show trails and news and travel beds. Big Gavin was already setting up the desk and gave me a reassuring grin. He could doubtless see the slight tension in my face.

Back in the basement studio it all seemed so logical, but now in the cold light of a live studio it all seemed a bit too much. Gavin was there to stand over me during my first solo outing on the desk. He would graciously answer my jittery questions and then just as I was about to push a flashing red button that would take all of the BBC south of Watford off the air, he would lean over my shoulder, calmly take my hand away from it and reach over and locate the correct one. We turned on the station output so I could hear the final minutes of Fi and Gid's breakfast show. As I looked round to my right, I could see through the large studio window into the control booth and then the other side of that through another window was Studio 1 and the breakfast show. They were in full flight with Nigel Barden who had brought in a range of cheeses that morning. Now there *was* a radio show that needed a drop of Beaujolais.

Gavin ran over the procedure for handover one final time. 'Right, so breakfast will hand to news, then it's during news we take control over from breakfast. Then you play the "news out sting" and go straight into your first record. Just like we did downstairs! It'll be fine.'

The 'news out sting' was the brief punchy jingle that you played out to signify to the listener that the news bulletin had finished and was an easy part of the process, as opposed to *taking control*. The simplest but at the same time most nerve-racking of all the myriad procedures I had been shown was *taking control*. Basically what you have to do is lift a small plastic flap and press the button underneath it. Pressing this button transfers broadcast priority from another studio to yours. This is a bit like changing channels on a telly, and you are only supposed to do it when there is a pause in speech. I heard breakfast winding their show up, Glover looked through the glass at me and waved.

'And coming up after the news Phill Jupitus with *Big Phill's Mixed Grill* – I can see him over there …'

My pulse started to elevate and I took a sip of water and weakly waved back.

Gavin leaned over me. 'Right, get news up on prefade and set the levels, put your two carts in and make sure they're wound to the start, make sure your first track is ready to go, and get ready to take control.'

I felt like the passenger who gets to land a 747 in an action film, with big Gav as the bloke in the tower talking me down.

The news bulletin was in progress as I eased up the flap over the control buttons. I listened keenly for a break in the news-caster's speech but he seemed to be deliberately not pausing just to wind me up. He wasn't at all, but it just sounded like that to me. A simple beat to inhale would not be enough for my needs that day: I wanted a big old Northern Line plat-form style gap before I was going to be pressing any buttons. I was going to choose my moment!

'Now!' said Gavin and I blindly pressed the button, my leaping heart closing off my throat.

And the moment I pressed that button I became a proper deejay.

OMG GLR

'Hit' – The Wannadies
'This Is Carboottechnodiscotechnobooto' – Bentley
  Rhythm Ace
'All-Nighter' – Elastica
'Delicious' – Sleeper
'Round Are Way' – Oasis
'What Do I Get?' – Buzzcocks
'Jatayu' – Transglobal Underground
'Babies' – Pulp
'The Name Game' – Shirley Ellis
'Wasted' – Hopper (Chopper Squad remix)

5
Employment

Having regular employment on radio, even if it was only a weekly show, dovetailed quite nicely with the stand-up work. If I was gigging on a Thursday night, I just had to make sure that I allowed myself enough time to get home and prepare for Friday morning's show. With 90 per cent of my comedy commitments being in the London area, this was rarely an issue. I very quickly slipped into a quite solid rhythm with doing the *Mixed Grill*.

At the end of every show, Suzanne would hand me research material for all the guests on next week's show, and then we'd go to the pub which was already heaving with the team from the breakfast show who had been going for a couple of hours. I could never fully embrace these boozy after-show sessions as I would always be working the clubs later that night. Weekends for stand-up comedians were the time when we would make all our real money for the week.

Midweek comedy gigs were small pub shows where you would be on a door split with the other acts. On such nights you could only expect to be earning £70 at most, but more often than not you'd be getting home with about

£40 bothering your wallet. But on Fridays and Saturdays the London live scene was positively heaving with work. The cream of the crop was the Comedy Store. In the mid-nineties a full weekend of gigs at the Store would net you £400, and you'd be playing there at least once a month. Add to this the fact that you could squeeze in another gig between the two that you would do for the Store on Friday and Saturday and you'd be doing quite nicely.

As GLR offered a parking space behind the studios I decided to drive up from Essex for the Friday morning shows. This tragically meant that once a week I had to negotiate the varied pleasures of the A13. Back when I had given up my civil service job, ten years earlier, one of the chief motivational factors was that I would no longer have to be a commuter. OK, so my position at Stanford Le Hope Jobcentre meant that while living at my mum's my 'commute' was only 500 yards of walking each day. But before that I had served my time on the grubby trains with all the other workers twice a day, every day, for forty-eight weeks of the year. Travelling on the Fenchurch Street line in South Essex doesn't exactly provide you with stunning vistas to absorb on your journey. There is a flat grey uniformity to the landscape. Factories and industrial estates smoothly give way to sickly hedgerows, and each new station seems even bleaker than the last. The horizon occasionally yields yet more estuarine wonders, oil refineries, container depots or the dull industrial north shore of Kent and what Dickens described in *Great Expectations* as 'the low leaden line' of the Thames.

I, however, would be driving. And so each Friday morning I would drag myself out of bed at around 6.30 to shower and prepare for the day ahead. As my children were commuting fifteen miles to their new school in Leigh on Sea, we were all up and bustling around the house at about the same time. The day before I would have compiled my selection of music and gone over Bernie's typed running order for the show. If I had any books that needed reading, I always tried to get through at least three chapters. This gave me enough to work with in an interview, and I'd always inform the author that I was looking forward to reading the rest. It was cheeky, but it always seemed to pay off.

In fact, with a cruel irony, the only time I had read all of a book written by one of my guests was when I had to interview John Pilger to discuss the reissue of his spectacular volume *Heroes*. I was in love with this book and a huge admirer of Pilger's. Sadly such enthusiasm and admiration do not make for a good radio interview. The whole encounter had the feeling of an annoying fan turning up at a signing and taking up too much of the author's time while other people were waiting. I was quite obviously pissing the man off, which seemed a touch unfair as here was someone who had gone toe to toe with the Khmer Rouge. I wasn't sure exactly what kind of a problem an ebullient enthusiast from the Home Counties could be presenting him with. I became aware that things were not going well with Mr Pilger when he answered each question as follows:

PRESENTER: 'What's the situation like in Cambodia now?'
PISSED-OFF AUTHOR: (*deep sigh followed by uncomfortable pause*)
'Look …' (*rolls eyes*)

It was the only time that a producer walked into the studio afterwards and looked at me and said, 'That really wasn't very good, was it?'

So after 'Pilgergate' I maintained a looser attitude when interviewing authors. For starters, only read part of the book, but read something! This will actually give you more to ask if you don't know what happens at the end. If it's an author you like, then prepare an extensive list of questions in advance. You don't want to be sat down just gurning at a stranger who ultimately you only really want an autograph from. Another ice-breaker with some of the starchier guests was to ask them about their favourite band and then go and fetch some from the library. This sweet little ruse took them out of the mindset of the promotional treadmill and got a different part of their brain working. Mind you, there was then the risk that they'd sit up brightly and go, 'Ooh yes, I absolutely love my music ... have you got any Phil Collins?'

Being a Friday show the *Mixed Grill* had a looser feel to it than Robert's Monday to Thursday stint in the same time slot. But then Elms was a widely travelled and experienced journalist and author whereas at this point I was ostensibly a clown. Writers, authors, comedians and musicians would come through the doors and leave with a cheery wave as I played another record. Being Friday, one of my regular segments was the film review with Angie Errigo.

Angie's name was already familiar to me from her excellent work in the *New Musical Express*, so to have her on the show did give me a bit of a tingle. Her looping American accent had a West Coast glamour, and of all the film reviewers I listened to she had the most considered outlook. There was no outlandish slagging off of films for its own nihilistic sake. She always strived to find the positive. I can only assume this stemmed from her time in film public relations when I'm sure she must have had to strongly advocate some absolute toss.

A good solid contributor in a show is a blessing when your skills as an interviewer are still being formed. My technique tended towards the friendly chat rather than bombarding subjects with preset questions. This was all well and good when it worked, but it was dependent on your interviewee being in a cooperative mood. It was easy to forget that, more often than not, you were just one of dozens of interviews that they were undergoing as a contractual commitment to whatever it was they were plugging. None of them really wanted to be sat in a stuffy studio on a nice afternoon. One advantage that I did have was that I had been the subject of radio interviews myself on a number of occasions so I knew how a bad one went.

My own all-time favourite bad interview of which I was the subject was so completely terrible that I actually started laughing in the middle of it. Professionalism and common courtesy prevent me from saying at exactly which station I was subjected to this bizarre interrogation because when you are on the promotional trail, you usually do most of the work ahead of any tour or project you are working on. But occasionally it is necessary to take part in a last-minute live afternoon radio show to give that evening's show a final push. Most of the larger towns in the UK have some kind of regional radio presence, be it commercial or BBC. There is a very different feel to these stations. The staff and deejays here aren't competing with other national stations. They have a contained and loyal listenership all in the immediate area. Local radio deejays are the perfect example of the big fish in a small pond.

These larger-than-life personalities can be readily identified by their regular appearances in local newspapers, opening fêtes or doing an outside broadcast from a boot sale. The best of the bunch can also be found appearing every Christmas in the local pantomime, billed just below the woman from *Home and Away* but just above the Irene Constantine Twinkle Toes School of Dance. They have a cool calm confidence, managing to stay just shy of outright arrogance, unless of course they work at the commercial station, where arrogance is apparently given to them with the station-branded silk bomber jacket and the mad-sounding fake on-air voice …

When one is going to appear on a local radio show, you know that the production team has been supplied with a full biography and performance details well in advance of the event that you are publicising. It is accepted that you will indulge in some friendly chit-chat and at the end of it all the presenter will say, 'Ha ha ha … well annnnnyway, if you'd like to see more of Phil Jupiter, why not go along to the Elms Theatre tonight. And I understand there are still *quite a few* tickets available.' It's gut-scorchingly uncomfortable on occasion, but it has become part and parcel of the whole touring experience.

One of the last regional interviews that I did was to promote a live show. I arrived at the station and a very lovely receptionist beamed at me as I walked into the lobby. She grabbed the phone and called upstairs while I wandered around looking at the promotional photos of all the local jocks. At least three of them were called 'Roger' unless Roger had three very different looks. This to me is a good solid radio name, nice and woody with an R at each end. When you say it, you have to sound butch and speak in a lower register. Try it now yourself, go on … *Roger* … *Roger* … *Roger* … Anyway, I wasn't seeing one of the three Rogers. I was on the afternoon show with a bloke whose name has mercifully been scoured from my memory by post-traumatic stress. I was taken into a uniformly bland regional radio studio and sat down in front of a slight, balding fellow, who was wearing headphones while nodding along appreciatively to Katrina and The Waves.

He smiled briefly and picked up a sheet of A4 and looked down at it. Now I am no scholar of psychology, but even I could tell from his yo-yoing eyebrows and pursed lips that this was the very first time he had read this information.

'OK, so … errrrm … you're playing in town tonight, and is this part of a tour of some kind?'

I thought that the fact that the gig we were discussing was highlighted in amongst a list of thirty-one other shows might be a clue there. But I have learned over the years that in the face of utter stupidity it is best just to smile and nod politely.

'Right, after travel we're back with you, then we'll have a bit of a record and do another bit with you and that'll be it.'

Smile.

Nod.

Katrina started to ebb and my slaphead nemesis eased the fader up on his microphone. 'Katrina and The Waves there and "Walking On Sunshine", not that anybody's going to be doing any of that today because it's still raining!'

(Pause, presumably to allow his listeners to recover from their hysterics over this top-notch comedy moment.)

'Time to catch up now with Margaret over at the AA travel desk. How are those roads then, Mags?'

Aside from the obvious bridling at being called Mags, an administrative assistant with the county's police force then read out a mind-numbing list of roadworks and told us we could expect delays during the rush hour. As if every other rush hour was apparently the time people chose to put their cars away and hide for the duration. She informed us she'd be back in half an hour, and my host tried to involve her in some banter.

'Anything planned for the weekend then, Mags me old mate?'

'No. Not really.'

'Right. OK. See you in half an hour!'

Then he played an absurdly loud travel jingle, the gravitas of which seemed to imply that to remain uninformed about travel delays could very well cost you your life … The jingle faded out abruptly.

'Now then, tonight a very funny man is going to be performing. You might know him from his appearances on *Never Mind the Buzzcocks* and *Gag Tag* or perhaps *Watership Down* where he played the voice of Dandelion, who was a rabbit!'

(Another pause for the imagined howling gales of laughter to subside.)

'Anyway, he's with us today, it's …' looks down at sheet '… Phill Jupitus. Hello Phill!'

'Hello.'

'Now, Phill … it says here that you used to work in a Jobcentre. What was that like?'

Ah, a nice easy opener … So I went into the usual description of my old day job, but as I did so I noticed that my interviewer was looking out of the window to his left. Had he seen something? I ploughed on nonetheless.

'I see. Now after that it says here that you then became a performance poet! What was that like?'

Once again I answered his question as succinctly as possible, trying to inject a little humour where possible, but these were very flat questions. Once in a while I'd leave a gap after a particular fact on the odd chance that he might want to do a follow-up question but he remained focused on whatever it was outside the window. I finished speaking and he looked back round to me.

'Right. Now after that you went to work for a record company! What was that like?' I had finally cracked his personal Da Vinci code.

Here was someone who from where I was sitting could not give a flying fuck about his job and especially his guest. He was perfectly happy to completely phone in what was passing for a radio show. This was a bloke who would never be invited to do pantomime, or go out on road shows, or sit in a bath full of jelly for Comic Relief. This was a bland, dull, average local radio disc jockey. The small fish in the small pond. Not even that, he was the frogspawn. And as he sat there completely oblivious to my presence, ticking off each subject as they slid by on the press release, I started to hate him. Well, not him personally, but what he and his kind symbolised.

Disinterested ex-hospital or student radio chancers don't understand the value of what they've got when they are given time during the day to broadcast to people on the radio. They have no obvious skills in any other direction, they aren't anywhere near good enough for national radio, they are too parochial or too old for the noisy young commercial sector, so here they drift, on BBC local radio, like castaways on a dull raft of their own stagnant disinterest, playing records they don't care about, talking to people they don't care about, and broadcasting to an audience that they don't care about. I never ever forgot this hellish encounter.

Having been on the receiving end, I decided that it would be an idea to only have guests on my show who I had, at the very least, some passing interest in talking to. And after the John Pilger nightmare experience I thought it best to avoid anybody I was too big a fan of. Suzanne was very understanding of this selection process. She also avoided booking the kind of guests who were too obviously 'doing the rounds', but if there was one who she thought I might get something out of she'd always manage to persuade me. Unbelievably there are still some producers who don't consult presenters about booking policy. Their base objective is to simply make sure all the slots are filled, regardless of who it is. Any warm body with something to talk about is booked.

One of my first guests on the *Mixed Grill* was the talented Irish actor Ciaran Hinds. Thankfully, he wasn't on the PR treadmill. He just happened to be appearing in Sam Shepherd's *Simpatico* at the Royal Court, which had been spotted by Suzanne and Bernie. So they managed to talk his agent into letting him pop in and chat about it ... He didn't strike me as an obvious booking, but it would be a chance to talk about Shepherd or his previous work with Peter Hall and Sam Mendes. The softly spoken Hinds talked amiably about his life in the theatre. As I looked round at the control booth window, Suzanne and Bernie were stood, transfixed and staring through the glass.

I looked at their liquid eyes and followed their unbroken gaze to the absurdly handsome Hinds. At which point I fully understood the real reason that he'd been booked. And so it was that every few shows I found myself chatting to somebody 'for the ladies'.

Live music was another regular feature of the show. The basement studio of GLR was a large open space containing just a few partition boards and scattered chairs. The window to the control room was set into one wall, and just below this were rows of sockets, which enabled the engineers to wire the whole room for sound. It was big enough to accommodate pretty much any band, so record companies welcomed the opportunity for exposure whenever any of their young charges were in town, to get them into a studio plugging the latest album and tour. For some reason the basement wasn't completely soundproofed, so as you were on air in the middle of a link the band would quite often launch into the soundcheck, causing you to raise your voice slightly before hurriedly going to a record. The usual drill was, at about twenty to one, there would be a live track from the basement. Then you'd play something from the latest album before they played their final live track.

It was unbelievably exciting to have a live band on every week. My first live guests were The Sneaker Pimps, who I had first heard earlier that year on Gary Crowley's show when he played their début single 'Tesko Suicide'. On top of the CD players there was a very old black-and-white video monitor, which was wired into a CCTV camera in the downstairs studio. As the bands played I would avidly watch the fuzzy screen, the camera eerily locked into one static position, the blurred figures ever so slightly tilted from the vertical. It was a niche TV channel with a demographic of one.

On rare occasions a live session in the studio wasn't possible, due to lack of an available engineer or a booking conflict. When this occurred, artists would play acoustically in the studio right in front of me. We had four microphones in the room, so could loosely accommodate one vocal and two guitars. To give these performances a little more ambience I was allowed to use the echo fader. Ah, the echo fader. Surely the most overused gadget in my presenting armoury. At the slightest excuse I would make my voice sound like I was speaking from the nave of St Paul's Cathedral. If anything even vaguely spooky was mentioned, I was in with the echo chamber. For those forced to work with me it must have been tiresome beyond measure.

The only time it kind of worked was when we had a visit in the studio from our twenty-twenty travel lady Sally Boseman. I'd been bantering on air with her for some weeks and when she was in the building catching up with everybody I insisted that she come on air. Having her there I proposed that we did live 'dub reggae' travel. I played a heavy backing track by Augustus Pablo while Sally went through her bulletin as usual, but I brought her in and out, her voice echoing, and added the occasional 'a riddly diddly bong' myself. I wasn't aware of how much I overused the echo fader until the GLR studios were dismantled in 1999 and Jo Tyler presented me with it, having removed it herself from the control desk. It sits in a cabinet in my front room to this day.

It was when performers were in the studio with me, armed with just a guitar and maybe some rudimentary percussion, that I was most moved. I sat transfixed while Nanci Griffith and Christy Moore sang the most heart-stoppingly lovely songs. All six of The Barenaked Ladies stood in a semicircle around a single microphone and delivered an amazing version of their single 'One Week'. But the most amazing musical experience I had in a studio was with the singing ensemble Black Umfolosi from Zimbabwe. The English of their leader was sketchy at best but between us we managed to discuss their history and plug that night's show. Then the seven of them stood up and began to sing. But to be accurate 'sing' is too inadequate a word for what they did …

I am not a religious man. The fact that people don't realise that the leaders of our dimwit ancestors had to come up with an explanation for everything, and so invented God and religion as a mechanism for keeping control, fuels my rage daily. I'm spiritual in as much as I like going somewhere quiet and pretty once in a while and taking a moment. But as I listened in the studio that day, I started to think that I actually might have backed the wrong horse. These men sang and danced three feet in front of me and the pure simple beauty of the sound they created made me spontaneously weep with joy.

My briefly bamboozled thoughts got back on track and I saw these men for what they really were, a testament to the maligned brilliance and creativity of humanity. That seven people could get together and create something like that was truly amazing to me. That day as I drove home I realised that the only good things about religion have been its contributions to art, music and architecture. Oh, and lest we forget, some of the hats are really funny.

Live music provided a nice raucous end to the show. If you timed it right, your last moment was often the final ringing chords of the band playing. More often than not, and for safety's sake, it was deemed prudent to finish shows with a record, so you weren't late going to the midday news show, *London Live*. By the end of my short Friday residency at GLR, I was a control desk driving machine, whacking the faders up and down with abandon while burning my own carts with idents and jingles, seconds before shows.

My first-ever celebrity ident was nabbed for me by Suzanne one weekend. Jarvis Cocker was standing in for Gary Crowley, and Suzanne was producing. I phoned her while he was on air and asked if he might consider doing one. The next Friday I slid the cartridge into the player and listened.

'Hi, I'm Jarvis Cocker the lead singer with the group Pulp and I'd just like you to know that you're listening to Phill Jupitus and he gives you twice the fat and half the taste.'

Such nuggets were ideal when kicking off a show or playing segues. I quickly realised that I could line up three of these carts to use in quick succession and often did. At the same time, I was cognisant of the fact that I didn't want to end up going down the wacky comedy clip route like former Radio 1 jock Adrian Juste. To quote Danny Baker, 'More is less.'

My Friday morning run finished, and I was transferred back to the GLR subs bench where I would be called on at any time to deputise for sick or vacationing colleagues. I was peppered throughout the week, rarely missing out on a bit of hot radio action. I did a few Sunday nights for

Bob Mills. Late night was fantastic because that was all your own music, no playlist. When Bob took a lengthy family holiday I had a three-week run. One of these shows I dedicated entirely to the work of Elvis Costello. Three hours of rarities, hits, live tracks, session tracks and cover versions.

That night I was in the hands of the wonderful Ray Paul. Ray had an insanely laid-back laissez-faire attitude to production, which I responded to. Somehow Ray managed to get me ten minutes on the phone with Costello in the middle of the show. When I wheeled round to him, my face alive with joy and asked him how the hell he had managed this feat, he simply smiled and shrugged. I know many other producers who wouldn't have even tried, but Ray was like a duck. The busy part was all beneath the surface.

There was one producer at GLR, however, who kept it all on the surface, and would help me completely change my attitude to making radio shows. His name was Phil Wilding …

Monkey Music

'Theme from *The Monkees*' – Rampage
'Mickey's Monkey' – Smokey Robinson and The
    Miracles
'Monkey Man' – Toots and The Maytals
'Run Red Run' – The Coasters
'Brass Monkey' – Beastie Boys
'The Monkey Time' – Major Lance
'The Higher the Monkey Climbs' – Justin Hinds and The
    Dominoes

'Monkey to Man' – Elvis Costello and The Imposters
'Monkey Wrench' – Foo Fighters
'The Monkey Speaks His Mind' – Dave Bartholemew

Chapter 6

Equally Cursed and Blessed

As the weekend earlies producer, Philip Wilding was the lucky soul charged with being the power behind the throne on my GLR Saturday morning show.

The vacancy that led to me being offered Saturday mornings was created by the departure of Fi Glover and Gideon Coe's *Pile of Cack Show*. Their excellent performance on breakfast had inspired management to give their two rising stars more of a free rein. So the Saturday morning slot gave them the chance to try a more overtly entertainment based show. The fact that they would be doing this in addition to their weekday breakfast show didn't really seem to be taken into consideration. Quite often, the decisions made at GLR seemed a little over-dependent on the goodwill of their dedicated staff. Anybody with an ounce of sense could see that this kind of workload would burn anybody out, and indeed the Saturday show proved to be a bridge too far, and Glover ended up leaving both it and GLR.

My plan for Saturday mornings was quite simple. Keep the music good and varied, keep the guests coming, and try to get a live band in whenever the budget allowed for it. I wasn't looking to reinvent the wheel. My rule of thumb was to make the kind of radio that once again I would be happy to listen to. I had always responded to the simpler formats as a listener, and so that's what I'd be doing on Saturdays. This suited Phil Wilding down to the ground as well. As the weekend morning producer he also had to be in for Jackie Clune's eight till ten slot just before mine, then when I came off air he played out GLR's pick-of-the-week-style show, *GLRs Greatest Hits*.

This being a time before email had entered our lives, I would call Phil periodically through the week to see if anything interesting had surfaced. Also working at GLR was one of my oldest friends, Jo Tyler. Jo had previously worked for Australian station Triple J and was now making radio at GLR. Getting guests to come out on a Saturday morning was always more difficult than booking the midweek programmes. The focus was to try and get some good solid well-known names in to close the show, while I'd make sure that I always had a mate in with me to keep me company for the three hours. John Mann, Andre Vincent and Mark Steel were the frontrunners for this gig, and they'd always turn up with a stack of papers and a few CDs and ideas for phone-ins.

Phil was a regular and prominent part of the editorial team backstage. I had first encountered him while doing the *Mixed Grill*, when his frequent barbed comments and his broad South Wales valley twang caught my ear in the office. On occasion he would be a contributor to the Friday show when the station's semi-resident architectural guru Maxwell Hutchinson would dispatch him along with an unfeasibly large mobile telephone to the exterior of a building due for discussion that morning. Max would launch into a lengthy and florid reverie about, say, the beautiful gothic exterior of the Natural History Museum, then we'd go across to the feisty Wilding who, in a howling gale and against the din of the passing lorries, would give his own impressions of what we had just heard described. You might think that a posh bloke talking about a building followed by a Welsh bloke describing the self-same structure is hardly the stuff of solid gold radio, but it worked beautifully. Hutchings was all historical facts and architectural context while Phil would paint a contrastingly vivid picture of a living, breathing London landmark.

This was one of Wilding's strengths. He never allowed himself to be anchored into office and studio life as so many of his peers seemed to prefer. As a trained journalist he was more than happy to go on outside broadcasts as a roving reporter, or help out when the news team needed somebody interviewed for a story. He was even coaxed into doing match reports for GLR Sport on a Saturday afternoon. That he came to be my producer when I was given the Saturday morning ten till one slot was just the icing on the cake. He was less a mere mortal and more a human Swiss Army knife.

After I had broadcast my final *Mixed Grill*, I did some deputising on nearly every other daytime slot. This was a great learning experience for me as I got the chance to work with just about every producer in the place. Now this was the kind of thing that provided a much better insight for exactly what it is that you need from your producer. The relationship between producer and presenter is skewed from the off. The pair of you are co-dependent, you do what your producer says, but they are also working for you. Each of you thinks that you are the one who is in charge, but you'd both be wrong. The relationship has to be symbiotic. All of the best producer/presenter duos I encountered were always quite obviously very close partnerships. Peel and Walters, Wogan and Pauly, Mark and Lard.

Radio producers are like snowflakes. No two are the same, and they are damp and cold to the touch. While some are happy to just hand you a sheaf of notes half an hour before you go on air and let you get on with it, others need to sit you down at length and go through each and every tiny detail of the show. When you are sitting in a room with one of these anal retentives, as they bombard you with questions about the approaching broadcast, what little confidence you had diminishes rapidly. Having said that, the languid, easy-going, 'Here you go mate, you're on in five!' dismissiveness of others can have you wondering if they just can't be bothered. In my experience, somewhere between the two was always my preference. I liked to have the feeling that the producer was at least engaged with the forthcoming show, but sussed enough to let me alone once I was on air. In the event that I started to stray or become self-indulgent, it was their job to put me back on track. In short my ideal producer was an avuncular, low-energy disciplinarian with a good sense of humour. If that reads to you like a lonely-hearts advert, then I'm not at all surprised. Finding a good producer is like finding your mate. Only in my experience there is slightly more dancing involved with finding a good producer.

During a show, some producers want to know what music you are going to play in advance, so they can do the music logging while others leave that all up to you. I think that to this day I'm fairly sure that I still owe Ray Paul a couple of logging sheets from some Bob Mills covering I did in 1997. The more 'hands-on' people were in your headphones on the talkback button all the time. I personally found having another voice in my headphones quite distracting. There was often a situation where I would ask my guest a question, and as I was listening to their reply, a loud voice would suddenly burst into my head, 'GOOD, NOW ASK HIM WHY HE ENDED UP DOING THAT WITH THE GOAT?' So while I was vainly struggling to gauge my counter-response, I was instead trying, and failing, to listen to two voices at the same time. On dozens of occasions, bemused interviewees must have seen my interested and attentive expression suddenly shift to one of complete distraction and then finally mild constipation.

As I had only been presenting radio for less than a year at this point, I was of the opinion that everybody in the room knew more than me. I would never complain if a producer was doing something that I disliked, because at the end of the day I was just the temp. I felt duty-bound to fit in with the working practices of others. What I didn't know at the time was that I was often working for people who hadn't produced a show themselves, and they were being tried out on me. This made for some interesting afternoons. Me thinking that they were in charge, while they were in fact making it up as they went along. Good times …

The entertainment radio producer walks a constant tightrope. At one end is a petulant, demanding, fragile egomaniac in constant need of reassurance for their actions. This is the presenter. At the other end is a collection of petulant, demanding, fragile egomaniacs constantly demanding justification for your actions. This

is the station's management hierarchy. The producer
has to shuttle back and forth, ministering to the varied
needs of both ends of his or her rope, while simultaneously juggling ideas, riding the unicycle of their chaotic
personal life, and all of this over a threadbare net of
dwindling self-confidence. Now I know this is a crappy if
extended metaphor, but it is as close as I can get to how I
always viewed the producer's paltry lot.

By and large, producers are a good deal smarter than most
presenters. But they have to be prepared to make it look like
it's actually the other way round. They have to take their own
ideas for items or interesting guests and great new music,
and then give them over to someone who at the end of the
day has a pleasant-sounding voice which appeals to women
aged 25–40 in the C2 demographic and who gets paid more
than they do. When a presenter does a good show the head
of the station comes in and thanks them, but if they ever
fuck up the producer is the one who gets bollocked. Another
thing that must really rub a huge number of hard-working
people up the wrong way is radio management's insistence
on referring to their presenting staff as 'the talent'. I think
that this is why a lot of radio producers don't do it for long,
and coincidentally why we should be grateful that there
are such stringent gun control laws in the UK.

I grew to admire Phil Wilding quite quickly in the
early days at GLR. His ready, scurrilous wit and take-
no-prisoners attitude wasn't to everybody's taste. But he
was funnier than most stand-ups I knew, he liked a drink
and he had lived a life and a half before finding himself in
Marylebone High Street. He had produced Mark Lamarr
on Sunday mornings, and understood exactly what it was
that made these kind of weekend shows run. Having also

done time with Danny Baker he knew how to 'feed the beast'. Mark and Dan needed no coaxing when it came to their choice of music, so he developed a keen sense of judgement when it came to picking out callers for the phone-in elements of their shows. Once a good idea surfaced on air, no matter how fleeting, it was Wilding's job to get it up on its feet and keep it going, and he was a master of this. So the thought of teaming up with him for Saturday mornings was an exciting one.

It's worth mentioning here that it wasn't just my eye that Phil caught while he was working at GLR. Charlie Higson and Paul Whitehouse were regular guests on the station and had therefore met Phil on a number of occasions. Whitehouse, being Welsh himself, got on with Wilding famously. So famously in fact, that alongside *Fast Show* writer Dave Cummings he developed a character for the show based on Phil. Those of you with long memories, or indeed *Fast Show* DVD box sets, may recall sketches featuring Whitehouse playing a long-haired, bespectacled, laconic Welsh sound engineer. That's Phil, that is …

A delightful side effect of taking the job at GLR was that it revitalised my love of music, which had become jaded by the time I had left Go! Discs. My discovery of international bands like The Wannadies and Man or Astroman along with domestic movers and shakers like Elastica and Blur slowly rekindled my passion. Not to mention the brilliant CD reissues put out by labels like Ace and Trojan. Friday evenings spent at Wendy May's Locomotion at the Town and Country Club in Kentish Town meant that I was spending money buying old soul reissues after hearing Wendy spinning them.

Now, working in radio I was getting new releases sent to me in the post. Much as getting a record in the post might seem fairly mundane, to me it was an industry affirmation of my new career as a deejay. I'm fairly sure that the first record I was sent by a record plugger was by Sleeper, but at the time that didn't matter to me. The important thing was seeing my name in marker pen on a cardboard envelope. I was on a mailing list! I was being sent free music! If I had gone back in time and confronted my fourteen-year-old self and told him that one day he'd be getting free music in the post, he'd have probably burst into tears and kicked me in the knackers.

The Saturday Morning Show on GLR was perfect for me. Myself and Phil Wilding swiftly developed a rapport. I knew that, no matter how outlandish an idea, he would rise to the challenge, and he knew exactly what kind of items would work best on the show. Upstairs editorial interference was kept to a minimum, and the listeners got it. As I was gigging the night before, I'd always arrive on minimal sleep, but the adrenaline of going on air and playing music was a better eye opener than a double espresso. During the week I was venturing into speciality record shops once more, and discovering new bands on an almost daily basis. I don't need to remind you that in a pre-MySpace world this required a fair bit of legwork.

Operating under management radar is always easier at weekends. Your superiors rarely listen to what you are doing, as they have their own lives to live. And having a slot between ten and one on a Saturday, you can be fairly confident that while you were doing your humorous phone-in about farmyard animal attacks your lords and masters were more than likely wandering the aisles of Waitrose. This imagined freedom enabled a fair bit of what people are wont to call 'blue sky thinking', but what myself and Phil just thought of as 'big ideas'.

'Big idea' shows were usually built around a single theme. The first time this happened was when, on a whim, the whole three hours comprised people's favourite cover versions. The week before, I had probably played a couple of fun covers and then said, 'I tell you what, next week, all cover versions.'

I'd glance through the glass to see Wilding squinting with his head tilted to one side, before holding both thumbs aloft in affirmation. A more organised station these days would do some kind of online vote, which would then enable them to produce the show as a kind of 'chart countdown' to 'the greatest covers of all time'. This sort of thing is frankly bollocks. That would have been far too grown up for us, not to mention far too democratic. I would put the show together myself at home by trawling through the racks and boxes, Phil would go through his own collection and the record library, and we'd throw the thing open to the punters as well. And with about an hour of *ad hoc* preparation we had a show.

This first tentative step towards a themed show would lead us to grander schemes. An article in *Media Guardian* accused a section of the shows at GLR of being 'too laddy'. I didn't have to look around to know that I was one of those shows. Our didactic and rather petulant response to this scurrilous accusation was to have an 'all lady' show featuring all female guests, all female callers and all female music. Again, this was another idea that was turned round in a week. I loved the immediacy of working at GLR. If a show on a national station wanted to do something like that, the sequence of events to make it happen would be mind numbing.

The presenter would have an on-air thought about doing a show, say all about dogs. Then the production team would be assembled to discuss 'ideas' for the all-dog show. These ideas would be typed up and shown to the senior editor. The senior editor would hum and hurr and say, 'We can't do a whole show about dogs because that would be stupid. Why don't we just have a few doggy elements to the show?' The cowering producer, rather than defending the idea, would agree wholeheartedly with their boss. Then they would go back to their presenter and moan about the boss and say that if they did do it they'd have to do the watered-down version. Then the show would be trailed for two weeks, they'd have a top ten dogs countdown, and do some funny schtick about interviewing a dog, using sound effects, and it would be crap.

Our *pièce de résistance* of themed shows came about from an innocuous bit of on-air banter. I had, without realising it, played 'One Monkey Don't Stop No Show' by Joe Tex and 'Monkey Man' by The Specials back to back. This led to a discussion about how many songs there were with 'monkey' in the title, or indeed about monkeys. The listeners, as usual, took the ball and ran with it, and within an hour I had a list of fifty such records. As I looked down, I realised that what I was holding in my hand was a show. I turned to Wilding, got the thumbs up and we were off and running. We had just a week to prepare the greatest simian-based radio broadcast London had ever seen.

During the week, I scoured every single disc in my collection for the word 'monkey'. By the time I got to Friday I had located thirty-six such tracks. Mind you, my collection was a lot smaller twelve years ago. Without even asking, Wilding was provided with a list from Laurence in the record library of their own contribution, and even people who didn't work on the show brought stuff in. By the time we had gathered everything together we had enough songs for six hours of broadcasting. It was staggering. The selection of guests was also tilted towards primates. Wilding phoned me in a state of some excitement to inform me that he had managed to snag us the head of the ape house from London Zoo. He had also found a very nice man called Peter Elliot. I cooed appreciatively about the man from the Monkey House, but confessed to not knowing anything about Elliot. 'He was the "primate choreographer" on *Greystoke*, you fool!'

The immediacy of the medium was seductive. But not everything got a green light. We were offered Manchester punk legends Buzzcocks for a live session. This would be something of a coup, not to mention right up the street of our listeners. But word came back that we didn't have resources in the budget for an engineer. BBC sessions always sound so tight because the engineers know exactly what's what in the studio and they are used to working fast because they work a nine to five. But anybody in a band will tell you that most of the best work in their own studios is done after midnight. One of the reasons The Clash never did a full BBC session was their slower than slow work ethic in the studio. Cup of tea, skin up, have a think about what you're doing, then just as they pick up their guitars the studio engineer is on his way home and asking them to turn out the lights when they leave.

The lack of money to get Buzzcocks on the show did rankle with me somewhat. So I asked Phil to phone the engineer directly and ask how much he'd want cash in hand to come down and do the gig for us. An odd look crossed Wilding's face. It may have been indigestion for all I know, but this may have been the first time he'd encountered a presenter sticking his hand in his own pocket to make a show happen. Having said that, I was on a decent whack as a stand-up, and so I was in the fortunate position of having the money. Most of my colleagues in radio were on sub Civil Service wages. As it turned out, I didn't have to spend anything, as Phil pointedly told management that I had offered to pay for an engineer myself, and this shamed them into opening the coffers.

Saturdays at GLR were the perfect side dish to life as a stand-up comedian. In the autumn of 1996 three GLR deejays, Mark Lamarr, Sean Hughes and myself, appeared on a new comedy quiz series on BBC2 called *Never Mind the Buzzcocks*. This ramshackle collision of humorous pop trivia and low-grade spite became a firm fixture in the BBC schedule and introduced me to another side of the world of pop music. GLR were delighted: having two current and one former deejay on such a high-profile show could only do good for the listening figures.

This didn't feel like a job to me. Playing records, drinking bad coffee and chatting with friends was something that we all did as kids. For many of us, pop music was our first inkling of the possibilities of a wider world. All over the country people formed bands when they first heard The Clash and The Sex Pistols. But it's often forgotten that these bands also inspired people to become artists, or designers or actors or poets. Listening to bands like The Members and The Specials first planted the seed in me that my life could take a different direction. For years

I thought that by not doing A levels or going on to study at university I had denied myself an education. But looking back, I can see that I was slowly educating myself anyway. And this piecemeal enlightenment had finally managed to get me a job which as a child I had dreamed of having.

Working weekend early shifts at GLR was taking its toll on Phil Wilding, and he approached management to ask if he could have one weekend off every six weeks. When they refused to entertain this he gave in his notice, and the following Saturday told me that these would be our last shows together. The loss of Wilding was quite a blow. We had got into an easy rhythm on the shows, our contrasting styles dovetailing perfectly in the ramshackle weekend format. We seemed to bring out the best of each other's qualities.

On one occasion, I persuaded Wilding to make an on-air cameo. I had been talking to the late Michael Sheard, who was known to some listeners as the fearsome Mr Bronson from *Grange Hill*, but was also beloved by sci-fi geeks as Admiral Ozzell from *The Empire Strikes Back*. He talked at length about how the whole *Star Wars* convention circuit had given him a new lease of life as well as a tidy revenue stream. As an actor he was kept busy enough on the British stage, but as a *Star Wars* cast member he got to travel the world signing autographs and having his photo taken alongside tubby asthmatics with bad skin.

Through gentle cajoling we persuaded him to re-enact his two key scenes from *Empire*, and we all gathered round the script that I had brought in. As he uttered the words we had all heard him say so often before on our well-worn VHS copies of the film, we all giggled like little children. However, the big moment came from my delib-erate casting of Phil as Darth Vader. He leaned even more heavily into his rich valley accent than usual, and the control booth dissolved into hysterics.

Phil's final show as producer featured a live session from Essex power pop trio The Sweeney. Little did he know that moves were afoot behind the scenes to give him a slightly unconventional send-off. The show trundled on as usual, and then in the final hour we all decamped into the basement studio to enjoy the live band. They sped through an incandescent version of their brilliant single 'Why', but then at the end of it they shifted gear into the shuffling grandeur of the Tom Jones epic, 'It's Not Unusual'. As they played, the spirit of the moment caught me and I moved the lead microphone across the room before announcing, 'Ladies and gentlemen, on lead vocals please welcome … *Phil Wilding*!' He only had time for his eyes to widen briefly before he was forced to launch into a definitive if halting version of the *de facto* Welsh national anthem. He left us wanting more, but not more singing.

I carried on with the Saturday show for a few more months, but the success of *Never Mind the Buzzcocks* and the desire to play the Edinburgh Fringe as well as trying a UK tour meant that carrying on at GLR would eventually start to get in the way. I reluctantly agreed to give up my Saturday slot. My last show featured a large gathering of all my friends, and as a guest we had former Clash front man Joe Strummer. It was a beautifully sedate way to go out. Joe graciously answered questions from the mob of comedians and deejays in the room, and when presented with Ronnie Golden's acoustic guitar he played a gentle buskers version of Junco Partner. Afterwards we all sat in the pub. Joe was with his partner and their kids and chatted along with us before checking his watch. 'Right, we'd better be going now.'

I wondered where exactly it was that he was off to. What is it that constitutes a family day out when your dad used to be the spokesman of a generation? So I asked him.

'We're taking the kids to see *Cats*.'

As ever with GLR, once they had you on speed dial you never really left, and from time to time I was asked to come in and deputise for various absentee deejays. One particular Friday I was filling in for Pete Curran, and Ray Paul was producing and phoned me up to say that we'd been offered an exclusive interview with Ian Dury. I didn't have to be asked twice as he was one of my musical heroes. We would be going to talk with him at his home in Hampstead and would be doing the whole two hours about him and his life and career as well as his battle with cancer with which he had been recently diagnosed.

The hour I spent in his company had an almost dream-like quality. His face was fuller than I remembered, a result of the steroids he had been taking as part of his treatment. We set up our microphones in his home studio and drank steaming mugs of tea and chatted about everything. His grace and good humour at such a difficult time was almost too much to take in. Every moment in his presence was like being in a big bath of loveliness. I never had another interview like it and I dare say I never will. The interview went so well that we put it out almost uncut. It was then that I realised an uncomfortable truth about what I was doing. You can't always plan great radio; sometimes it just falls in your lap. You just have to be on air at the right time.

'If it ain't broke, don't fix it' is a phrase that seems to carry very little weight with OFCOM and the BBC. Despite being a firm favourite with listeners, in 1999 GLR was put in the frame for a total revamp. Out would go daytime music in favour of a much more talk-based format. The audience went spare. They started a website, petitions, had meetings at Conway Hall, bombarded BBC management with letters of complaint and generally got quite cross. Their rage was given full vent on 17 September when Jane Mote, head of BBC Regional and Local Programmes, went on to the Robert Elms show to discuss the changes. Dozens of increasingly irate callers kept coming and coming and none of them, not one, was in favour of the BBC plan. As enjoyable as it was hearing an executive squirm under pressure, the *schadenfreude* was short lived as the restructuring was a *fait accompli*. Under the terms of its remit GLR wasn't really doing its job as a local radio station. Oh, sure, it was playing lots of great music and it was a laugh, but it wasn't addressing a huge chunk of its potential audience, and so the curtain fell on a great radio station.

At this time I was far too busy with my stand-up and various television gigs to do too much for GLR. Anyway, I was naturally enough a bit suspicious of the new regime. Like the listeners, I preferred GLR the way it was, and was no fan of talk radio. I had never really understood the appeal of listening to people bickering as a form of entertainment. I mean, if it was so appealing then why weren't there audience sections at every post office counter in the country filled to capacity on pension day? What I had heard of talk radio seemed to thrive on the 'presenter' starting the 'show' by saying something contentious and then sparring with a few irate callers, who themselves would cause others to call in and take issue, and before you know it you've filled an hour of airtime with what was, at the end of the day, a fake argument. Not my kind of thing at all, but popular with millions of listeners all over the world.

Despite my misgivings the new controller of the soon-to-be-defunct GLR, Dave Robey, invited me in for a coffee and managed to cajole me into doing a two-hour Friday afternoon show. I was given free rein with my choice of music and guests, and would be looked after by Jo Tyler who had been working with me since I first started on radio. This meant that she knew exactly what kind of guests to book for the show. It seemed to be a good deal to me. I got a couple of hundred quid, I would be in town for whatever gigs I had lined up on the Friday and I was free of any managerial interference. And just like that, I was back on air to the people of London once more. Well, I say the people of London. GLR had an audience somewhere between 350,000 and half a million on a good day. So if you say as a ballpark figure London and its environs constitute about 8 million, then over 7½ million people couldn't really give a toss if I was on air or not …

As part of the relaunch of BBC London, the Marylebone High Street studios were being refitted for use as the new headquarters of the Corporation's London news operations for both radio and television. So in the meantime the radio station had a temporary move to Bush House, at the eastern end of the Strand, the home of the BBC World Service. To me, Bush House is even more impressive than Broadcasting House itself. Its huge arched doors and the never-ending procession of broadcasters from all over the globe, making programmes for their home countries, seemed to perfectly embody the words of the BBC's motto 'Nation Shall Speak Peace Unto Nation'.

For those of you who don't know it, the BBC World Service is the global arm of our own dear Corporation. Broadcasting on various wavelengths and frequencies and at varying times, it is like a last sigh of the old British Empire. The fact that you could be in the middle of Nome, or Buenos Aires, or Lusaka, and if you had a radio and some patience, would be able to pick up a plummy English voice bringing you the news, every hour on the hour, always tickled me. I was always a great admirer of the World Service, even if I wasn't a listener. The idea of your words being relayed around the globe for those who wanted to listen still appealed to my inner child. Whenever I was in America I would always fruitlessly search for it by tuning up and down the dial on my walkman radio, but to no avail. The constantly shifting frequencies of the service were not for the faint hearted. You needed patience and an accurate radio schedule to locate it, something I could never be bothered to get together when I was supposed to be relaxing. Most of you who listen to Radio 4 and leave your sets on at night will catch the four or so hours of the World Service which is broadcast just after Radio 4 has played 'Sailing By' and given out the last shipping forecast of the day.

Those few months driving to Bush House would be my last at GLR or BBC London or Radio London. To be honest, I'm not exactly sure what the station was called towards the end. The team were crammed shoulder to shoulder into various spare offices scattered around the West Wing of Bush House, while the studios were a five-minute walk and a ride in a lift away in the East Wing. This was a real change for broadcasters who had been so accustomed to being right next door to their producers. While you were on air people were always about to lend a hand and you were no more than forty feet from your own office. Meanwhile at Bush House if you forgot a book or a record, because you left it in the office, it would be ten minutes before you could get hold of it.

I did the Friday afternoon show for a few months but was growing bored. The station was going in a new direction and I wasn't. I loved being on air, and the shows were fun, but I felt like I was doing it for its own sake. Leaving GLR happened pretty much the same way as when I started there, by accident. One Friday I just decided not to do it any more. I don't think I even said anything on air about my departure. I drove out of the Bush House car park for the last time, phoned them up on the Monday and that was it. Me and deejaying were done.

Until, that is, I got that call from Addison.

Wilding's Things

'Girls, Girls, Girls' – Mötley Crüe
'Thousand Dollar Wedding' – Gram Parsons
'The Closer' – Marah
'The Trees' – Rush
'My Wife's Nightie' – Lord Kitchener
'Motorcycle Emptiness' – Manic Street Preachers
'International Velvet' – Catatonia
'The Man Don't Give a Fuck' – Super Furry Animals
'Passenger 24' – Melissa McClelland
'It's Not Unusual' – Tom Jones

Now We Are Six

Having been made an offer to do something genuinely new and different in radio, to launch the breakfast show on a brand new digital station, how could I possibly turn it down?

I now had to give some serious thought to the overall shape of the show but more crucially the people I wanted to help make the pipedream a reality. It would be important to assemble a team that I trusted enough as radio professionals, but who were also just daft enough to come along for the ride. I had two names from my broadcasting past, and I intended to ask both of them. With the best will in the world I had no desire to be lumbered with the BBC's choice of producer.

The best kind of relationship between a presenter and producer is a symbiotic one. With it being a new station, chances are that I'd be given some young careerist hot shot constantly shooting random feature and guest ideas at me. If that happened, then in the fullness of time I would probably end up taking hostages before shooting my way out of the place. But by the same token I didn't want somebody on the back foot who would constantly be asking my approval of what was needed for the show. To make the thing work I would need to be around a team who would both understand me and more importantly know when to disregard my inevitable bullshit. So I quickly made two very important phone calls.

Jo Tyler was squirrelled away on the fifth floor of Western House, already in the employ of Auntie Beeb, archiving thousands of hours of old session tapes. James Brown, The Beatles, The Who ... she had unfettered access to an Aladdin's cave of musical history. When I phoned her with the exciting news about my job offer she was completely unsurprised, which did strike me as rather odd. A little later I went up to her office, plonked myself down in a chair and told her all about the corner office meeting with Big Jim and Lesley and their 'secret' job offer. She nodded, smiling, and turned back to the stack of boxed quarter-inch tape reels in front of her. Again she seemed less than impressed with my bombshell, which did start to rankle slightly. Seemingly unable to make any impression, I decided to cut my losses and change subject. 'So what have you been up to in here then?'

'Oh, you know, archiving these old recordings and stuff. We've also been working on the new digital station for Radio 2 ... Funny enough we had a meeting about possible presenters last month.' She paused and glanced up at me over her glasses. 'Your name came up ...'

It then became glaringly apparent that the very reason I was called in to see Jim Moir was the woman sat in front of me. I hugged her like a slightly embarrassed bear.

Decision-making at the BBC, like most corporations, is usually done on a committee basis. Firstly, a number of staff members are gathered together in a stuffy little office and, over the course of what usually turns out to be a very lengthy conversation, various decisions and ideas slowly emerge. These gems are then written down and taken forward to yet another committee with slightly fewer but more senior figures at it, and so this process repeats itself. Eventually the 'refined' idea reaches someone senior enough and it gets a final yes or no. Then at this stage of proceedings another meeting is convened in the stuffy little office with the original group of people to discuss exactly how to implement the idea that came out of the previous meeting. I'm sure you can agree that the circle of bureaucracy is a beautiful thing.

One of the unfortunate by-products of this kind of system is that nine times out of ten anybody who comes up with an idea will lose it to somebody higher up the food chain. These amoral weasels will then gleefully take all the credit for something that is not theirs. That is the sad truth about managerial hierarchies in almost any organisation. If you really want to advance up the corporate ladder then you will have to be prepared to be a bit of a thieving twat. I dare say that if you gathered everybody who was in on the inception of 6 Music, and individually took them into a corner, at least one of them would say something like, 'Well, I was at home one night watching *Buzzcocks* and I thought, Hey! Why not Phill for breakfast?' Another might go, 'Well, I was chatting with an old mate from GLR and we were talking about your old Saturday show, and I thought, Hey! Phill Jupitus at breakfast!' And on it would go. Certain areas of BBC management have taken a lot of stick in recent years, which is unfair. Some should at least be applauded for their unwavering commitment and consistency in taking credit for other people's ideas.

Knowing that Tyler was on the ground floor at this new station gave me a real boost. She was a shrewd woman who understood the day-to-day workings of radio and the tricksy machinations of the BBC better than anybody else I knew, plus she was a mate. It would be advantageous to have somebody I could get a straight answer from if things started to go tits up. She filled me in on some of the details I hadn't got from my initial meeting with the bigwigs. Andrew Collins and Stewart Maconie were on board. Collins and Maconie were both published authors with keen minds and an exhaustive knowledge of music who would make fascinating radio presenters. Gideon Coe and Chris Hawkins were old faces from GLR and real dyed-in-the-wool radio heads, two music lovers who both had distinctive presenting styles. I was much more intrigued by these names than the clutch of celebrities I'd been told about in Jim's office. Craig Charles would be doing a funk show, Brinsley Forde was going to be presenting a specialist reggae programme at weekends. Even Suggs, the lead singer of Madness, was in the frame for a Saturday afternoon request show. On hearing this news I just stared at Jo and she closed her eyes and quietly nodded. Timekeeping wasn't really Suggs's thing, whereas Friday nights were …

Jo then went on to explain that my first order of business would be to get a team together and decide on a rough format for the show. Then in the month before opening the station would run a 'white network', which is basically having a fully functioning radio station with everybody working but not broadcasting any of it. Then when it comes to your first day you've already been running the show for a month or so. As yet I didn't have an exact start date, but I knew it would be February or March of the next year, 2002, which gave me around four months to ponder the wisdom of my decision and to find people to work with. I did have one person in mind.

Starbucks at the northern end of Wardour Street in London's Soho was quite busy that October morning. People too cheap to spend money on London offices held business meetings over poorly concocted cappuccinos. World-weary Christmas shoppers braced themselves for the horrors of Oxford Street with a quick caffeine hit. Doughy muffins disappeared bite by bite into eager mouths, washed down with rich foamy lattes. And I sat at a table waiting to ask someone to go back into the lion's den.

It is fair to say that Phil Wilding was an occasional bridge burner. When leaving employers he was known far and wide for arranging leaving parties where he would outdrink everybody present before going on to tell them a few home truths about themselves. It was usually complete carnage. Indeed the last time Phil left GLR I was invited to his farewell drinks session. Unfortunately I already had a few gigs booked in town, but worked out that between them I could nip to the pub and raise a glass, just before closing time, and still make the late show at the Comedy Store. With the unpredictability of West End traffic, my timing was a little off, and as I walked through the pub door the bell for last orders chimed. I scanned the bar and saw that only a small clutch of GLR staffers were hovering at one end of the room, all preparing to leave.

To one side, Phil Wilding was apparently amiably chatting with a young lady. I wandered over to him.

'Sorry I missed it, mate.'

His head slowly turned towards me, and eventually his red-rimmed eyes caught up with his face. At this point I noticed that his body was gently swaying, like a stalk of wheat on a summer evening.

'Wrghrfghaaarghmmmmmph … shhhhhhwaaaaaah …' was all that I heard, but as he was smiling I assumed it was something positive so I smiled back and nodded.

As I looked over his shoulder I noticed that many of those departing looked haunted, deeply troubled even. As we stepped out of the pub into the fresh night air, Fi Glover, who was marginally more sober than the rest of the bunch, stepped over to me and started to explain what had transpired over the course of the evening.

'He said some things. A few people got a bit upset and left early … but now I think he might turn on the rest.'

I nodded sagely. 'Well, they all know sometimes he can be a right b—' I began.

But before Fi could get to hear what Phil Wilding could be, I was struck with great force and sent barrelling into an enormous pile of black binbags full of God knows what, on the pavement outside the pub. In retrospect it's probably a good job that they were there, as the next stop would have been the tarmac and buzzing traffic of Marylebone High Street. As I struggled to regain my composure in the glare of the sodium street lighting and the dozen or so startled onlookers, I looked down and in amongst the crumpled glossy sacks, my flailing legs and the general chaos was the unmistakable haircut of Phil Wilding. He looked up at me from the floor, bloodshot eyes rolling, winked and said, 'Ha-hah!'

It was a slightly shorter but still stylishly unruly mop atop a much more sober head that came wandering into Starbucks.

'Alright fella!' he grinned in his charismatic valley brogue. It was some time since I had last seen Philip, but he seemed to be thriving. Despite an externally laissez-faire demeanour, here was a man with a rigorous work ethic. He had been working as a freelance journalist and radio producer since leaving GLR in a cloud of D&G, tears and recriminations a few years previously. He filled me in on his intervening years. A spell working with 'the Dans' (Danny Baker and Danny Kelly) on TalkSport, stints with Chris Evans and producing content for Virgin Atlantic's entertainment channels, as well as occasional freelance writing for *The Times*, *Classic Rock* and others. Like I said, work ethic.

As a producer he possessed a rare gift. Most of the radio producers I knew somehow seemed to operate in isolation. By this I mean that they had an awareness of what was required of them by the show and by management. They would come up with ideas, and features and guests that would work very nicely for the show. But they could do all this while hardly communicating with their presenters. Wilding knew that you would ultimately get better results by finding out more about the person who was actually presenting the show. This was probably why his superiors remained wary of him throughout his career. He was never *their* boy, he was resolutely his own man, and was always very protective of presenters, but at the same time was more than willing to bollock them when they fucked up.

Years previously at GLR I had comedian Steve Bowditch on the Saturday show. He had brought in a record that he had made with some mates 'as a joke'. He said that they'd failed abysmally as a pop group so decided to try and actively court the Satanist market. This seemed eminently reasonable to me so I gave the tune a spin. It was dreadful, a swirling mess of guitars and drums and the low growling of Steve's voice. I thought it was funny. It had been on for just five seconds when I heard Wilding barking in my headphones. 'Get this off!' I looked round at him, shrugging with confusion. He came onto talkback a second time. 'Get this off *now*!'

I pulled the fader down and turned up my microphone.

'Well, I'm sorry ladies and gentlemen, apparently we aren't allowed to play certain kinds of music on this station.' And swiftly but petulantly I put on some inoffensive indie pop track.

As it began I heard the click of the talkback a third time and the Welsh admonition, 'Hey you! Don't work angry!'

It's a small example, but illustrated one of the reasons I liked working with him. He took no shit. Phil's more hands-on approach to presenters meant that he had a greater sense of what would inspire them to do better work. When there were phone-in shows at GLR he had extraordinary instincts for exactly which callers he should put on air – skills which served him brilliantly during his tenure at TalkSport with the Dannys. Wilding knew what worked on radio because he loved the medium.

I bought two absurdly large mugs of coffee that looked more like desserts, sat down opposite him and just cut to the chase, telling him as much as I knew about this new gig: a breakfast show hosted by me on a brand new network with a music policy to match, and access to the BBC music archive! How would he like to produce it? His dark eyes grew wide and he made an odd face. I wondered if he might be having the same kind of 'Peel Sessions moment' that I had experienced in Jim's office. I dare say for an individual like Wilding the notion of going back to the BBC for a third time held a kind of perverse allure. But then, I was just as prepared for him saying that he wouldn't touch the job with a bargepole.

I shrugged, gave a weak smile and added, 'I dunno, it could be fun for a couple of years!'

He looked at me and arched his eyebrows, and I could almost hear the unsaid words that his look conveyed. 'If we last that long.'

He thanked me for the call and said that he'd have to give it a bit of thought, which was understandable. As much as I love working for the BBC it is at the end of the day a corporation, and as such it operates in a very proscribed fashion. Management structures are just as constrained as those in high finance or industry. Just because the end result is a creative one, doesn't mean that the business side of it was any less ruthless. Having never worked regularly at the BBC during the week, I rarely encountered any problems with 'management' because they weren't there on Saturdays and Sundays. At my new job I would be doing the show within a two-minute stroll of the network controller's office and his number two. I'd also only be twenty yards down the corridor from the station editor and the programme controller.

At this time I really wasn't sure that Phil would agree to take the job. The look on his face as we talked about the Beeb made it clear enough that he thought he would personally be taking a big risk going back there. And he had yet to be approved by the superiors. I had done as much as I could at this point. I had two good friends who were on my side. Now I had to give serious thought to what the show would sound like.

Ironically that was the one thing that I didn't really know. As I have previously explained, I almost couldn't see the point of trying to compete when Wogan and *Today* were already out there. My blue-sky notion of a Peel-style show at breakfast time was all well and good but maybe there was a reason that nobody had done a show like that in the first place. The only concrete idea I really had was what I didn't want it to sound like. And I didn't want it to sound like any of the existing shows available. Local BBC was too entrenched, Radio 1 was too chart-based, and commercial radio was too ... well ... *commercial*.

In terms of style and content our closest rival was Christian O'Connell on XFM breakfast. He was sharp, funny and had a good, consistent show. But on the downside he had to play about fifteen to twenty minutes of adverts every hour, and was hamstrung by a very restrictive playlist. If we were going to nick anybody's listeners, we'd ideally want a few of his.

Speaking of playlists, I hadn't really had any kind of discussion with Lesley or Jim about my somewhat jaundiced attitude to playlist-based radio shows. In retrospect it might have been wise to ask if somewhere in my contract it could be stated that a guaranteed percentage of the show's music was free choice. I am stunned that modern radio is still so reliant on computer-selected, pre-programmed playlists. I can understand the appeal of this on a chart-based radio station, but what was the point of hiring somebody with an extensive knowledge of music as well as a none-too-shabby record and CD collection and then not let them use either facility? This fundamental difference between how I saw the show and how management viewed it would be one of the most common sticking points for disputes during my time there. Ironically on a station that would be called 6 Music which when it started had a poster campaign that said 'We Play What We Like and Nothing Else', I would be regularly carpeted for playing too much music that I personally liked.

I had a couple of months before I would have to start working properly on the show, which were smattered with all of the usual workday distractions for the average jobbing stand-up comedian.

The freedom of life as a stand-up comedian is not to be sniffed at. You generate your own material and get to play anywhere from small arts studios right up to 2,000-seat theatres. The bigger acts are now regularly filling arenas like the O2. With the exposure I had been granted by appearing on *Never Mind the Buzzcocks* I could pretty much be guaranteed a decent audience anywhere in the UK. It was a privileged position that I wasn't really very good at taking advantage of. Having recorded a decent live stand-up video, *Quadrophobia*, I didn't see the need to repeat the process. My own lack of ambition, coupled with short-sightedness, kicked my stand-up career completely in the knackers. But on the positive side, the varied toolbox of skills that I had acquired by doing stand-up comedy over the previous seventeen years would serve me well in radio. Especially when I had to get up and do a show daily.

And there of course was perhaps the biggest lifestyle change I would have to face in taking on the job: getting up early in the morning. As a live performer, your body clock becomes skewed towards the end of the day. Your mental processes and the surge of energy and adrenalin you require are customarily let loose somewhere between eight in the evening and midnight. If you are playing the clubs that have late shows at weekends, then you can often find yourself going onstage at two in the morning. Thankfully those days were behind me and the gigs that I took were usually done and dusted by eleven. But that still meant the focus of my daily energies was the night-time. This suited my natural rhythms down to the ground. Since childhood, the late night has always been my favourite part of the day. Back then television would sedately grind to a halt at just after midnight, sometimes even later at weekends. These being the pre-video days, you would watch anything that was on TV late at night. The Open University, *The Sky at Night*, rubbish foreign cinema, the George Hamilton IV Show, I mean anything.

As a stand-up comic working in London you'd cover a great deal of ground over the course of a busy weekend. Minicabs and tubes ran you from show to show. Before I could drive, I would stay with friends in town. Once I learned to drive and was able to commute into town and ferry myself about, I'd usually get home at gone three in the morning. To shake the gigs out of myself, I'd settle down with a Jack Daniels, and watch the night's telly that had been videotaped. Ending up with a career that played to my naturally nocturnal bent was mere good fortune. After a job where one existed in noisy, crowded rooms, these quiet, solitary small-hours moments were a relief.

Presenting the breakfast show would necessitate getting up at around 4.30 in the morning, five days a week. This was around the time that I went to bed during the old stand-up days. My first taste of keeping such insane hours was when

I worked for two weeks on *The Big Breakfast* on Channel
Four. They sent a very lovely man to pick me up from home
at 3.45 a.m. every day. I'd get in the car and start reading
the day's newspapers, looking for gems to use in the news
round-up in the first hour.

This was my first experience of trying to force my owl-
like sense of humour to work before the sun came up,
and it was tough going. Your body physically rebels when
you force it to act against its natural patterns. Headaches
and sickness were common. I was going through a kind
of cold turkey from what I realised was a crippling addiction to sleep. Thankfully there were an accomplished
team of writers and producers on *The Big Breakfast*, who
more than filled in the gaps for my physiological weak-
nesses. Not to mention I was co-hosting the show with the
insanely beautiful Melanie Sykes, a warm, bright, funny
presenter and quick to learn. Also, deep down when you
know that the gig you're doing is just for a fortnight that
takes some of the pressure off.

I had to seriously consider the long-term effects of
time-shifting my life for two years. I tried to imagine what
it would be like to ply my trade at the opposite end of the
day. At home, I'd have to go to bed before the kids, which
they would doubtless find hysterical. I wasn't too keen on
disturbing the missus, but as we had a spare room next
to the bathroom it actually meant that she was about to
get some decent rest for the first time, as I snore like a
bastard. If I could stay awake on the journey in, then I
could read the papers in the car and get some notes done
for the show. Having a daily programme, I thought it
would be daft not to use the newspapers as a source of
material. I would usually start live gigs by taking a wander

through the local newspapers, which always seemed to go down well. It was a quick and fun way to kill a bit of time. I opened my ring-bound notebook and turned to a clean page. At the top of it I wrote 'breakfast radio' and underlined it. Then I wrote a number 'one', drew a circle around it and wrote 'newspaper review'. In picking up that biro and writing something on a piece of paper, I had officially started to put together the show …

Up Late

'Harlem Nocturne' – New York Ska-Jazz Ensemble
'Let's Spend the Night Together' – David Bowie
'A Rainy Night in Soho' – The Pogues
'All Night' – Sam Phillips
'Nightlife' – Kenickie
'I Want You' – Elvis Costello and The Attractions
'River Man' – Nick Drake
'Take Me Home' – Holly Cole
'Small Hours' – John Martyn
'In the Wee Small Hours of the Morning' – Frank Sinatra

8
Waiting

As the start date for the new radio station drew ever closer, I was having more and more impromptu meetings in coffee shops with Phil and Jo. The station was still sorting out its accommodations so we didn't have our own space where we could close the door and hide from management and play 'office volleyball' with a screwed-up copy of the *NME*. We had all previously worked, got hideously drunk and had arguments together before, so we just needed to clarify that we could still do the first thing. The station, which still didn't have a name yet, was slated to start broadcasting on 11 March 2002. Over the next few months we would consume more cappuccinos than the population of Milan as we regularly convened and tried to work out what we wanted to achieve with our breakfast radio show.

During one of our very first brainstorming sessions, I eagerly reached into my bag, took out my pad and read from the page that I had written on six weeks previously. 'How about a paper review?'

The two of them looked at each other, then back at me like I was some kind of idiot. At that point in time even I had to concede that I demonstrably was. With the kind of smile you would give a slow child you had just caught eating soil, Jo addressed me slowly. I think she wanted to be certain that I would properly absorb the information.

'Well, Phill, we kind of assumed that you'd be wanting to do that.'

I craned my neck and noticed that both of their lists featured the words 'newspapers' at the top. They also had a lot more things written down than me. I casually nodded and carefully slipped the pad back into my bag and tried to pretend that nothing had happened.

Jo filled us in on some of the features that had been suggested for all of the daytime shows on the network. There would be a dedicated music news service on the half hour in addition to world news bulletins, which in breakfast would happen every thirty minutes. There would be an album of the day which would have one track played out on each show. These particular long players would be chosen by the head of music at first, but eventually listeners would be encouraged to pitch in with their own suggestions. After all interactivity with the audience would be a large part of what the station would be about. There would also be one or two archive BBC session tracks put in the running order. A playlist of current music would be ironed out at a weekly meeting and classic tracks would be chosen by computer.

I had a look at this rough running order for the show to see how many tunes per show I would be able to choose for myself. I scanned the flimsy print out for the words 'presenter choice' or 'free play' and eventually located them. In a single three-hour show, these words appeared just once an hour. This was far from what I had hoped for, but I didn't want to launch into an argument with management before I'd even started doing the job. Besides, in fairness I hadn't seen what kind of 'classic' stuff the system was going to throw up for me to play. With the broad remit of the station, there could potentially be some absolute gems. The more items that cropped up on Jo's show list, the less it would seem that we would have to do. I leaned back in my chair and smiled to myself, ignoring the pounding caffeine headache that had just hit my temples.

As for the name of the network, I had been asked to email any ideas I might have to Lesley Douglas. This would surely be an absolute cakewalk. At the age of thirty-nine I had already named two children and a number of pets so a radio station should be no problem at all. Back in the old days, you would preface the name of your station with the word 'radio' so people knew what they were getting. I'm sure this was eminently reasonable at the time. If deejays in the 1960s had gone on air and said, 'You're listening to Caroline,' you might have assumed that you had tuned in to listen to a girl with a large record collection and a ship.

At the time there was a vogue for giving radio stations a punchy one-word name, which would capture the imagination and was much more easy for branding purposes. One of the first stations to beguile the listeners by just having a noun for its name was Heart, previously Heart FM. In marketing terms this was a perfect choice. The heart is synonymous with rhythm, beat, life, romance, not to mention centrality, so it worked on a number of levels. However, if you actually listen to the output of the station you don't really hear 'Heart'. The words that come into your head are 'lightweight', 'flimsy', 'insipid' or 'your mum'. There are times whilst tuned in to Heart that I have mistakenly been under the impression that I was either in a lift or had been put on hold by the bank. Much as this kind of broadcasting infuriates me for its lack of spark, what enrages me more is the massive demand for it. It is radio that is specifically designed to be on in the background. It asks absolutely nothing of the listener, save the occasional phone-in. I have always found it sad to think that this is exactly what some listeners want from a radio station, a bit of background ambience and nothing to think about.

I started to toy with a few random words that might speak to the remit of the new station. 'Choice' was already taken, as was 'Melody'. 'Beat', 'Pulse' and 'Rhythm' all seemed a little too on the nose somehow. 'Noise' could be construed negatively, as could 'Racket'. I thought BBC Free might be a goer, until it was pointed out to me that one of the new digital television services was going to be called BBC Three, which might lead to some confusion in London and the South East:

''ere, did you 'ear that BBC free yet ...'

'Yeah! I watched it as well, you wanker!'

I put the problem of the name to the back of my head for the time being, having faith that inspiration would strike at the right time.

One important fact that had been finally cleared up was that we had been told at what time the show would be running. The daily schedule was still a moveable feast. I didn't know the exact start time of my show, and yet I had still agreed to do it. In retrospect this seems a touch cavalier. It was entirely possible that they might be thinking about trying to change the listening habits of milkmen or farmers and my shift might be five till eight. Mind you, they were talking about courting real music fans, so breakfast time for those hippies is more like ten till one! At one initial meeting I remember there being talk of a six a.m. start, which I must confess made me throw up in my mouth ever so slightly. Some wag mooted eight as a possible start time, which might have been nice, but all of our competitors would have already been on air for an hour or two so we would have been like the last princess to the ball. We would go on air at seven o'clock and run for three hours.

The audience on breakfast shows traditionally shifts over the course of the programme, with varying peaks and troughs of listeners depending on the time people leave for work or school. We started to play with the idea that we could structure our show with three distinct and different-sounding hours. The first hour would have to hit the ground running. Plenty of punchy music and not too much chat in the first half hour, then after the news a couple of talk-based features and one of the session tracks and the birthdays. The second hour would have a bit more in terms of prepared comedy stuff and a regular feature contributor and the album of the day track, then the last hour would slow down a bit and have a couple of featured items in the first half hour and then in the last twenty-five minutes of the show we'd have our guest. The three of us quite liked this shape. The laid-back approach to shows we had done previously wouldn't really sit well at breakfast time. Audiences responded to regularity. The features would have to happen at the same time every day. Papers at half seven, contributor at half eight, guest at half nine. Those would be the main beats of the show with all the other features as a kind of backbeat.

Listener competitions are a major component of all entertainment-based breakfast radio. They provide a bridge between the show and its audience. A good caller to a radio show is pure gold because for many broadcasts it is the only time that anything spontaneous can happen. People like to call in to radio shows so they can feel part of the gang. Not to mention that there is nothing that listeners like more than stacks of free shit. Phil and Jo had always been consummate prize blaggers back at GLR and because of this we would go on to have a bulging sack of goodies at our disposal on the breakfast show.

Having said that, over at Capital Radio Chris Tarrant would occasionally give away tens of thousands of pounds, while Christian O'Connell would pay off your credit card bill, and Heart were always giving away holidays which were very popular. But to be honest, it's the ideal prize for them because listening to Heart would give anybody an overpowering desire to flee the country. Being at the BBC is a bit of a pain in the arse because you're not allowed to give away too many freebies because it can be seen as commercial endorsement. So the majority of our go-to competition prizes would end up being promo copies of CDs, DVDs and books, which suited our lot down to the ground really. Competitions were in!

In the months leading up to the launch we had plenty more of these twitchy, java-fuelled get-togethers, throwing ideas about, chatting about potential guests, speculating about how many listeners we might get. As the start date drew ever closer, I quietly went about finishing off the various gigs, TV and radio shows and corporates in my diary. My last proper stand-up show was on 8 November 2001 in the Channel Islands at Jersey Opera House.

Had I known that I wouldn't be doing stand-up like this again I might have taken more trouble to absorb every single moment. It certainly didn't feel like a goodbye show, it was just business as usual. I went onstage, took the piss out of the local newspaper, took the piss out of the occupation tapestry, told a few gags about Battle of the Flowers, sang a song and left. It was a fun evening and the audience were lovely, but the last thing I felt was any sense of finality.

If there was one thing I could have changed about my whole breakfast radio experience, then it would have been finding a way to continue doing stand-up comedy. Working in radio the audience is an unknown, amorphous thing. We had no idea of the size of it or if we were doing anything approaching what they wanted. We were, to coin a phrase, whistling in the dark. The worst thing about doing radio as a live performer is that you have no immediate reaction to feed from. If you have an idea onstage and it dies, then you know it was a bad idea straight away. On radio you can be running with something for an hour or more before it slowly dawns on you that it's got no legs.

As a live stand-up comedian, you are working within a forum for the dissemination of whimsical ideas. You can decide to say something on the spur of the moment and you are completely free of any editorial constraint. You can just throw it out there and see what happens. This kind of interactive spontaneity had been an important part of my creative life for years. You know the bit in *Jaws* where Chief Brody is sitting on the back of Quint's boat and he's just chucking fish guts and blood into the sea to try and attract the shark. That was pretty much how I did stand-up. 'Comedy chumming' had served me well for nearly twenty years, but had I known I was about to give it all up I might have gone about things very differently, but as we all know hindsight is a fucker.

A few days after that last stand-up show I went down to Brighton, to the Theatre Royal to appear as a guest panellist on the Radio 4 comedy show *I'm Sorry I Haven't a Clue*. For me this is the comedy equivalent of being asked to sit in on guitar with The Rolling Stones. ISIHAC or *Clue* is a British radio institution, which is now in its fourth decade. Barry Cryer, Willie Rushton, Graeme Garden and Tim Brooke-Taylor had been given silly things to do by Humphrey Lyttleton with Colin Sell at the piano for years until 1996 and the untimely death of Rushton. The decision was made to continue doing the show, with a roster of younger comics taking it in turns to fill Willie's vacant chair. Amongst the regulars for this privilege were Jeremy Hardy, Sandi Toksvig, Linda Smith, Stephen Fry and Andy Hamilton. I had previously done a show in 1999 at Milton Keynes and so this would be my second time with them.

When you perform comedy for a living, perhaps the trickiest audience members you will ever have to face are your parents. Unless they are in showbiz as well, it is almost impossible to explain to them in any meaningful sense how you have been able to turn your ability to be a smart arse into a regular income. You have to understand that it was the same part of my brain which once made them say 'Shut up Phillip!' or 'Go to your room!' that was now making me a quite comfortable living, so they had trouble grasping the concept. My sister would often go round to their house and turn the television over to *Never Mind the Buzzcocks,* and they would sit and stare at it and not make a sound.

Phill Jupitus

Then after thirty minutes of silence they would say, 'Very good. Phillip is looking well these days,' or 'What a lovely shirt he had on.' So their favourite thing about my career over the previous ten years had been down to make-up and wardrobe. But appearing on *Clue* was something they could grasp. They had been listeners to the show since it began in 1972. My mum had been a fan of Humph's music since the 1950s, so in her mind me doing a gig with him heralded my arrival in showbiz!

I booked them both in at the Grand on the seafront, trying desperately and failing to book Mrs Thatcher's former room and bombsite as they are diehard Tories, and I think would have appreciated the gesture. The gig was a delight, and as usual when appearing on *Clue* you tend to find yourself watching more than participating, but why not? Sitting just to the right of Tim Brooke-Taylor for that gig is the best seat in the fucking house. Mum and Dad came back afterwards, glowing with something that I couldn't really work out at the time, which I assumed to be the menopause (Mum) and the house red (Dad). I subsequently realised that the rosy hue about their faces was actually down to parental pride. It would be some years before I saw it again, but to be fair, some people never see it at all.

In our preparation for the breakfast show, we had many discussions about music. The three of us had broad and cosmopolitan tastes, and wanted the show to reflect that. Many hours were spent putting together a list of the core artists and tracks for the station. This list would go on to form the basis of a massive database of sounds from which we could draw material. It was in effect like having a really really big iPod. As you searched down the list

133

there was a wealth of material by an astonishing range of artists. But it was by no means complete. We wanted to be able to plug the gaps in the database with what we drew from our own music collections.

Phil and I were big fans of American guitar pop/rock and bands like The Replacements, Wilco and the early work of REM who were all represented on the database. But by the same token we loved lesser-known artists like Marah from Philadelphia, The Detroit Cobras and Pete Yorn, who weren't. Yorn had released his début album that year, *Music for the Morning After*, and it was quite simply stunning. As he was unheard of in the UK, his record label were quite surprised to hear from us asking if he'd be coming over to the UK at all.

Pete's début gig was at the tiny Water Rats at King's Cross in London on 17 January 2002. The venue comfortably holds a band, but anything beyond that gets a bit snug. Phil and I could barely contain our excitement and indeed on the night we went on to ruin the gig for many of the audience by singing every single song incredibly loud from our spot right in the middle of the room. Some months later at his next London show, a man came up to me with a minidisc.

'I thought you might like to have this, mate. It's a bootleg of the Water Rats show.'

I thanked the man profusely, but when I eventually got home and listened to it all I could hear was me and Wilding bellowing like drunk warthogs during every song. Well, at least we were passionate about something.

We were now close to starting the two-week 'white network' run for the station, which now had a name. We were quite looking forward to what had been decided after such a lengthy consultation period. Indeed, everybody had been asked to put ideas forward, so we were on the edge of our seats. So the new name for the first new radio service from the BBC since the launch of Five Live was going to be … 6 Music! The BBC had decided to stick with the whole numbers thing, which had served them so well previously. Radio 4's digital service would be called – wait for it – BBC7 so I assumed that the Radio 1 station would be eight, but *no*! They were going for the far more radical 1xtra. Please note the 'xtra' as opposed to 'extra'. You see young people have such busy lives these days that such inconveniences as spelling and grammar have been culled in order to allow them more time to drink Breezers and spread chlamydia. Radio 1 of course desperately wants to be 'hip' and 'now' so of course went for '1xtra' which is certainly 'of the moment', not to mention 'zeitgeisty', and in no way at all comes off like a desperate uncle in his forties trying to pander to his thirteen-year-old nephew.

Armed with our sassy new name we started to try and come up with some features based around it. At the time I wish we'd had some sort of deal that the first person to suggest 'Six of the best' should be beaten about the head with hardback bound copies of the BBC charter. The only feature that we came up with was a direct rip-off of Dave Letterman's Top Ten. In this long-running feature on his show, he would take a big news story and do ten quickfire gags around it, which he would then read out in a chart run-down style, building up to the funniest of the ten. Our 'spin' on the Letterman idea was called Six Musings, a name suggested by Jo Tyler. We had a musical bed called Peter Gunn Mambo by the Jack Costanzo Orchestra, which was two minutes and twenty-seven seconds long. This was a perfect length for the piece, which we would usually place just before the last track into the 8.30 news. This gave us a chance to do more formulaic straight gag writing and suited me and Phil down to the ground.

After the nine o'clock new bulletin we had a feature called 'the double whammy'. In this we would play two tracks back to back that had some kind of musical connection with each other. This kind of feature was more often than not turned over to the listeners for ideas and we made sure to play stuff that was as removed as possible from the straight daytime format. The double whammy served well as a fanfare to the different pace of the final hour. We had wanted to develop a different ending for the show that would be the same every day, and we came up with 'What have we learned?' This would be a list of about eight random things we had discovered over the course of the previous three hours and was a good way of recapping the best bits of the whole show for the listeners. On a Friday this feature would become 'What have we learned this week?' This feature stayed with the show from its inception in March 2002 and proved so popular that a well-known national Sunday broadsheet stole the idea. Serves us right for nicking Six Musings from Dave Letterman, I suppose.

Thinking about the approaching 6 Music show occupied most of my time from January. I hosted both the Empire Awards and the Q Awards that year, which were two of the last gigs I did before starting. At the Q Awards, as well as hosting, I had to present a lifetime achievement award of some kind to John Lydon who came up to the stage like Napoleon returning from Elba, flicking the Vs and giving the finger to all and sundry as he promenaded up towards the stage. As he came towards me and I held out his award, he leaned in to me grinning and in his low North London drawl said, 'It's a fucking laugh, isn't it.'

He then went on to tell everybody in the room that they didn't deserve to be there apart from Kate Bush who was a genius. Just like Napoleon, when you think about it. It is worth pointing out that Ms Bush was only about ten feet to my left when she accepted her award and after the standing ovation from the crowd had subsided, gently whispered into the microphone, 'I think I've just come …' Ten feet. Ten. Feet.

After some gentle negotiations it was agreed that we would only have to do two weeks of 'white network' before going on air. For me this was enough of a run up to the main event. But first they had to teach me how to use the kit. Julian and Jim were our tech gurus at 6 Music. Anything to do with the equipment was their domain, and, like anybody with real knowledge of how things work, they regarded mere presenters with cold-eyed scorn.

It is understandable, I suppose. You spend months trying to meet the needs of a demanding management and you are launching a brand new broadcasting system, so you build a technically intricate set-up. Then a big lummox comes along and eats over it, filling the faders with muffin crumbs and nearly spills a pint of Um Bongo in it one morning. I completely understood their mistrust. Like most radio desks, the Dalet playout system we were using was connected to the database and a couple of CD players to allow some element of free choice. This entire system had been jerry rigged in a tiny office on the fifth floor of Western House. In here we would be attaching flesh to the skeleton of our ideas.

Our editor, Anthony Bellekom, was a tall, taciturn and approachable fellow who had spent several years of his life working with the legendary eccentric Viv Stanshall. I feel certain that the time he spent with Viv served him well throughout the remainder of his career because to Anthony no idea was ever too bonkers. Everything that you came to him with was given due consideration. Having looked at our running orders for the show he nodded sagely.

'Yes, they look fine. We'll just run those as is for two weeks, then we'll be off.' Then he'd drift back down the corridor with his hands behind his back like some visiting RAF air flight marshal.

Our programme controller, John Sugar, was a very different fellow. A talented producer in his own right, he had been making great radio for years, with some of the biggest names in the business. But the time had come to spread his wings and progress up the ladder. 6 Music proved to be John's baptism of fire. His casual demeanour and matey office chat almost immediately rubbed me and Wilding up the wrong way, and our relationship with John never got the chance to settle at a mutually agreeable place. We remained wary of each other right up until John's unexpected departure from 6, which in retrospect is yet another rueful keepsake to tie a ribbon round and delicately place in 'Phill's Big Box of BBC Based Regrets'.

The full team for 6 Music Breakfast was myself, Jo and Phil and our broadcast assistant (BA) Jacqueline 'Jaffa' Wood. The four of us would arrive bleary-eyed in the mornings and then slowly drift into our various roles on the show. Working at that time of the day becomes quite organic, as you are struggling against your own physiology, which is screaming, '*What are you doing up at this hour?*' Your tasks as you arrive tend to be kept quite repetitive so you almost perform them as a kind of reflex action.

My pre-show ritual when I first started at 6 Music was to read the newspapers and highlight any amusing nuggets. I would then flag the page with a post-it note. I only used the four main broadsheets to plunder and we also took *USA Today* so I could get baseball news. I ignored the tabloids as I didn't read them in real life, so why read them on the show? Initially I would dig out at least half a dozen stories, but the problem with that was that you did far too much jabbering between records. Also as it was still early in the morning for me, my editorial faculties were a little off beam. My judgement for what constituted a 'good' news story for my kind of low-impact badinage seemed to be impaired by lack of sleep. I would often read out hellishly dull news items after saying, 'Here's a good one,' only to look up and see the incredulous gazes of Wilding and Tyler.

In those two run-up weeks prior to the start of the show we relied heavily on the goodwill of a number of friends we had made over the years to come into the studio and be guests on radio shows that would never be heard. Amongst the musical guests were Pete Shelley of Buzzcocks, Tony Wright from Terrorvision and Nicky Tesco from The Members. Those who came in the first week were perhaps the most disappointed, as they were quite obviously being interviewed in a storeroom. Fair enough, it was beautifully appointed with all the gadgets and trappings of a proper radio show, but just behind their seat was a teetering mountain of redundant stationery, filing cabinets, non-swivelling swivel chairs, broken desks and dusty bulletin boards. It felt like we were running a pirate radio station out of the loft of a branch of Rymans. One sneeze and we could have lost the man who wrote 'Ever Fallen in Love'.

One problem with making radio that you know nobody apart from management is listening to is that it's very difficult to gee yourself up into making it sound anything other than that. Part of the mystique of radio is that even though you don't know how many people are listening you are fairly sure that somebody is, and that gives some focus to your work. These demo shows were great practice for using the gear, but beyond that they lacked the spark of a real live radio programme. When they did start to come to life was when we had guests in with us. More than willing to pitch in was Linda Smith, whom I had known for many years from our time doing gigs together. She was a fellow West Ham fan, and in love with the blunt charm of the area. I recall sitting chatting after a gig with her and her partner Warren one night, when Linda launched into a random observation.

'I was reading our local paper the other day, the *Newham Recorder*, and I was about three pages in and I thought to myself, I don't know why they don't just have done with it and call it *The Newham Murderer* ...'

Part of this dry-run process gave us the chance to practise what we would do in the event of sudden and tragic news from the world of music. To that end, on the Wednesday of our second week of dry-run shows Anthony Bellekom phoned up Jo Tyler and said, 'Lou Reed's dead.'

He wasn't really, but from our point of view for the next three hours he was ostensibly dead. The music news team rapidly threw together the story with whatever details of Mr Reed's *faux* demise they had been fed by Bellekom. With it not being a real death it was massively tempting to speculate wildly over the cause of his death. 'Details are sketchy at the moment, but reports are coming out of America about the death of Lou Reed, who we believe got into a knife fight with Noam Chomsky.'

We dragged up all of the Lou Reed music we could, and the show carried on in an oddly muted fashion, even though we all knew he wasn't really dead. Sadly the experience of this dry run grimly paid off before the end of the year with the sudden death of Joe Strummer in December.

One day during the white network period I was as is customary wandering aimlessly through the West End of London. Soho is a funky warren of bakeries, record shops, cafés and recording studios, so I spent quite a lot of time there. If I was making my way from Wardour Street to Broadcasting House, my regular cut through would involve walking up Poland Street. I always enjoyed walking up here for the nods I'd get from all the bears smoking cigarettes and nursing pints outside the gay pub The King's Arms. I was later told by our showbiz contributor Neal Sean that I was once number one in a chart of 'breeder bears' which was kept on the wall of the bar.

As I was about to turn onto Oxford Street I noticed a familiar figure on the corner. Just finishing up a call on his mobile was the man who launched Radio 1 in 1967, Tony Blackburn. Tony had been a guest on *Never Mind the Buzzcocks* some years previously. When I found out he was coming in I brought in my copy of *British Motown*

Chartbusters Volume 2, which Tony had written the sleeve notes for, and I eagerly asked him to sign it.

'Hello Tony!' I said to him, and he looked up a little startled. I was hoping that he would still remember me after such a lengthy gap.

'Hey Phill, hello, how are you doing …'

'Not bad, mate. What are you doing round here?'

'Oh, you know, I've just been doing some recording round the corner. How about yourself?'

'Funnily enough I'm working on one of the new BBC digital stations and we're launching next week. Not on the same scale as you launching Radio 1, but you know …'

Blackburn paused and thought for a moment. 'Yes, digital, I read something about that. Which one are you doing again?'

'6 Music. It's a kind of indie station, you know …'

'That's it, 6 Music yes, I've heard of it. Well, good luck with that.'

'Thanks, Tony. To be honest it's a bit of a change in lifestyle for me, working at the other end of the day …'

'Yes, yes … it can take a while to get used to.'

We said our goodbyes and went our separate ways. I took it as a good omen that I had bumped into one of the people who defined breakfast radio in the UK the week before launching a new breakfast radio.

Our second week of dry-run shows took place in the actual studio we would be using for 6 Music on the fifth floor of Broadcasting House. Much as I wished that I could get to walk into work through the legendary Portland Place façade every day, our murky little entrance was round the corner in Hallam Street. From my point of view this was quite a body blow. Walking into the main entrance of BH was like stepping into another era: the high ceilings of the lobby and uniformed commissionaires made you feel like you'd just walked into a John Buchan novel. Indeed, Richard Hannay, the hero of *The Thirty-Nine Steps*, had rooms on Portland Place. But the Hallam Street entrance had automatic sliding double-glazed doors that reluctantly whined open as you walked in, giving you more of a vibe of doing a walk on in *Blake's Seven*.

As launch day for 6 Music approached I finally started to feel the frisson of nerves that I had been anticipating for the past four months. Indeed, working around Broadcasting House meant that I was constantly bumping into broadcasting legends, some of whom would chat, and proffer advice. Terry Wogan was part of the furniture at BH, and whenever I bumped into him, his cheery smile and warm handshake would give me a lift. The man is like a human form of Prozac.

In the week leading up to the launch of 6, we met in the lobby of Western House. After he had administered my RDA of Wogan, he asked, 'How's it going up at 6 Music then?'

I shrugged by way of response and scratched my head. 'Yeah, it's alright. We're ready to go, I think. Got any advice?'

Although this request was said in a jocular fashion, I really did want to know what he had to say.

He paused briefly. 'Don't do stuff out of the papers, everybody and his dog does that, and try not to fill the show up with features. Just play the records and talk to them. Keep it simple.'

I smiled weakly and thanked him for his time, got into the lift and looked at my running order for the show. Two chunks of newspaper review and eight separate features every day.

Well, it's not like Terry could ever listen. He was busy.

On the Blocks

'Panic'/'Life on a Chain' (live) – Pete Yorn
'Thunderbirds Are Go' – The Rezillos
'Fake Plastic Trees' – Radiohead
'Cool Collie' – Hopeton Lewis
'These Boots Are Made for Walkin'' – Nancy Sinatra
'The Happening' – The Supremes
'It's Time' – Elvis Costello
'Got Odd' – Gouge
'Celebrity Hit List' – Terrorvision
'Like a Rolling Stone' (live) – Bob Dylan

We're Not Happy Till You're Not Happy

Halfway through the process of writing this book I realised that I was operating on a set of out-of-date preconceptions. Here I was writing about what kind of radio I liked and didn't like, but I hadn't actually listened to any radio that I *didn't* like for years. Quite so! Why would one waste one's time by spending the first few hours of the day in listening hell? It would put a kink in the start of your day and I imagine that one would subsequently walk around in quite the mood.

Despite my fondness for it, even my show of choice, the *Today* programme on Radio 4, has those odd moments which infuriate me. Robert Peston, interviews with George Osborne, Robert Peston. My real anger is reserved for those occasions when they have had some quite hard-line evangelists appearing on their regular feature, 'Thought for the Day'. Every day at around 7.50 a.m. a representative of one of the major faiths hits us upside the head with a snatch of wisdom plucked from whichever philosophy they live their life by. And we listeners are supposed to take this nugget and somehow apply its wisdom to fit the needs of our day. As a lifelong atheist, this usually means that the postman finds me out of sorts and glowering as I sign for my Amazon packages. If he's reading this then I am truly sorry, it's not you, it's religion.

Britain is by and large a secular society, so I don't really understand why we have to have five minutes of multi-denominational rubbish shoved down our throats every day at ten to eight. I am of the opinion that until they actually prove that god exists, then 'Thought for the Day' should be shared on a fifty-fifty basis with a completely secular thought. Rabbi Lionel Blue strikes me as some-one who seems to be quite aware of the inherent contra-dictions of modern spirituality and his contributions are usually the best of a very patchy bunch. But having said that, as the first openly gay rabbi, I imagine that over the years he's learned plenty about compromise. But imagine just how brilliant it would be if on the Monday we had Lionel talking about love for our neighbours, but on Tues-day a bloke coming on suggesting that people try just a smidgeon of Marmite on their toast before putting peanut butter on it or someone advocating a good walk. That's a thought I can get my head round!

I have often fantasised about what my own contribution to a more secular thought for the day might be should such a thing ever come to pass ...

EVAN DAVIS: Now on Radio 4 it's time for 'Thought
                 for the Day' with Phill Jupitus.
JUPITUS: Thank you, Davo ... You know, I was
                 on my way to White City today and
                 I suddenly thought to myself that all
                 the dickheads in the world should just
                 stop it. Now when I say dickheads,

> you know who you are. So please just
> knock it off! Alright!

JIM NAUGHTIE: That was 'Thought for the Day' with
> Phill Jupitus. The time is nine minutes
> to eight …

The reason people maintain such fierce loyalty to their morning radio shows is that they want, nay, *need* it to be a completely predictable experience. Then it can form an intrinsic part of their daily routine. No surprises, just a nice easy listen, a bit of travel and weather and then they can leave the house at that same moment every day and go off to work, hopefully with a spring in their step. I have always found that irritating radio shows seem somehow even more irritating early in the morning. I suppose it's because you've been asleep for hours and waking up is more often than not quite a stressful situation. The last thing you need when you have to get up is to have to cope with something jarring or unpleasant that you have to listen to.

As I am now approaching my fifties, I have learned over the years exactly what I like to listen to at breakfast time. Actually that's not strictly true. I'm more acutely aware of exactly what I *don't* like to listen to. Here's a checklist of the ten things that I don't want to hear first thing in the morning:

- advertising
- artificial presenter voices
- bad jokes
- boy bands / girl bands / Coldplay
- showbiz news and gossip

- really grim actual news
- sexual innuendo
- stupidity
- fake sincerity
- hysterical listeners phoning in

Now as I look back at this list it does make me wonder why exactly I decided to spend four precious hours of my life listening to an entire commercial radio breakfast show. In fact I can honestly say that by the halfway stage of the show, the presenters had violated nine of the ten breakfast listening no-no's listed above but only because mercifully nothing had exploded in Helmand Province that morning.

Another thing worth pointing out is that commercial radio really isn't in the business of chasing the elusive forty-seven-year-old radio snob demographic, which I inhabit. Its job is to make fun, disposable radio for listeners with disposable income who are aged between sixteen and thirty-five. Such shows have a good, loyal following and are very popular. Although well aware that this kind of radio is not intended for me, I thought – 'What the hell!' As I was writing a book about breakfast radio, why not make the effort to listen?

And while I'm listening perhaps I could try to fathom exactly why it is that whenever I hear such shows I lunge frantically across the room and turn the radio off without hesitation, and usually while swearing quite loudly. I decided to write my reactions down in real time, to give a sense of what I was going through emotionally. Unfortunately these shows are paced so fast that I would occasionally miss some elements, and I suppose that's my loss, but I'll live with it.

On the assigned morning my alarm went off at 5.45. I set out some muesli and a bowl and some milk, ready for breakfast. I set up my laptop on the table and had the radio remote control by my side. As the clock approached the top of the hour, I tuned in and braced myself for what was to follow …

* * *

6.00 a.m. The news headlines come and go quite quickly followed by the weather, which is brought to us in association with the NHS. I feel sure at this point that anybody unable to get an appointment with a hospital would feel glad that medical funds were bringing us the bloody weather. I haven't even heard the presenters yet and something has already annoyed me, which does not bode well for the next four hours. After the weather a chirpy jingle lets us know who we are listening to, before making way for a record whose name eludes me. Somebody is singing 'Lady Starlight' but a quick Google search tells me that this is either a sassy New York deejay or a song by The Scorpions and to be honest it sounds like neither. Then in true deejay style, Male Presenter bursts onto the airwaves, talking all over the end of the record. This for me has always been one of the prime indicators of deejay lameness. The more of the record that is playing that they talk over, the bigger a tool they are.

His arrival on air is sudden and loud. His accent darts all around but it has that heavy fake diction. If he spoke to his mates like that down the pub, I dare say they'd tell him to fuck off. I, however, have no such recourse. Male Presenter tells us not to mess with his mojo. This seems a shame, but nevertheless I delete 'mess with mojo' from my to-do list. His co-host then pops up with a similar amped-up style of delivery and straight away they start talking about the weather. It is quite an icy morning and has snowed in recent weeks, and she is concerned that we might be running out of grit for our roads. Male Presenter also expresses his concern at a possible lack of grit: might there be a market for stolen grit taken out of the yellow containers at the side of the road? They continue talking about gritting roads for a minute before he remembers that as a child he used to shovel the snow off people's paths. Then he tells me it is eleven minutes past six and they play …

RECORD   'The Fear' by Lily Allen

They do not play all of this record, and in fact talk over both the introduction and the end. I am now assuming that this is their 'style'. Male Presenter is now asking us, 'What did you do for money as a kid?' and thinks back to his own childhood. Apparently he went to the posh estate to shovel driveways. I'm sure that he wants this to illustrate to us what a savvy operator he was as a child, but to me the subtext is: 'Fuck you, poor people! Shovel your own driveways, not that you can afford driveways!' I start to giggle at the thought of him knocking on the doors of 'the big houses' asking to shovel their driveways in his booming radio presenter voice. 'Hello mate! Shovel your driveway for you? It's coming up to ten to eight!' It is quite telling that my first laugh of the day is self-generated. Sadly, he can't remember what he charged for his shovelling skills.

'Have you ever worked for yourself as a child?' he asks us listeners, and briefly I ponder sending in my story about painting a steamroller. But I worry that if I join in I might become one of them.

Female Presenter tells us that she had a paper round and worked in a newsagent. Also she wanted a horse but couldn't afford one so would groom horses and muck out at a local stables. This provided all the thrill of ownership without any of the cost. Male Presenter takes this as the cue for one of his comedy flights of fancy:

'By the way, there are no serial numbers on horses, so why not just have a go on one in a field or steal them, although hang on a minute, can you still be hung for horse theft?'

While this odd legal equestrian poser hangs in the air, a nice man comes on the radio to tell us about the traffic, before Male Presenter gives me the bad news I have been hoping against hope not to hear. Tragically, they will be playing some Coldplay in a moment. We then discover that their usual travel man is on paternity leave, having just had his first baby. This prompts both presenters to move into darker territory …

FEMALE PRESENTER: My brother told me that only real men have girls when they have kids …

MALE PRESENTER: Well of course you know that after conception we all start out as female but then become male at a later point …

FEMALE PRESENTER: Well that certainly explains your hair in the eighties!

As I listen to this odd little exchange, I am reminded of words that Graeme Garden once said to me: 'You know, Phill, that wasn't really a joke. It just made a noise like one ...'

ADVERTS	T-Mobile / Renault / *Love Lift Us Up* (CD) / Blockbuster Video / Barratt Homes
RECORD	'Viva La Vida' by Coldplay

As Christopher drones on I have the time to observe that my cafetière is broken and, in a moment of improvisational genius, ram down the filter with a spoon. This bit of frontier thinking makes me feel like I'm in an episode of *MacGyver*. As Coldplay fizzle away, Male Presenter tells us that one day *he* will rule the world. Before the full horror of a world run by a regional radio deejay takes hold, Female Presenter spares us all with a succinct, 'No you won't.' I always thought that the point of another voice on the radio was to give a show a more naturalistic, conversational feel. These idiots, however, seem to spend most of their time immediately contradicting each other, then trying to build some kind of banter on blindly adopting a contrary position, which is a completely arse-about-face way of doing things. It's a bit like listening to a couple of toddlers jacked up on Red Bull who also need the lav really badly.

Then Male Presenter heads for a rich seam of comedy gold. 'By the way, I had to buy a battery for my van at the weekend. I couldn't get to it, you know, so I left it for a couple of weeks, and as it turns out I had to buy a new one, and that got me thinking about batteries. Why do kids' toys have so many batteries these days? Why can't they just make everything rechargeable, like mobiles?'

I'm not sure if he has thought about this before he says it, or he just has one of those completely free associative brains that can just pluck stuff out of his arse and start riffing on it. But it seems a fair point: why aren't kids' electrical toys rechargeable? Female Presenter responds by saying that nothing in her house has batteries. This prompts Male Presenter to guffaw mightily before inferring in a none-too-subtle way that she must have batteries in her house! We the listeners are then tacitly forced to think about her theoretical vibrator. I push my muesli untouched to one side. Yes, at just before 6.30 a.m., a dildo gag before trailing the quiz. Good grief, I'm going to hear some of the people who listen to this every day! By now I am starting to get a headache.

ADVERTS	Chlamydia testing kit / T-Mobile / supermarket / Bird's Eye Foods / Inspire.com / Blockbuster Video
6.30 a.m. NEWS, WEATHER, JINGLE	
RECORD	'The Promise' by Girls Aloud

It is worth pointing out here that they have now been on air for thirty-five minutes and only played four records. After this delightful toe-tapper, Male Presenter returns to the theme of other jobs he had as a kid. Presumably aware of the limited seasonal nature of his other childhood money-spinner, he tells us that he also used to caddy at a golf course. 'It put me off golf, though ...' I find this surprising as with his lame jokes and terrible attitude to women he's like 90 per cent of all golfers I've ever met.

Good Morning Nantwich

Then we move on to the competition, and the prospect of some banter with the callers. The first can't remember having a job as a child. They gamely try to bait this caller but she's got nothing to give. Finally she gets a question wrong and they play a funny noise which symbolises her abject failure. The next caller tells us that she walked dogs as a child, which prompts Female Presenter to ask if she was like the Dog Whisperer with lots of dogs. The lack of response indicates that the listener has no idea who or what the Dog Whisperer is, so on with the question! Incorrect answer … funny noise … next caller.

The caller sounds mid-sixties and rural and says, 'Hello to you and your crew!' He's delightfully perky with an alluring countryside twang but he still gets his question wrong and so the rollover goes to £4,000. At no point does anybody explain the mechanics of the quiz, which I'm sure their regular listeners are more than familiar with.

6.43 a.m.   RECORD   'Pray' by Take That

Once more Male Presenter crashes the vocal to tell us '… they sounded better with Robbie!' Then he goes on to tell us how it was a vodka-fuelled night that led to the Take That reunion. This gives him the opportunity to dip into the wig bag and give us his funny drunk voice. Again this leads them to asking the listeners, 'Has anything funny happened to you after a night's drinking?' The likelihood of something funny not happening to you when drunk being fairly minimal, I sense they may get some feedback. Female Presenter then informs us that 'Nothing good ever came out of being drunk!'

154

Then the travel gimp disagrees before saying, 'I went out on the beer one night and woke up married with kids!' which causes Female Presenter to dissolve into hysterics, while Male Presenter goes a bit quiet.

6.47 a.m	TRAVEL	
	ADVERTS	Tesco's / Brit Awards competition / sponsor jingle / Renault / T-Mobile / film ad 'He's Just Not That Into You' / jingle
6.52 a.m.	RECORD	'I'm Yours' by Jason Mraz

I'm coping a bit better than I thought. The first hour is nearly done and I haven't smashed anything. I have a coffee with double cream in it which is dark, rich and tasty. Mr Mraz's little ditty is quite charming. Maybe this show isn't so bad after all? Alas, I have spoken too soon, as Male Presenter has found a 'funny asylum seeker' story in one of the tabloids. Apparently a group of people fleeing whatever war-torn, disease ravaged shit-hole they and their families were slowly perishing in smuggled themselves out in a lorry load of chocolate. He then says something I don't quite understand.

'I tell you what, we should just cover all the asylum seekers in chocolate. It would be *great*!' How or why such an act would be 'great' eludes me. I am struck with the possibility that Male Presenter is a closet Dadaist. Meanwhile Female Presenter wonders aloud if it was loose cocoa powder or in boxes. Male Presenter, however, is not listening because he's building up quite a head of steam.

'They come over here and get free houses and free cars! Talk about your land of milk and honey!' I'm sure that in his head, he thinks that 'land of milk and honey' is hilarious, and in some way dovetails with the chocolate motif. But it makes no sense. He then repeats his theme but in a slightly more forceful way.

'They *mumble mumble* (i.e. 'fucking') come over here getting free cars and free houses – now we cover them in chocolate!'

I am staring at the radio open-mouthed. Male Presenter is obviously pursuing the ignorant bigot demographic, which is a tough task on a breakfast show as they're all busily getting ready to call Jeremy Vine later.

	ADVERTS	Blockbuster / Trust a trader.com / bed sale for … Dreams
6.59	TRAVEL	
7.00	NEWS AND WEATHER	
7.02	ADVERT	Churchill Insurance
	JINGLE	
	RECORD	I know it but can't remember. Waiting for chorus. It's a bloke singing … Hang on … It's Ronan thingy! 'Life is a Rollercoaster'!

They name-check the record and tell us the time before moving on to showbiz news. Angelina Jolie is trying to get pregnant!

'Doesn't she need Brad involved?' Male Presenter asks.

They then talk about fertility tests and there is a couple of minutes of smutty nonsense between themselves. They then play a clip of Angelina Jolie who talks about playing with kids. This annoys Female Presenter for some reason.

'She reckons she's all that just because she plays with her kids!' The conversation grinds on relentlessly. 'Do you have much to offer your kids if you're, say, an accountant?'

This is a springboard to ask for calls and emails.

>RECORD   'Single Ladies' by Beyoncé
>
>TIME CHECK 7.14.

The team are still discussing what can you offer your kids? Male Presenter starts into Angelina Jolie again. Apparently in the interview she also talks about how she and the kids play pretend games. This has quite obviously infuriated Female Presenter.

'Why does she think she's all that? We all pretend with our kids! Artists' kids love drawing! You can impress kids with your skills. As a DJ you have nothing to offer your kids!'

Male Presenter leaps in with an affirming 'She's right!'

7.15   TRAVEL

I am noticing that Female Presenter is laughing more loudly as the show progresses (strictly speaking that should be *regresses* ...) and it is becoming a very *very* annoying laugh. We then have the weather from Male Presenter.

>ADVERTS   Tesco / sponsor jingle / Horlicks /
>   T-Mobile / Barratt Homes / 'quote
>   me happy' Norwich Union / jingle
>
>RECORD   'Mercy' by Duffy

A couple of emails have come in, one from a woman who works as a nanny. Female Presenter wonders if when you got home from work as a nanny you'd want to play with your own kids as you'd been playing with kids all day!

At this point I shout '*Oh fuck off!*' out loud. In apparent response to my outburst Male Presenter says we're going to be hearing some Leona Lewis in a minute ...

ADVERTS	Chlamydia testing / Horlicks / Renault / Barratt Homes / Audi / T-Mobile
7.30	TRAVEL FOLLOWED BY NEWS

Here is the note I actually wrote at this point of the show:

> '*I have two and a half hours of this shit to go. I'm not sure I can manage it. It's just so vacuous. There is no intelligence behind any of the comments. They are just talking because they can! These fuckers have such a tightly scripted show in terms of the time they know they have to fill, why can't they be bothered to be even slightly engaging? Why would people settle for this crap? It's just mind numbing. A fucking chimp could do this show. There is nothing to think about at all ...*'

Reading those words I now realise that a lot of people love this show for that very reason. It demands absolutely nothing from the listener. While I find it offensive, ignorant garbage with mostly unlistenable music, their audience find them fun, inoffensive, and the music quite delightful. I am forced to remind myself once more that this show is not supposed to appeal to effete liberals like me. Two and a half hours to go. Let's do it.

WEATHER

7.33   RECORD   'Run' by Leona Lewis

It is the day after the live ITV coverage of a vital football match cut away to an advert during which Everton scored the only goal of the game. Male Presenter is not a football supporter but uses this story to crowbar in talking about the old pitch-side hoardings advertising Brut that you used to see. They take this as a cue to talk about old perfumes. Male Presenter is stunned to discover that they still make Brut! He starts to reminisce about Henry Cooper and the old Brut commercials. This gives Female Presenter the green light. 'Do *you* wear Brut? Text in!'

7.41   RECORD   'Torn' by Natalie Imbruglia

As Male Presenter comes back, he is wackily mimicking the guitar solo. He then name-checks the tune. (I have to say that he is very good at name-checking artists, I was always absolutely terrible at it ...) They then have a caller: who wears Brut and he's on the phone! You can tell that the room thinks that he's a laugh! He tells us that he smells like a smooth operator. He tells us that his girl-friend can't leave him alone. He tells us Brut doesn't make you smell like 'pot pourri'.

Another caller thinks Brut is totally overpowering. He was a seventies skinhead and wore Brut. He's actually quite an interesting geezer. Until the presenters start chipping in and start laughing too loud at themselves, and before you know it, he's gone.

TRAVEL

Then it's sincerity time as Female Presenter bigs herself up for aiming to do a half marathon for their charity in under two hours! Male Presenter asks her what her time was last year and it was 2.26.

'That's a lot to knock off!' he pipes up. 'And it's a lot of time as well.' That doesn't even mean anything …

| ADVERTS | Chlamydia testing / trail /sponsor jingle / Renault / Comfort / double glazing / jingle |
| RECORD | 'No Air' by Jordin Sparks |

7.56   We are subjected to yet more Brut banter.

'Isn't it champagne?' says Female Presenter. She has been to the Brut website and reads it out and laughs as she reads. She then talks about women wearing Charlie. Which leads to yet *another* obvious joke from Male Presenter. 'Nothing wrong with a bit of Charlie!'

So this paragon, this jester, this prince among men has now done jokes about asylum seekers getting too many benefits, vibrators and cocaine, and we are not even half-way through the show. An overly keen caller uses the phrase 'Go for it!' That is their demographic. The kind of people who still say, 'Go for it!'

Female Presenter worries that when kissing a bloke she smells of aftershave afterwards. Male Presenter talks about legwarmers and the fact that he can get his legs behind his head. The reason for this odd swerve in the banter is that they are now plugging an eighties disco that they are doing and they want all the men attending to wear old fragrances! This causes them to laugh at themselves some more.

7.59	ADVERTS	Autoglass / BP / Renault
	TRAVEL	
	NEWS	
	ADVERTS	Vicks vapour rub / jingle
8.05	RECORD	'Whenever Whatever' by Shakira

Male Presenter gives us a time-check before talking about pan pipes ... The mailers and texters are talking about old scents ... He feels the need to say 'Splash it all over!' quite a bit, too much in fact.

Then there is quite a sudden subject change initiated by Male Presenter. 'Let's talk about bail-out Bill, an American guy who gives money to people ... How would you get money from bail-out Bill?'

This is the cue for him to do some pre-prepared comedy. He plays the old Simon Bates 'Our Tune' theme while talking about wanting cosmetic surgery. Female Presenter is laughing even more now than she has been in the earlier part of the show. These two incessantly laughing at each other is starting to sap my will to live. It's not necessarily what they're saying, it's the moronic contrivance of it all.

| | RECORD | Anon swing beat R&B track ... not sure who it is. |

Here are my 'live' notes from this point in the show:

> *'This is the laziest radio I have ever heard. There is a set formula that they do not deviate from … It is what EVERY music show does in the commercial sector. A few tunes, calls, competitions, mail-ins, stories out of the tabloids, fake enthusiasm, I'd love to know what their audience figures are … I'd imagine the main competition for them is Johnny Vaughan who can do this sort of thing BUT with charm, wit, intelligence and personality.'*

Male Presenter is now talking about 50 Cent and his recently launched line of grooming products … Travel gimp is in the studio and says that it should have been called Fifty's Scent. The fact that this bloke has come in and is funnier seems to irk Male Presenter. The fact that he doesn't like it means that I enjoy it very much. Male Presenter then reaches once more into the deep dark recesses of his soul and – I shit you not – does 50 Cent in a funny black voice, you know, like Jim Davidson used to *in the nineteen fucking seventies*! Does OFCOM know about this?

8.18   TRAVEL

Female Presenter tells us that there is a road-show style quiz coming up which features eight blokes against eighteen women. At the mere mention of men and women Male Presenter's sleaze reflex springs into action. 'I like those odds!' This is followed by a smutty laugh. He says, 'I'm a dozen men on my own,' which prompts Female Presenter to respond with 'What, size wise?'

They both laugh heartily at themselves while I wonder where these two cheeseheads are broadcasting from and what the statutory sentences are in the UK for actual bodily harm if you haven't got any previous form.

	ADVERTS	BMW / Norwich Union / T-Mobile / Blockbuster / jingle
8.24	RECORD	A ballad that sounds like a bit like Sting, but isn't. Apparently it's not on the playlist. And it does drone on a bit …

Male Presenter has been reading the *Sun* again and wishes to draw our attention to a story about a young lady with tattoos who has sliced her name into a fellow's back with a blade. Harrowing stuff indeed, but he feels the need to add his own comment, and as he's telling us about it he refers to the young woman as 'this psycho bitch'. Delightful. Somebody new has come into the studio to enter the fray. I think he is the producer of the breakfast show. Male Presenter does a frankly dreadful joke about chlamydia which causes both Female Presenter and producer to laugh exuberantly.

	ADVERTS	British Heart Foundation / Ski Plus / Renault / Autoglass / Barratt Homes
	TRAVEL	They are running a minute late at least
	NEWS	Late
	WEATHER	
8.34	JINGLE	
	RECORD	'Breathe Slow' by Alesha Dixon

8.37   As Ms Dixon fades out Male Presenter tells us
that 'She's scrummy' while Female Presenter counters
with 'She wears really short dresses.' They are now
going to talk about the fiasco that is Todd Carty on
Dancing on Ice. Male Presenter says that the public 'are
out to sabotage these shows by voting for clowns!' The
producer pitches in that these shows are supposed to
be about entertainment. Male Presenter uses the word
'pants'. As in 'I was watching Todd Carty on *Dancing on
Ice* and he was really pants!'

    RECORD 'I Get the Sweetest Feeling' by Jackie
           Wilson

After only 2 hours and 43 minutes they play a record
which I actually own. I am starting to get quite angry …

8.48 TRAVEL

    WEATHER

    ADVERTS Tesco / Renault / Blockbuster /
         Energy Saving Trust act on CO_2 /
         jingle

8.53 RECORD 'The Loving Kind' by Girls Aloud –
         the second outing for Girls Aloud in
         one show, for *fuck's* sake

Male Presenter once more crashes the vocals but as it's
Girls Aloud I really couldn't give a fuck.

8.58 ADVERTS Blockbuster / Homebase / Bird's Eye

9.01 TRAVEL   Still late …

9.02 NEWS   The newsreader is apparently a bit
         fucked off that these dickheads are

coming to her two minutes late. She has adopted a 'tone'.

ADVERT   Churchill Insurance

They then have one of those lame spot-the-year things where they play a load of records and you try to guess the year. As this means that they won't be jabbering between records I think I'm going to enjoy it! Apparently your reward for identifying the year is 'a mention on the show'. I am hugely tempted to call in but manage to resist as I know that, if I talk to them, somewhere a fairy dies.

RECORD   'Jump' by The Pointer Sisters
RECORD   'Against All Odds' by Phil Collins
RECORD   'Ain't Nobody' by Rufus and Chaka Kahn

Male Presenter pops on to tell us that there's going to be some George Michael. I hope against hope that he doesn't use this as a springboard for a massive arsenal of anti-gay material.

9.16   TRAVEL

Male Presenter is very taken with the quality of the introduction to our next record, which is …

RECORD   'Careless Whisper' by George Michael
9.22   RECORD   'Somebody Else's Guy' by Jocelyn Brown, the best record of the show by a country mile

9.26   RECORD   'Stuck on You' by Lionel Ritchie

After three and a half hours of sheer audio torture I am in such a state of rage now that I am trying to stay away from cutlery for fear of self-harming. I have realised that part of the function of the feature between 9.00 and 9.30 is to enable the presenters to take a dump. (I don't blame them at all. I would play 'Ghost Town' by The Specials for the same reason.) Ironically they have been dumping meta-phorically in my ears for the past three and a half hours. Just ahead of the 9.30 ad break Male Presenter bursts back on air and indeed sounds a little 'lighter'. He calls Lionel Richie 'Lionel Rich Tea'; Female Presenter laughs at this gem before telling us that the year was 1984! Which oddly enough is how I have felt for the past three and a half hours. Like I was in George Orwell's 1984 in Room 101 with a cage over my head and rats running round and round doing racist gags and shitting in my ears.

ADVERTS   Autoglass / Bath stores / Specsavers / Renault / Chlamydia testing / Blockbuster / Trail

Here are the somewhat disjointed notes from my last half hour of listening.

RECORD   R&B thingy unsure what it is … baby um … I don't like living under your spotlight … no idea … it is now 9.37… have come too far to give up now …

	RECORD	'The greatest day of our lives' … that anthemy pop crap … stay close to me … It's Take That! It's called 'Greatest Day' … don't feel so angry as the lads do not pretend to be The Beatles and are all very pleasant … M namecheck Spotlight Jennifer Hudson … spews out station branding …
	ADVERT	Brits / Chlamydia / ambulance chasing / Energy Saving Trust / Blockbuster / BP / At Cost again
	TRAVEL	
9.47	RECORD	Dunno … is it … James Morrison with Furtado? Yes it is …

The last hour has hardly any of them in it, which is a small mercy …

	RECORD	It's that lovely LA backing singer lady … 'I'm All out of Love' I googled her … she's called Anastacia … Just eight minutes to go … I am tired and depressed by this experience …
	RECORD	'Footsteps' ('Teardrops') by Womack & Womack
9:56		They are done for the day … His sign off is 'Have a brilliant day!' I get the sense that this last half hour may be pre-recorded … Have a brilliant day? He can fuck RIGHT off!
9.56	ADVERTS	Audi / British Heart Foundation / Barratt / Blockbuster / Bird's Eye
	NEWS	

When it was all over I stood up and closed the lid on my laptop and took a shower. As I stood under the cascading water I almost felt violated. This is the first time I have re-read the notes I made in over a year, and even just re-reading them I felt a sense of anger building all over again.

The main question I have to ask myself is, 'Am I overre-acting?' Not all radio has to be intelligent, challenging and edifying. There is a strong argument for saying that the job of the breakfast radio show is simply to keep people company at the worst part of their day, which is getting up in the morning. As much as what they do is not my cup of tea, they are obviously very efficient at it. They play the records, make with the saucy banter and deliver a target audience to their advertisers. People really like what they do. They raise money for charity, they are cheerful, entertaining, consistent and have been on air longer than I managed.

But why do shows like this constantly have to play to the lowest common denominator? Is it that difficult to make a show that still uses the contemporary zeitgeist as a springboard to *thought* rather than simply *reaction*? When they were ripping the piss out of Angelina Jolie, why didn't they think to themselves, 'Well, of course she's just going to spoon feed them stuff about the family that isn't too challenging. Interviews are a fake conceit in the first place.' Their show seems to delight in taking abso-lutely everything it deals with on nothing but face value without any forethought.

And there it is. I had my answer. The reason that I hated this show was that nobody seemed to think at all before they opened their mouths. And as a result of this they delivered four hours of radio, which was mostly negative in its outlook, occasionally offensive, quite often wilfully ignorant and, in my view, with no redeeming qualities whatsoever. It is the worst radio programme I have ever listened to in my life. And in mitigation it's not just them, there are *dozens* of local shows that use the same tiresome bloke/bird template up and down the land. And the reason that an audience is perfectly willing to settle for this is because at the end of the day it's only a radio show and nobody takes radio that seriously!

Yes they fucking do …

Anger Mismanagement

'We Hate It When Our Friends Become Successful' –
  Reel Big Fish
'Bodies' – The Sex Pistols
'Gay Bar' – Electric Six
'Nazi Punks Fuck Off' – Dead Kennedys
'Cheney' – Brakes
'Staring at the Rude Boys' – The Ruts
'All My Life' – Foo Fighters
'Phone-in Show' – The Members
'By the Time I Get to Arizona' – Public Enemy
'Fuck You' – Alberto Y Lost Trios Paranoias

10
New Morning

My children laughed like drunken gibbons when I said, 'Right, I'd better be going to bed,' at eight in the evening on Sunday, 10 March 2002.

'But Daddy, it's only eight o'clock!' said Emily.

'What time do you have to get up?' said Molly.

I gave them both a level stare. 'Quarter past four.'

They looked at me with blank stares of incomprehension. I was getting up so early that it was completely beyond the realms of their understanding. 'Well, goodnight anyway, Daddy. Have a good show ...'

'You gonna listen?'

There was a pause before they said, 'Yes, Dad ...' Neither of them can bear my taste in music. The pair of them kissed me and ran into the other room, and thirty seconds later I heard the opening strains of *The Lion King* on the DVD.

'Turn that down, please,' I shouted out straight away. *'I have to sleep!'*

As things turned out I didn't really sleep all that much anyway. Once their shrill laughter had subsided, I hauled what was left of my shattered pride upstairs and went through the standard routine of getting ready for bed. Usually one pays scant attention to such minutiae, but somehow tonight felt different. Each moment had a bit more weight to it. This routine was going to be repeated a lot over the next few years.

Firstly I had set up two alarm clocks on my bedside table, just in case one went wrong. I was paranoid enough about waking up to briefly wonder if I had a third kicking around some place. I set them both for 4.15 in order to give myself plenty of time to get ready. Shower, then dress, have some breakfast, then leave. The car would be arriving to pick me up at around 4.50. What little music I did bring to that first show was rattling around in the old BBC programme box I'd first been given at GLR.

The box had been extensively customised in varying stages over the intervening years. On one side the three letters of the BBC logo had been changed in the same italic font to read 'SKA'. On the other side the logo was covered over by a large grinning cartoon animal face, courtesy of the Mambo store in Covent Garden. The rest was festooned with various stickers, airline tags and back-stage passes which I had acquired over the years. I thought it looked 'cool' but the overall look was more like 'tatty'.

I decided to wear an aquamarine suit for this auspicious occasion. There would be cameras, of course, but I did feel more comfortable in a suit anyway. I had a dim recollection that besuited and elegant BBC announcers in the 1930s always wore dinner suits and bow ties in the studio. Why on earth shouldn't I try and revive this custom? I stood in my kitchen nursing a still full mug of lukewarm tea as I leaned against the wooden work surface. I looked up as Shelley, bleary-eyed, wandered into the room and kissed me.

'Have a nice time,' she said, her eyes squinting against the glare of the lights. 'Try to enjoy yourself.'

She gave me a sleepy hug, did an about-face and trudged back up the stairs to bed, as I poured my untouched tea down the sink. I wished I was going with her.

I looked out of the living-room window and saw the waiting car. It was an Astra. I briefly thought to myself, I bet Terry Wogan's not in a fucking Astra! I picked up my case, opened the front door and went to work like a normal person for the first time in seventeen years.

As we cruised westwards along the almost deserted London Road I looked out of the window at the shops and houses of suburban Essex fleeting by. In my youth there was a small part of me that thought I should try and avoid doing the very thing I was doing right now. The whole notion of being a bloke in a suit with a case and commuting to London was something that other people did. And yet here I was. We hit the base of Bread & Cheese Hill then picked up speed out of Thundersley at the Saddlers Farm roundabout. After that it was a straight run all the way to London down the A13.

The landscape that slides past you as you drive along is industrial. The flaming 'Catcracker' chimney of the oil refineries at Coryton, the jutting arrogance of the Queen Elizabeth II bridge at Dartford, then the rectangular aluminium mountain ranges of the container depots all around Dagenham. These all serve to remind you that you live adjacent to the Thames. And every day we would follow its snaking route into the centre of London.

The last couple of miles took us partly along the Victoria Embankment. There's something about all rivers, but the Thames is special. I loved it best at high tide, driving past the high bows of the boats moored along its northern bank, the imposing beauty of the Oxo tower, then the dull concrete pile of the National Theatre and the Royal Festival Hall with the slowly shifting colours illuminating the Millennium Wheel beyond. The only thing I hated about my journey to work was that it made me take these incredible sights for granted. As I stared at the rippling grey waters I thought of the words at the end of the chorus of 'London Calling' and silently mouthed them as we sped along: *'I live by the riverrrrr ...'*

At 5.45 a.m. in the Western House offices of 6 Music, everybody was subdued. We exchanged stilted 'good mornings' but they were just for show. The importance and true meaning of today, which had eluded us all for the previous four months, now came into sharp relief. We were about to launch a new radio station for one of the world's oldest and most trusted broadcasters. Everybody just avoided each other's eyeline and we spoke to each other in truncated monotone sentences. There was little of the raucous laughter, or easygoing bonhomie, which had characterised the two weeks leading up to this point. I picked up the enormous bundle of papers which we had delivered to reception every day and found a quiet corner to try and eke out some comedy from the hundreds of pages of newsprint. I couldn't imagine that the chuckles would come that easily today. It all felt just a bit too serious.

After I had spent a good forty-five minutes just staring at papers like a tranquillised dog, Phil Wilding tapped me on the shoulder, a bundle of documents in his arms.

'Shall we?' he asked.

I looked back at him imploringly and mumbled my response, 'Let's not, but say we did!'

He shook his head and wandered off. I made a meal of standing up and followed him on the five-minute walk to the studio. As we emerged from the lift on the fifth floor of Broadcasting House there was a clutch of smiling BBC PR officers milling around with a few selected journalists and photographers.

Lesley Douglas wandered up to me with a friendly 'Are you all right then?'

At this moment I think the true answer to this question might have upset her, so I settled for the more diplomatic response of winking, smiling and nodding silently. This fantastically adaptable gesture would get me through the morning.

Glancing up at the clock. Fifteen minutes to seven. How could that really be the time? I'd only just got up!

In the studio, Jo Tyler was chatting to Julian the engineer, and the pair of them had the audacity to be actually laughing about something! John Sugar and Anthony Bellekom were quietly wandering around as well. This moment for them was the fruition of years of work behind the scenes. But they looked positively calm! The pair of them had the kind of good-humoured casual bearing of a couple of kindly uncles. Once again I heard laughter, and they looked over towards me.

'There he is! You all set, mate?'

Wink. Smile. Nod. Move away. Glance up at the clock. Ten to seven! How the fuck was it already ten to seven? I'd only looked at the clock ten seconds ago and it was quarter to! Why was time suddenly accelerating? If it continued at this pace, by the time we got to the end of the show I'd look like Jimmy Young.

While this thought occupied me I sat in my chair by the control desk and looked up at the clock, and it was now five to seven. Great. It's my first day at my new job and time was speeding up. According to Einsteinian theory I think that meant that I was apparently being pulled towards a black hole.

I looked at the clock itself, rather than its quite unreliable data. It wasn't a normal clock. It didn't have the big hand, little hand and second hand I had known all my life. This was some bizarre LED hybrid nightmare clock. The time was in digits at the centre of its circular face so it looked like a really big, really old digital watch. The seconds ticked along in the illuminated red digits, but around the outer edge of the face a single tiny red dot also counted out the seconds.

I felt like Tom Skerrit crawling around the air ducts of the *Nostromo*. The dot was moving closer and closer and I was getting more panicky. The dot represented my doom. And as I stared at it, a funny thing started to happen as we drew closer and closer to seven o'clock. Time, which had sadistically sped me towards this moment, suddenly and for no apparent reason slowed down. If only there had been a bumble bee hovering in front of my face then I could have filled my time by counting the individual beats of its tiny wings.

The glowing red dot moved another second up and I felt my heart whacking the sides of my throat somewhere around my tonsils. Opposite me sat Phil Wilding, while Jo Tyler stood just behind me, her eyes fixed on my hands, my clumsy, massive hands, which were now starting involuntarily to vibrate ever so slightly. It would be her responsibility at this auspicious moment to ensure that I didn't suddenly play the wrong track or fade up the wrong microphone. In the past she had often reached over my shoulder and taken my hand in hers just as I was about to do something spectacularly dim-witted. I could feel her calm stare burning into the skin on the back of my hand. Burning the words 'Don't fuck it up *now* ...'

I glanced back up at the clock and the tiny red dot deigned to move yet another second closer to 7 a.m. and I stared back down at the button which I would need to press in five seconds. My saliva glands had given up the ghost a few minutes previously so my mouth felt dry and uncomfortable. Cottonmouth, they call it in America. It didn't feel like my mouth any more. My tongue was a lolling, unfamiliar thing sat behind my dreadfully maintained teeth awaiting orders from my brain, which was now completely under the influence of my own somewhat overworked adrenal gland.

It's a funny old drug, adrenalin. It's almost as if your body in times of extreme stress insists on heightening your senses and speeding up all of your autonomic nervous processes just in case something dreadful happens. Why it would decide to give you a powerful stimulant at such a time is beyond me. I can't imagine that the best thing to do when you're already feeling panicky is the physiological equivalent of a line of cocaine. Conversely when people undergo a punishing

exercise regime or run a marathon the body produces
endorphins, which are like a kind of self-generated
opiate. Surely running a bloody marathon is when you
need the whizzy stuff! I was feeling incredibly stressed,
so why wasn't my central nervous system telling some
crazy gland in the brain to administer a slight tranquil-
liser? Nothing too mad, just the equivalent of a stiff
brandy, or a quick drag on a one-skinner.

But no, apparently my body wanted me wide awake
for this car crash moment in my life. As it transpires, the
human body is somewhere between a complete sadist
and an incompetent pharmacist. It wants you to remember every single millisecond in 5.1 Dolby Stereo 3D HD
clarity. The human body is obviously a complete fucking
bastard.

This assortment box of negative thought sped through
my mind in just less than one second. I shook it off and
refocused on the task in hand, and gave some thought
to exactly what I was about to say. But would I say the
right words? How difficult could it be to simply press
a button, slide a fader, say good morning, then press a
second button which starts a song so I can then take the
next three minutes off to read a newspaper and take a
sip of my refreshing beverage? Something I would do for
forty-four weeks a year for the next five years without as
much as a flicker of consciousness now seemed almost
Herculean in its difficulty.

Back at the bastard clock, the bloody red dot pushed
me a second closer to the moment I now assumed that
I would press the wrong button, yank up the fader,
accidentally say 'Fuck' on air, start the wrong record
and effectively end my broadcasting career all in three

action-packed seconds. This would be a shame, but if one is going to crash and burn, then I always thought you should do it with a certain *élan*. And why not go the whole hog under the baleful glare of the Director General of the BBC and a clutch of senior managers? And if we're going for uncomfortable and judgemental, why not throw in my mum and my first girlfriend for good measure, eh?

Through the control room window to my left I could indeed see the smiling anticipation of the DG himself, Greg Dyke. He looked like a very nice man. He had a lovely suit on and had a winning smile. From what little I knew of him he seemed to be somebody who knew about what people liked in their broadcasters. Unlike many of his predecessors at the BBC he definitely had the common touch. He was also fiercely protective of his staff, which at the BBC sat well alongside those key qualities you needed to be a truly effective head honcho. Integrity, vision and the kind of big brass knackers it takes to diplomatically tell the *Daily Mail* to go and take a flying fuck at a rolling doughnut.

Next to Greg was controller of network radio, Jenny Abramsky. I didn't have an awful lot to do with her during my time at the BBC and in fact wasn't even sure if she liked me. But she was always pleasant whenever we bumped into each other in lifts and never bollocked me, and once she took me to Wimbledon, so I can only assume everything was cool. To her left was controller of Radio 2, Jim Moir, who was looking at me with a cheery, kind of 'I told you so' face on. Beside him was Lesley Douglas, who would occasionally bollock me, but as she'd always do it over a very posh breakfast it never really felt like discipline as such.

Throughout my life I've never responded particularly well to authority. Now I don't mean that in an arrogant 'Ooh, look at me, I'm a maverick' kind of way. I simply don't like people who have it within their power to tell me what I can or can't do. I feel very uncomfortable in their presence, simply because they have control over me. The balance of power is tilted in their favour. I'm on the back foot even when they're saying something nice. As feelings go, I can only assume that it's akin to a kind of mild claustrophobia. The thing is, though, I can do exactly what they want to a T, but not when they're all staring at me. It seemed quite ironic that four BBC executives, who had gone to all the time and trouble of hiring me to launch their lovely new radio station, would then proceed to stand there and do the one thing that would make me knob it up completely. I tried to ignore their piercing managerial stares and looked around the room for some form of distraction that wasn't the fucking clock.

This is not as easy as you might imagine. It's very difficult to find anything particularly distracting in the décor of your average BBC facility. The drab institutional greys and beiges of the seventies have been augmented by the occasional ill-considered pastel shade or heavy-handed primary, none of which is helped in any way by the near-permanent neon lighting. The furniture, such as it is, belongs to the '1970s dentist's waiting room' school of interior design: cheap and unyielding tubular metal sofas upholstered with the thinnest of synthetic sponges, which are set at insanely obtuse angles that serve to baffle even the most flexible of spines. The subtext of this kind of furniture seems to be, 'Oh, by all means feel free to wait, but not for too long, eh.' Variation in textures ventures no further than the occasional sound-baffling sheet of dark blue hessian stretched over laminated MDF.

Occasionally through a Broadcasting House control room window you will see the reassuring green baize of the tables in the studio booths. These lofty, sanctified chambers are the preserve of 'proper' broadcasters, i.e. Radio 4. All their honey-voiced continuity announcers need to do is utter words like 'North Utsiera', 'Dogger' or 'Archers' and all seems well in the world. On a Thursday morning the broadcaster Melvyn Bragg fills just such a room with a dizzying array of challenging thought and opinion. Even though I would imagine that the average person rarely understands a word of *In Our Time*'s high-octane intellectual sparring, you simply have to keep listening. It's like a long, hot, cerebral jacuzzi. In these kind of rooms John Humphrys or Evan Davis give captains of industry and politicians of the day a sound going over and maybe a few hours later Kirsty Young will say 'Record number four?' Such rooms are the stuff of broadcasting legend. I was not in one of *those* rooms …

The studio we were in was a temporary facility, just intended to be used while we got the network up and running and they finished the construction of our proper studios over the road in Western House. As events transpired, this 'temporary facility' would be our home for the next four years. Perhaps that's what I found reassuring about working at Broadcasting House. When I worked for the civil service there was a minimal style, which twenty years later was mirrored in these sparse surroundings. Admittedly every once in a while there would be a framed photograph of Ken Bruce, presumably so you knew you weren't sat in the DHSS. The idle whimsy of this thought briefly tickled me before my eyes reluctantly fell back to the clock and my red glowing nemesis moved me a second closer to the grave …

I looked back to the people in the room with me. Wilding was scribbling away at his ever-present notebook, and stubbornly refusing to meet my gaze. From the tilt of his head I could tell that he knew full well that I was looking at him, imploring him to just quickly glance up and give me a wink or a smile or anything to break the tension. But he wouldn't do that because he felt exactly the same as me and wanted no part of my growing paranoia. If our eyes met it would be a tacit admission of the potential oncoming disaster. Somehow the whole thing would then be our fault just because we looked at each other. A couple of BBC and press photographers, who looked less than pleased at having to be up at this hour, idly tinkered away with their massive cameras, waiting to capture the moment when my career actually struck the waiting iceberg. Two seconds to go …

Why was I sat here? I had a perfectly serviceable career as a stand-up and resident captain on a TV pop quiz. At this moment it seemed odd to now be throwing a spanner in the works by becoming a deejay. DJ – I mean have two letters in the alphabet ever prompted more scorn and derision? This was not a noble pursuit. This was not trading in the fun and rhythm of language, which I had done as a poet. It wasn't putting pen and brush to paper to create new images, like I had when I was a cartoonist. It wasn't playing with new ideas and thoughts and shaping them in new ways to make thousands laugh, like I did as a stand-up. I was a deejay. Appallingly

I realised that I now had something in common with Bruno Brookes, aside from us both having an endocrine system. I had thus far managed to avoid having anything in common with Mr Brookes but now I was a member of that rarefied club. Travis, Bates, Blackburn, Juste and (shudder) Edmonds: I was one of them. My mind was assailed by doubt and insecurity. The biting lyrics of 'Panic' by The Smiths thrummed in my ears. *'Hang the deejay, Hang the deejay, Hang the deejay …'* And to be honest it wasn't really an ideal moment for that to be happening, no matter how good an idea it seemed. My eyes darted up at the clock. One second to seven …

My heart was a jackhammer in my chest. I swallowed nothing and stared at the pearl white button beneath my hovering left index finger. The recalcitrant digit was vibrating with its own nervous energy, counterpointed by my almost hummingbird pulse. I had not felt this nervous in years. The first time I had to go onstage with The Style Council at the Apollo in Manchester in 1987 was about as nervous as I'd ever got, but once I was actually up there and saw Paul Weller and his dad John in the wings watching me, it all went away. Today I was being stared at by an impassive cadre of powerful BBC executives, all of whom I knew were thinking, 'Now I wonder who we can get to replace him when he fucks up?' Somewhere in the ever-expanding space between 06.59 and 59 seconds and seven o'clock exactly, my mind became a total blank. Brilliant.

In Mexico it is called *'El loco luz roja'*. In France it is known as *'La folie du feu rouge'*. In Germany, it is simply *Radiofernsesprecherscheisenfest*. But everybody who works in radio knows about 'The Red Light Fever'. It was Phil Wilding who had first told me about this curious affliction which some unfortunate individuals are sadly prone to. Normally intelligent, sane, rational, articulate people go into a radio studio to promote their book or sitcom but, once in front of the microphone, the split second the red 'on air' light goes on they turn into gibbering idiots, prompting you to wonder how they ever got the book deal or sitcom in the first place. What if I had suddenly developed red light fever? Maybe I'd somehow contracted it from the phalanx of evil BBC executives through the glass.

I was now free associating about the wide range of potential disasters which might be about to befall me. What if I spontaneously developed Tourette's and at the moment the microphone went live screamed at the listeners to 'FUCK OFF AND FUCKING LEAVE ME ALONE YOU FUCKING FUCKERS!' What if my nerves got the better of me and I puked nothing but my own blood and bile over the control desk? What if one of the photographers had some kind of rare Bolivian river parasite that had been incubating in his brain ever since he got back from La Paz eight years ago and it hatched right now, making him go totally psycho and beat me to death with his Nikon? The insistent thumping in my chest and ears now attracted my full attention. What if I was about to have a massive heart attack, which, let's face it, was not entirely out of the realms of possibility?

I pressed the button, the jingle started. As it finished I pushed up the fader ...

'Good morning and welcome to BBC 6 Music. I'm Phill Jupitus and this is the record that you voted for to launch our station.' I pressed another button, leant back and reached for the *Guardian*. 'This is a fucking doddle,' I thought, and asked Jaffa for a cup of coffee ...

Six in the City

'Little Bitch' – The Ordinary Boys
'First Day' – Futureheads
'Glamorous Glue' – Morrissey
'Big Pimpin'' – Jay-Z
'Contact' – Roy Richards with The Baba Brooks Band
'Junior Kickstart' – Go! Team
'Johnny Appleseed' – Joe Strummer and The Mescaleros
'Stupidly Happy' – XTC
'Murray' – Pete Yorn
'Don't Falter' – Mint Royale featuring Lauren Laverne

11

What Once Were Vices Now Are Habits

One of the more surprising things about my long-dreaded transformation into 'a morning person' was the speed with which it happened. Within that first month of broadcasting I slowly but surely began to actually enjoy the abnormal rhythms of the very early nights and stupidly early mornings. Fellow newcomer BBC7 was in its infancy as well and had an interesting assortment of archive light entertainment on tap. I became quite the fan. The Goons were on a lot, as well as the somewhat less enthralling *Clitheroe Kid*. The wonderfully subversive *Round the Horne* was regularly aired and still retains its power to shock, even now. It felt odd yet comforting to be listening to the same kind of radio programmes that Dad first heard during his National Service in the fifties – shows that he then made me listen to repeats of back in the late 1960s.

For those of you who have never had the experience, preparing for a radio show the next morning is a pretty sweet way to finish off your day. The usual routine was that I would listen to BBC7 in the evening while getting everything together for the next day. I'd just cruise up and down the shelves, rifling through thousands of CDs looking for any I hadn't heard in a while. I'm not quite sure how grateful our small digital audience was when I successfully tracked down my copy of 'The Revolution Starts at Closing Time' by Serious Drinking, but it cheered me up. One of the most attractive things about being a deejay is the ability that you have to introduce people to something exciting and new or to remind them about something they've forgotten that they love.

Just as punk was in its ascendancy, my mates and I would usually hang out round each others' houses. It was suburban Essex and we were too old for the playground and too young for the public bar. There was simply nothing else for us to do, so life revolved around our record players. Clive and Mark were apprentices at Marconi Electronics in Chelmsford, while my other mates Brian and Dieter worked in the City. This gave all of them an income, and access to record shops. Also around this time, Brian's older brother John worked for the record label United Artists, who had just released the début Stranglers album *Rattus Norvegicus*. Brian subsequently had a pre-release white label copy, which to a collector is quite a valuable item. However, Brian borrowed Clive's finished copy and wrote out the track listing in felt pen on the plain labels, rendering it pretty much worthless. What did we know – we weren't collectors or purists, we were just kids in love with music …

Not having any income of my own, I would remain completely dependent on my mum for occasional handouts. It was a baking hot summer when the focus of my spending slowly switched over from fishing tackle to pop records. I vividly remember going with Mum to Godfreys in Basildon to buy a copy of *Never Mind the Bollocks*. There's nothing to make you feel quite so un-punk rock as getting your mum to go up to the counter with that in her hand. The only other way I could get hold of new music was to record bits of the John Peel Show off Radio 1.

Dad had recently been working with an American company in the Gulf and, mostly due to boredom and lack of booze, he had acquired a wide range of electrical gadgets he really had no use for. A couple of gems were the mosque-shaped alarm clock, which would call you to prayer, and the Casio 'biorhythm calculator'. One of the most practical was his large Panasonic boom box. I somehow managed to appropriate that for myself and it sat in my bedroom up on the double radiator underneath the pin board.

Every night just before ten I would insert a blank 'Soundhog' C90 cassette, then would press play, record and pause altogether. There would be just a couple of minutes of Radio 2 to negotiate, then we'd be good to go. Trouble with bootlegging Peely, though, was that while you were intending just to tape the music you'd end up keeping his whimsical between-song chit-chat as well. I remember taping some great stuff by Bethnal, Penetration, Siouxsie and The Banshees, The Fall and The Bonzo Dog Doo Dah Band. It was only when listening back to these tapes years later that you realised that some of the best bits about them were of John, wittering on between tunes.

Our late-night music sessions down at Brian's or Mark's were always the same. We'd have a few cans of cheap lager or cider and talk crap about girls who we had no chance at all of doing anything with. The only really positive thing about our lives was the music. Stuff would be on and off the record player constantly as we searched through the record boxes looking for other stuff to play. Clive and Mark had access to Parrot Records in Chelmsford, so had a much better collection of stuff. I first heard bands like 999 in Mark's front room just as I first heard The Stranglers' epic 'Down in the Sewers' round at Brian's.

It's funny to think that we were all just sitting there and listening, then occasionally looking round at each other and going, 'This is brilliant!' Then you'd put it on all over again and repeat the process. It was exactly that magical feeling which I always wanted to try and recreate as a deejay, that mutual discovery of something new. Hearing something special or unique for the first time that you can't quite put your finger on. Breakfast radio listeners had previously been seen as passive; I wanted ours to play a more active role. I wanted elements of the show to be a bit like those days round my mates' houses ...

Whenever I scanned the racks that covered my office wall, I was always looking for at least two or three tracks I could drop in that would create that kind of reaction. More often than not it would be old rather than new music which would do this best. Great new music was all well and good, but if you played something from the fifties or sixties, the reaction was more like, 'I can't believe I've never heard this before!' The best music for this was some of the lesser-known instrumental ska tracks by groups like The Skatalites. On our playout database there were maybe three or four original 1960s ska tunes. At home on my shelves I had hundreds and hundreds of these gems, and wanted to play them all.

I also liked peppering the occasional jazz, Latin and Northern Soul cuts throughout the week. The BBC granted me more freedom than any other breakfast show, but still I wanted more. I was a spoilt bastard.

As time went on, I noticed that the same classic tracks kept cropping up on the playlist, which after a time started to rankle. If we had songs from artists like The Jam or The Clash or Elvis Costello, nine times out of ten it would always be hit singles. Now there is nothing wrong with that, but why did we have to play singles all the time? At home I had pretty much everything ever recorded by these three artists. Why be so conservative with our selections? Instead of 'Oliver's Army' by Costello, why not play the fast version of 'Battered Old Bird' or the acoustic demo of 'Green Shirt'? Instead of 'Eton Rifles' by The Jam, why not their version of 'Heatwave' or 'Running on the Spot'? Instead of 'Should I Stay or Should I Go' by The Clash why not 'The Right Profile' or 'Something about England'? Listeners to 6 Music weren't the kind of people who would mind being thrown the odd curve ball once in a while. But in my enthusiasm for the job I didn't realise that I was second-guessing the audience, which was an insane thing to be doing when we didn't even know if we even had an audience yet.

Once I'd prepared for the show, there would be at least fifty CDs to choose from. Sadly we didn't have a record deck set up to play vinyl on the station, nor indeed would we have one for another four years. There was naturally enough a bit of resistance to playing anything that might have crackles on it over the lovely clean digital airwaves. After all we'd spent millions bringing digital broadcasting to the nation, why fuck it up by running the risk of fatty putting something on at the wrong speed? But if this station was for music fans, do you think they would really get upset just because we were playing analogue copies rather than a digital format? It was one of those fights that you'd start to have and then realise halfway through you were talking when you should have been listening.

The only other thing we had to do was to write 6 Musings. This would involve me getting home and sitting on the BBC News website trawling for a story that we could wring half a dozen decent one-liners out of. I'd do this in the afternoon, and then send the likely contenders across to Phil, and we'd then both write the gags between us, ping-ponging emails back and forth until it was done. On a good day this would be all done by teatime. Occasionally we were still writing them just before we read them out, but part of the fun of having to do it every day was the discipline.

Once I was in bed for the night, I would switch over from BBC7 to audio books. My two go-to storytellers were Garrison Keillor reading the abridged version of his novel *Radio Romance* or Elliot Gould's sonorous reading of *The Lady in the Lake* by Raymond Chandler. Their soothing accents from the other side of the world would have me asleep in a matter of minutes, so my knowledge of the plots of any of these books is far from complete. I'm not sure I ever heard it as far as the hard-boiled LA gumshoe Philip Marlowe actually finding the lake, let alone the lady.

The process of waking up in the morning was the trickiest part of the operation. Let me tell you this: the 'snooze' feature on an alarm clock is a false economy that early in the morning. The reason for this is that you are in a state of very deep sleep indeed, so at 4.20 a.m. the alarm goes off and you hit the snooze button, desperate for just a few more seconds of sweet repose. But you don't really 'snooze' so much as plunge straight back into the deep sleep from which you were so cruelly yanked. And then after what feels like only a split second the fucking alarm is going off yet again, and you blindly repeat this process over and over. It's like alarm, snooze button, close eyes, alarm, snooze button, close eyes, alarm, snooze button, alarm, get up. The previous sixteen minutes of fractured slumber feel like three seconds and you are immediately in a very bad mood. After a few mornings of this you switch tactics.

On hearing my first alarm, I would immediately sit up, cantilever my legs round, put my feet on the floor and remain hunched over for a moment, hating myself for even taking the job on in the first place. Once this brief period of self-loathing was done, I would slowly stand up, then pad gently across the landing to the bathroom trying my very best to be quiet. Now, when you weigh 22 stones and are naturally clumsy, you can't really do quiet. Your large body may have a lower centre of gravity, but you have more volume, and you are in a near coma. You aren't designed for stealth in any way, shape or form. Think about this for a moment. There are no fat ninjas and the Victorian burglar Raffles didn't nick pies.

The powerful hiss of the shower, accompanied by me coughing, farting, knocking over the 'Miss Matey' and dropping the shampoo bottle, probably woke up the entire family and the neighbours most mornings. But it was a small price to pay for consciousness. For me, the shower is the only wake-up call that has ever really worked.

Once I'm wet and soapy there is no turning back. Like it or not, the day has begun. Getting up in the dark and jumping straight into a shower wasn't ever what I would describe as a 'pleasant' experience. I know many people absolutely love a nice hot shower. It's bracing and refreshing. What I was doing in this instance was more like waterboarding myself into a state of wakefulness. And if I also accidentally got shampoo in my eyes as well, then that's just a bonus. Nothing says 'good morning' quite like searing eye pain …

As my regular driver Harry drove us towards London each day, I never failed to get a certain thrill from the deserted streets and the way we would breeze past the sparse traffic on the A13. My favourite part of the journey remained those final few miles, when we would pass dozens of iconic London landmarks. But an essential something was missing from them. It took me some time to realise exactly what it was that was absent. They looked just as they did on postcards and from the hundreds of television programmes and films, but somehow unfamiliar. Initially I thought it was that I was seeing them in a more fragmented sense as we breezed by. It was only after months of making the journey that I realised the thing that was missing was people.

Deserted London is a haunting and wonderful thing. Occasionally before the show I would leave my music box in the office, then go back out of the building and walk the hundred meandering yards or so back to Portland Place, one of the main thoroughfares running from the Euston Road into the heart of the capital. By the time our show finished at ten, this road would be jammed with cars, taxis, vans and motorbikes. Its pavements would be busy with fast walking pedestrians making their way into Soho. At a quarter to six in the morning it was almost completely silent. The steady thrum of what urban noise there is becomes more distant and faint at that hour. The sudden diesel growl of a black cab rounding a corner is the only interruption. As you walk along, the only steady noise is the echo of your own footsteps. I would walk to the centre of the road and just stand there looking around at the façades of the buildings. The black silhouette of the spire of All Souls Church pointing into the sky where I would see the first suggestion of the day's light approaching from the east. On the occasional mornings when I did this, the idea of one of the most vibrant cities in the world being in this form of stasis struck me as being so absurd that I would often end up laughing on my own. In the middle of the deserted street.

I'm sure for some of you this next statement will be hard to believe, but breakfast is something I can never really face until I'm properly awake. At other times of the day I more than make up for this reluctance, but at that time of the morning food just seems like the most awfully crass idea. In the very early days I would force myself to have something. Anything. Marmite on toast or cereal were the easiest options at the time. But I just didn't want them. So then I'd try and eat different things. I'd go through odd early-morning eating fads for weeks at a time.

One particular favourite involved soaking muesli overnight in orange juice then adding plain yoghurt in the morning. That actually isn't as bad as it sounds. Pickled herring was another winner, but possibly not for anybody who had to be in close proximity to me. For a short while, I used to make extra portions of dinner the night before, and have that when I woke up. Nothing gives a kick-start to your day like forcing down cold lasagne at 4.45 a.m. Absurd as it seems, once you realise that you don't actually need to eat when you're not hungry, the whole thing gets easier. Until you have to decide what to drink.

You don't anticipate falling into bad habits when you take on a new job. You are eager to make a good impression, and keen to do well. I imagined that the regularity of the hours and the lack of anxiety about where my next pay cheque was coming from might ultimately calm me down. To an extent this was true, but what I didn't anticipate was my crippling dependence on the demon bean. I think if I was a tea drinker the unpleasantness might have been avoided. When you're a tea drinker your options are limited. The only real variables are sweetness, strength and whether or not to have milk. Simple. I started to drink coffee, quite a bit of coffee, quite a bit indeed. At first we would get our Java-fix from the seventh-floor tea bar at the BBC. It wasn't really what you could call drinkable. It was a warm brown liquid that smelled like something trying very hard to be coffee. It was like a *Stars in Their Eyes* beverage. 'Tonight, Matthew I'm going to be a cup of coffee!' And everybody applauds, and they go, 'Oh bless it for having a go! It looks just like a cup of coffee!' But everybody in the room knows it isn't.

Sadly, when you actually tasted it you realised it had failed in its lofty ambition. The most it could manage was hot and wet, and sometimes even the former eluded it. We needed to establish an alternative supply for the show. Our first thought was that we would do it ourselves. However, having made some tentative enquiries, we were prevented from having our own coffee machine, as all electrical equipment had to be first approved by BBC safety inspectors. I suppose that in the long run it might have been worth the effort if we'd got a really good one, but the very idea of endless form-filling and bureaucracy put us off from the start. It was the same reason that I never submitted an expenses form while I was at the BBC. I simply could not be bothered. So quite early on we started sending out for coffee.

We couldn't do this at any old time. We would have to wait for a quiet moment in the show when we could spare our BA and then ask them ever so nicely if they could nip down the road. As you couldn't send them out all the time, we tended to have our corporate beverage moment somewhere between 8.00 and 8.30. By this point in the show we were properly awake and had been on air for an hour. So it was less a beverage and more a reward for a job well done.

It's hard to believe that once I would simply order a regular cappuccino with no chocolate on top. Such a simple coffee order seems almost laughable now. Within days this proved to be not quite enough somehow, and I said so to my colleagues. Jaffa suggested that I did have the option of having a bit more espresso in it, so I found myself asking for the same order with 'an extra shot'. Just to give it a little bit of a zip. Little did I know that I was upping the ante of those early stages of my addiction. We'd take it in turns to get 'a round' in, and would always include whoever was out on the news and music news desk. Oh it was a jolly old time, turning all our colleagues into hopeless coffee junkies.

Occasionally, Jaffa would return with an unfeasibly large muffin for her breakfast. As I sipped on my coffee I'd look over to my left and see her through the glass, breaking small ladylike chunks off and popping them into her mouth. My reaction to this was sub-Pavlovian: having seen a muffin, I now had to have a muffin. So now my order increased to a small cap, extra shot, and a skinny raisin bran muffin. Reasonable enough.

Well, you can probably see what's coming now. A small cap doesn't have enough liquid to help you deal with the sweet, doughy, cloying texture of the muffin, so I had to increase the order once again to 'medium cap extra shot, raisin bran muffin'. This sufficed for a short while, but then having the muffin with the coffee took a bit of the caffeine edge off. So I bumped the order up to medium triple cap and a muffin right up until the moment that I saw Phil Wilding eating a cheese and marmite panini.

What had started out as a quick mid-show pick-me-up had now escalated – or degenerated, depending on your nutritional viewpoint – into a full-scale meal with a dessert. I dare say if somebody had suggested I have a bag of crisps or a brownie as a starter I'd have gone for that as well. At its ludicrous peak, my standard order from Starbucks was: a large *venti* cappuccino with three extra shots, two cheese and marmite paninis and a muffin. Between the sugar, fat and caffeine I'm not sure how I didn't have a stroke while I was working at 6 Music. I dare say if I hadn't left the station in 2007, by now I'd be on a quart of espresso and two trays of Krispy Kremes.

One truism about those who make breakfast radio is that they are a law unto themselves. They arrive at the office before anybody else and prepare for their shows in isolation. Not for them the bustle and banter of the office that everybody else at the station works around. We settled into the rhythm of doing the show with no bother at all. The only time I ever found it difficult was if I was made to stay up late the night before doing a show. In our first week it was decided to have a launch party for staff and listeners. Well, I say listeners, I think we might have just invited anybody who emailed in the first week. John Sugar asked me if as the presenter of the breakfast show I would host the evening. I pointed out to him that as the host of the breakfast show, maybe I wasn't the guy to be rattling around a gig at eleven at night. But he remained adamant, so I booked a hotel not too far from work.

The launch gig took place at Sound on Leicester Square and featured quite an eclectic mix if you liked guitars. Kicking the evening off was a new young singer from Wales called Amy Wadge. She was gigging and promoting herself tirelessly, so this opportunity was a big deal for her. I remember having to write her name on my hand, so as not to forget it, but spelling it with an 'o' instead of an 'a' so there was no ambiguity about the pronunciation. Amy's a tiny little thing who plays a big old acoustic guitar, which is visually quite striking. As I watched her on the stage, I couldn't help but think of The Sour Grape Bunch, two diminutive children with guitars who sang mariachi songs on *The Banana Splits* show. As I giggled to myself, I woozily thought, 'Hang on, it's only half seven and I feel completely thrashed!'

The sudden onset of tiredness at the time when not so long ago I would just be thinking about getting ready to go out became a common feeling. It affected all of us who worked on the show in varying degrees and manifested itself in a variety of ways. I would get either giggly or grumpy, and on occasion a delightful combination of both. More often than not I would just become surly and uncommunicative. Not ideal for somebody about to go onstage.

The rest of the bill at the party was a good cross-section of the kind of stuff that 6 Music played on a day-to-day basis. Pete Yorn, Kelly Jones from The Stereophonics, Embrace and rounding it all off Lenny Kravitz. I introduced each of them to the stage with a grim economy. Each act had to perform half-hour sets and as the evening wore on I became more and more tired. The only time I managed to generate any enthusiasm was when Yorn played his set. This was now the third time I'd seen him live in a month. As he played the beautiful 'Life on a Chain' I sang along, sipping on the bottle of water I carried around with me. If people thought I was in a bad mood that night, they should just count themselves lucky that I wasn't drinking on top of the tiredness. Jones and Embrace did their thing and at around 10.30 I had to introduce Lenny Kravitz. Fact is I'm quite a fan of his loose funk rock, but that evening the only thought going through my mind was *'For the love of God, please let me sleep!'* I could have been introducing the reanimated corpse of Elvis doing a duet with Janis Joplin and I'd still have just wanted to get to bed.

Putting on live events was something that 6 Music would do all too infrequently in its freshman year. But budgetary constraints meant that they couldn't go crazy. Meanwhile over at 1xtra they were regularly doing outside broadcasts at clubs and venues all over the UK. Like us they had a niche listenership but they were thinking a lot more laterally about ways to expand that. It would be a couple of years before 6 Music started to tie itself in with regular live events such as Leicester's Summer Sundae Festival and its Glastonbury coverage.

From my point of view, a lack of live gigs was just peachy. Anything that cut into my new sleep regime was viewed with suspicion. I was still adjusting to the early nights, and so the week I started I was suffering from a mild form of jet-lag.

The first year was a learning experience for both us and our small but growing band of listeners. We were in uncharted but very exciting waters. Listeners were more than keen to give us feedback, despite our inability to receive texts at this point. I found this quite galling as 1xtra pretty much existed on its heavy text traffic. The text-speak generation would have to wait three years before they could use their huge distended thumbs to contact 6 Music. In the meantime, email filled the breach admirably. We'd get requests, greetings and comments steadily throughout the shows. Once a new listener cottoned on to our free-and-easy play policy we'd get some fairly odd requests.

Whenever people asked me what kind of music the station played, I could never sum it up in a nice simple sound bite. I would usually just end up telling them ten records that I had played on the show that morning. I think the indefinable nature of 6 Music is why it was so difficult for us to build a large new audience. If you ask most people they will say they like music. They would probably go on to observe that there's a very wide range of music available on Radios 1, 2 and 3 so why the need for another music station?

Just after 6 Music started broadcasting, all staff members were issued with sleek black DAB tuner rack units that they could plug into the spare channel on their stereo. I suppose at the time I should have really asked where they came from. But this was a freebie, so in those situations I find it best to just nod, say thank you and take whatever it is out of their hands and then leg it. It was very nice of them to provide them, and I suppose quite a practical move. DAB was a completely new arena for British broadcasting and I suppose they wanted us to hear what else was out there, and these tuners would be our window on this new world.

My relationship with electronic equipment is an uneasy one at best. The only wiring I can cope with is the bit that has a three-pin plug at one end and goes in the wall. Once it was out of its box, I set it on the floor and stood back. It was a matt black, fourteen by ten inch rectangular unit, which looked uncannily like the monolith from 2001 and was only marginally less sinister. My little Sony midi hi-fi unit was a perky, brushed aluminium affair with lights, LEDs, dials and a friendly demeanour. Plugging in this strange new gadget into the auxiliary channel at the back of it seemed like some kind of violation. As I looked at the two pieces of mismatched technology it felt like one of my young daughters had come home with a six and a half foot tattooed Goth. Not a problem as such, but I just felt rather uneasy.

I plugged this strange new machine in, not knowing what might happen. I can only imagine that it is how Bill Gates must have felt on New Year's Eve 1999 as he sat in his bunker surrounded by water and non-perishables, clutching a shotgun. Would the thing hum into life go 'beep' and cause an EM pulse that would shut down every electronic device in Europe? Would arms and legs suddenly shoot out of it, just before it pinned me to the ground and tried to get me pregnant with its evil half-human, half-electronic cyborg baby? I plugged the audio leads into my poor little stereo and connected the device's antenna. Now I say antenna, but what it looked like to me was eight feet of plastic-coated copper wire, so the word 'antenna' was gilding the lily somewhat. I took a deep breath, eased the plug into the socket, closed my eyes and pushed the power switch to the 'on' position.

Nothing.

I hesitantly opened one eye. The lights were still working, outside the window birds chirped and the sun shone. Life was going on as usual. I stood up and walked over to the unit. I could see that the display screen was now glowing with a strange pinky-blue light, which as I looked at it turned out to be the word 'welcome'. Well, it seemed rude to ignore such a chirpy greeting, so I consulted the manual to see what I should do next. Perhaps it would like a camomile tea and a rub down.

The manual told me that I should press the button marked 'scan' in about a dozen languages, and at this point who was I to disagree with the manual? It could have said, 'Now run yourself a nice hot bath and then go and fetch a toaster and an extension lead,' and I would have done it. So I meekly obeyed, pressing the button, at which point the word 'searching' started to flash at me on the small display screen. 'searching … searching … searching …'

What could it be searching for, exactly? As its mysterious search progressed, four tiny empty rectangular boxes on the screen started to slowly fill up with light. One … two … three … aaaaaand … 'search complete'.

I was so stunned by this message that I forgot that I had already set the stereo to its auxiliary channel so my speakers suddenly burst into life, and the volume was set rather too loud. As a result of this, the very first words that I heard coming out of my brand new DAB tuner were 'YES! TOMORROW MORNING ON THE RADIO 1 BREAKFAST SHOW ...'

So I was right after all. The new radio *was* evil!

Tasty Treats

'Java Jive' – The Ink Spots

'Mick's Blessings' – The Style Council

'Comedy' – Shack

'The Snake' – Dodgy

'The Model' – Kraftwerk

'Cheeseburger' – Gang of Four

'The New Workout Plan' – Kanye West

'The Pop Singer's Fear of the Pollen Count' – The Divine
   Comedy

'Scooby Snacks' – Fun Lovin' Criminals

'Delicious' – Jim Backus

12
Pleased to Meet You

Having eased into the new job, the first hurdle to negotiate was the thorny problem of repetition. I was aware
that I had never been involved with any long-term daily
form of entertainment previously. So just how does one
do the same thing every day for a year and keep it fresh?
The best entertainment broadcasters can make a virtue
of going through the same features and the same style of
delivery for years and years. And that repetition is exactly
what their audience wants. If Terry Wogan had ever
opened his breakfast show with a shrill, 'HEY EVERY-
BODY, GOOOOOOOOOOD MORNING AND ISN'T IT
A GRRRRRRRRRREAT DAY OUT THERE!' there would
have been some kind of insurrection, albeit a quite slow-
moving one that would have stopped every half hour for
tea and biscuits and to moan about the young people.

The regular beats of the show were offset by the two
constantly shifting factors, the new music and the daily
news. After the first record out of the 8.30 news, we would
pick up on a few small news stories that might give us and
the audience a laugh. Before the show we would scour
the newspapers for any items that might be gag worthy.

We made a conscious decision not to use any stories from the tabloids, as they were already in the business of presenting small whimsical news items as entertainment. We'd look through all the smaller stories that would give us something to chat about before the next record. On some mornings there was an embarrassment of riches and on others it was just an embarrassment. But that was the nature of the beast: whatever you had, no matter how lacklustre it might be, you still had to run with it. But it didn't faze me as I was already used to doing topical stuff on the radio.

By the time I had started working on 6 Music I was being regularly booked into guest slots once or twice a series for *The News Quiz* on Radio 4. The usual line-up would be Simon Hoggart in the middle chair, Francis Wheen and Jeremy Hardy sat out on one side and more often than not I'd be sat next to the ever-present Alan Coren. My grasp of current affairs was sketchy at best, but as with all of those panel games it's not about writing jokes. You need to listen to what's going on and occasionally pick up the ball and run with it.

Usually the one-liners I had prepared in advance would customarily die on their arse, whereas what would make the edit would be what I came up with on the night in response to others. I would make reams of notes in the early days and would nervously sit there waiting for the topics I had revised to come up. And revised is an appropriate word because doing *The News Quiz* was like being back at school, only in this case it wasn't possible to look Simon Hoggart in the eye and say, 'I'm sorry sir but the dog ate my jokes ...' It took two years of doing *The News Quiz* before I had the balls to go onstage at recordings without notes. After doing the show a few times, I relaxed and set the comedy barometer a little lower, and I was only ever really satisfied if I'd made Coren laugh.

Now 6 Music breakfast was fully up and running, we had to get word out about the station. I was corralled into a number of interviews with the press, but the jewel in the crown was my booking on *Friday Night with Jonathan Ross*, a real chat show. With viewers!

The British have always had an uneasy relationship with television chat shows. This is in part born of the fact that we initially went at it from a journalistic rather than entertainment perspective. Our kings of chat in the 1970s were Michael Parkinson and Russell Harty, both former journalists. It is worth noting that both their most famous interviews involved the pair of them being physically assaulted by their guests, one by a ridiculous-looking, googly-eyed bird with a long neck, the other by Rod Hull and Emu.

Sadly Russell Harty is no longer with us but Parkinson got the chance to emerge phoenix-like from his own ashes and slap down young upstarts like Ross and Graham Norton with his elder-statesmanlike interviewing style. But the thing is, the audience had changed. His low-ball style of questioning was absolutely perfect for the film legends of the forties and fifties. The Parkinson interviews with the likes of Peter Sellers, Fred Astaire, Richard Burton, James Stewart and David Niven were quite brilliant. These stars had an aura of genuine Hollywood mystique.

But these people and those like them were now all dead. We were in a new millennium, where contemporary American film stars live and breathe by appearing on at least half a dozen zingy high-profile network and cable chat shows at home. Parkinson should have come out of retirement with a completely new style of show: one-on-one interviews conducted on location without a live audience. Coming back twenty years later and doing the same show all over again just reminded you how good it was in the 1970s. Exactly how many times can you get Anthony Hopkins to do his Tommy Cooper? The post-modern nadir of 'new Parkinson' was Robbie Williams gurning into the camera lens saying, 'Look, Mum, I'm on Parky!' Michael deserved better.

Jonathan Ross, however, is both an interviewer *and* an entertainer. That is something that should be noted by all those who go, '*He's not as good as Parkinson! He's always making jokes!*' He is a comedian without portfolio who has one of the most agile minds in modern television. I know that his probing, cheeky and often salacious style isn't for everybody. My mother can't stand him on television or on the radio, and indeed when the infamous 'Sachsgate' incident took place it was for her a final savage indictment on Ross.

When the *Daily Mail* (mother's paper of choice) was in full apoplectic flight about the Brand and Ross furore, she would merely gesticulate in the direction of the front page whenever I was around her house, and arch her eyebrows. This mute assertion was her way of telling me that she had been right all along about Jonathan.

Then she moved into realms of militancy that made my work at Miners' Benefits in 1985 look like small potatoes. 'I don't see why I should pay my licence fee if it's going to him …' I didn't even look up from the newspaper; I took a sip of my tea and picked up a nearby biro.

'He doesn't get any money from you, Mum.'

She looked at me quizzically. 'What do you mean?'

I entered a 7 into the grid of a sudoku. 'You live in Essex. The licence fee is apportioned on a regional basis. Jonathan is in light entertainment, which is principally funded by the licence fees from London, Manchester and Glasgow ...'

'What do I pay for then?'

'Well, Essex outside the M25 comes under East Anglia so that covers *Antiques Roadshow*, *The Archers*, *Springwatch*, gardening programmes and David Attenborough ...'

I'm not sure I've ever seen her more delighted.

The breakfast show had been on air for nearly three months when I made my first televised appeal for listeners on *Friday Night with Jonathan Ross*. At the time one particularly pithy industry gag about the station was that we shouldn't have been called 6 Music, we should have been called 6 Listeners. Indeed, the occasional TV spots featuring a wedding being spoiled by the deejay playing 'Fell in Love with a Girl' by The White Stripes were certainly noisy and stylish, but they weren't exactly hoovering up the potential faithful. We were still hamstrung by the nascent technology. There simply weren't enough DAB radios available in the shops. I made a habit of checking in with my local electrical goods retailer in Leigh-on-Sea on a bi-monthly basis.

The first time I went into the shop to ask about digital radios he said, 'Yeah, we've got one here ...' and took me over to a standard AM/FM wireless which had a digital display.

'No, no ... a *digital* radio ...'

He looked at me and slightly narrowed his eyes, looked back round at the radio and slowly pointed again at the liquid crystal AM/FM readout.

I sighed and tried again. 'No, mate, the new radio format, digital audio broadcasting, DAB!'

His eyes widened and he smiled. 'Oh … *digital* radio … right, I gotcha … No. We aren't stocking them.'

I smiled weakly, closed my eyes and enquired as to the reason they wouldn't be embracing the new technology.

'Well, we mainly stock Sony and Panasonic audio kit, and the last time I heard anything they aren't planning to release any models. If the big manufacturers don't pick up on DAB, then their competitors probably won't bother making one, and if that happens it'll end up going the same way as Betamax.' I had been in my shiny new job for just under two months, and here in this small suburban electrical retailer a little man in a blue shirt was foretelling my doom.

The appearance on Jonathan's show and the chance to address his several million viewers was an opportunity to garner some new listeners. The show was recorded the day before transmission, so on the morning of Thursday 30 May, after coming off air, I popped my head around the door of John Sugar's office.

'BBC Publicity got me booked on telly with Jonathan Ross this week, John.' I smiled and gave him a cheeky thumbs up. He beamed in response.

'Excellent, mate. It's good to get out there and spread the word.'

I turned to leave and as I did there was a hesitant, 'Oh … and Phill …'

I looked back round to him.

'Try not to do anything about us not having any listeners, eh?'

I gave John my most reassuring nod. 'No problem, John. I hadn't even given it a thought, John.'

But I was thinking about it now.

* * *

Also booked on the show were ironic housewives' choice Dale Winton, Welsh legend Tom Jones and the Red Hot Chili Peppers. I was incredibly excited. I could get my copy of *Blood Sugar Sex Magic* signed, share a pint with Tom Jones, and fend off the delightful advances of the saucy Winton. I had always retained a fondness for Dale, ever since quite early in the life of *Never Mind the Buzzcocks* Mark Lamarr took me to one side. 'Jupes, I was at a BBC do the other night, and I tell you who fancies you …'

I closed my eyes, hoping for either French or Saunders.

'Dale Winton!' said Mark, and my joy ebbed temporarily. But to be honest at the time I was nearly forty so I had to take my admirers where I could find them.

'He came up to me,' Lamarr went on, 'and said, "Here, Mark, I'll tell you who I fancy on your show …" and I said Sean (Hughes) 'cos it's always Sean they fancy, and he goes, "Ooh no, not him, the big one, Phill!"'

I had my first celebrity crush. I had truly arrived in showbiz now.

I would occasionally bump into the delightful Dale at various TV and radio studios and would go up and tease him about how he was my bitch. He would giggle girlishly, and tell me to stop it. One time I was flicking through the racks at HMV and there was a tap on my shoulder. I wheeled round and there was Dale. Brilliant white teeth, jet black hair and satsuma glow. "Allo, Dale. How are you, babe?' I hugged him and he giggled and flushed ever so slightly around his cheekbones. He had a shopping basket full of Northern Soul compilation CDs. The boy was and is a very knowledgeable soul enthusiast.

'I'm alright. What are you doing here?' he said.

'Just picking up a few bits for the show …' and I brandished the half dozen albums I had in my hand.

'You don't pay for them, do you? You should call the labels and ask for them. What's the bloody point of being on the radio?'

'Oh fuck off, I'm rubbish at blagging.'

He giggled some more at my filthy mouth and I teased him relentlessly with a little peck on the cheek. He moved close and whispered …

'I tell you what I like about you.'

'What's that, Dale?'

He moved a little closer and dipped towards my ear and rubbed his hand on my large stomach and looked into my eyes. 'I do like a balcony over the playroom.'

I burst out laughing so loud that several startled punters turned towards us. And just like that, he was gone.

Still, my relentless flirting with a national treasure aside, the show was a laugh. Tom Jones arrived with his son who is also his manager. A keen as mustard runner approached the two imposing Welshmen and asked if they would like anything to drink. Tom looked down at her and in his perfect valley accent said, 'You 'aven't got any bitter, 'ave you, love?' As she dashed off to the BBC bar to fulfil his request I was almost disappointed that he didn't shout after her, 'LOVE! CAN WE HAVE BRAINS S.A. IF THEY'VE GOT IT! TA!'

To be on a show with Tom Jones and Jonathan Ross was an odd moment for me. In 1996 I was commissioned by *GQ* to write a piece on one of my favourite people in television and I picked Jonathan Ross. At the time he couldn't get arrested. He'd walked away from his production company Channel X, and was presenting the lamentable *Big Big Talent Show* for ITV. I made the point that here was Britain's first media polymath. Ross was just as funny as many of the guests he had on the show, but never billed himself as a comedian. He was the first British chat show host to embrace the American template of doing a few shows a week and keeping them pacy and irreverent.

His first show, *The Last Resort*, was one of my favourite television shows. Indeed on one episode his guests were Dawn French, Terry Gilliam and Tom Jones. For me this one episode is probably my favourite half hour of British television. French came on set and proclaimed herself 'moist' at the thought of being on the same show as Jones. When Terry Gilliam came on set he dropped to his knees and sniffed the seat of the chair, which had only recently been vacated by French. At the end of the show Jones sang 'It's Not Unusual' with the skinny and tone-deaf Ross backing him vocally as an obviously aroused Dawn French rubbed herself up and down the huge letter 'T' of the 'TOM JONES' backdrop which they had brought in. For one simple visual gag, it must have cost them thousands of pounds. But it was the 1980s and Channel 4, so the wasting of money was almost *de rigueur*. Now that might not sound like much, but to me in my early twenties it was like looking into a magic kingdom.

About six months after seeing this amazing moment, I applied for a job as researcher at Channel X for the next

series of *The Last Resort*. Having absolutely zero television experience I typed out a letter of application pointing out my keenness. When I read it back, I noticed that
the thing was absolutely crammed with spelling mistakes
and grammatical errors. I grumpily took up the red felt-
tip pen and proceeded to correct each one. At the end of
it I looked down at the resulting mess and wrote, 'Do you
seriously think you'll get a job in TV with this standard
of typing?'

I looked again at the scrawled overtyped sheet and
pondered for a moment. Then I folded it up, slipped it into
the envelope and posted it. Two thousand young hope-
fuls applied for the opportunity of working for Jonathan,
and I was one of twenty who got an interview. Sadly my
complete lack of television experience was a lot more
apparent to the lady behind the desk, as I am absolutely
terrible at interviews. I just mumbled how much I liked
the show and how much I'd like to work with Jonathan,
before saying 'I dunno' in answer to a string of production-
related questions. I was not at all surprised to receive a
curt 'Thanks but no thanks' rejection slip.

I remember thinking about that just before I walked
onstage to be interviewed by Jonathan on his chat show.
Doing television with Jonathan Ross is, for the performer
who understands him, a sheer joy. He is generous, while
at the same time fully prepared to joke at your expense.
At the same time, he can take it just as much as he dishes
it out. As long as you realise that there's no malice in the
man you'll get on fine.

He introduced me and I strode out onto the set, grinning to the usual applause. I seemed to be dressed
in a sartorial style I can only describe as 'midlife crisis

toddler'. All that was missing was the Farley's rusk. The interview was the usual light banter about my beard and size and the fact that by sitting next to Tom Jones I was now pregnant. I also talked a bit about Dale, which forced the vision mixer to keep cutting to him in the green room where he giggled and went pink. The worst bit of the interview was when Jonathan asked me to describe 6 Music and how it was different from Radio 1 and Radio 2. I was always legendarily crap at plugging my own stuff but I gave it a go.

Sadly, Jonathan then asked me how many listeners we had and my self-deprecating humour got the better of me.

'To be honest, Jonathan, if I drove through the West End of London with the cab window open and shouted at people, I'd get more listeners.'

Ross laughed and the crowd laughed and I laughed but at the time I thought to myself, 'I'm not joking, you know ...'

RB Shot JR

'Fame' (live at the BBC) – David Bowie
'Resurrection Shuffle' – Tom Jones
'Higher Ground' – Red Hot Chili Peppers
'Secret Love' – Billy Stewart
'That's Me Trying' – William Shatner
'Love Me' – Dudley Moore
'Television Drug of the Nation' – The Disposable Heroes of Hiphopracy
'(I'm a) TV Savage' – Bow Wow Wow
'Shame and Scandal' – Clint Eastwood and General Saint
'Rocks Off' – The Rolling Stones

13

Impossible Broadcasting

One of the regular things that happened during the time I spent at 6 Music was an odd little verbal exchange I would have with Phil while we were in the studio. We never ever said the words on air, I assume because we both thought that by saying it out loud in front of the audience we would somehow be jinxing ourselves. And we said it to each other a lot. It would usually be uttered when we were playing a brilliant record for the first time ever, or we'd had a particularly good link, or a spectacular guest had just said goodbye. The moment would go like this: I would press the button to start a tune and settle back in my seat, as the record would start to pound out of the studio monitor speakers. Then I'd look over the desk …

'Phil!' No response. Raise my voice. '*Phil!*' Then he'd look up at me with his alert gaze. I would lean towards him with a slightly raised voice.

'Mate, this is seriously the best job I have ever had!'

Then he would nod enthusiastically in response. 'I know, me too. I fucking love it!' If we said that to each other once, we said it a hundred times over the five years.

But looking back, I have very little clear chronological sense of what happened when. That is the problem with doing the same thing every day. Repetitive elements subsume the extraordinary moments beneath the gloss of routine. When I first tried to write about my years at 6 Music, I did so chronologically. I took a large A4 ring-bound notebook, and got out my engagement diary and tried to note down events as they happened, dovetailing them with my own recollections. Sadly the somewhat minimalist diary on my computer contained such taciturn entries as 'Belfast' or 'Glasgow'. Not really a lot to go on as far as what I actually did during these trips, so I would try to remember, and generally the only thing that I can remember with any clarity from any of the outside broadcasts that we did is getting heroically drunk.

In the early days of the show, drinking in the evening was practically impossible. Entering my forties I had discovered that my tolerance for alcohol had diminished. In my teens and twenties, Herculean amounts of light and bitter and vodka and lime did their level best to upset my constitution, to little avail. In my entire life I was only actually paralytically drunk on one occasion. This occurred when I was twenty-one and visited a friend at Loughborough University. I wasn't overly taken with a beverage they had up there called 'Mild' and less than impressed with the bitter with heads so creamy and dense I was always surprised not to see the bar staff stick a Flake in them. A friend started drinking something called a 'Purple Nasty'. This was a pint of snakebite with a Pernod and blackcurrant chucked in it at the last minute. I had eight of these things. And spent the night on the floor of a student bathroom, wide awake but completely immobile for six hours.

There was initially an unwritten agreement between Phil and myself not to drink the night before a show. This was no high-and-mighty moral crusade on our part. We just knew that we had to be up at four thirty the next morning, which was a grim enough idea without alcohol being factored in as well. This 'rule' lasted us for most of the first year. Indeed for several long stretches I didn't drink at all. My wildly fluctuating weight was never easy to maintain when I was drinking too, so I always quite enjoyed the teetotal months. The drinking came into its own from the point when we regularly started to do outside broadcasts. Phil is from the Welsh Valleys and had been on the road with Motley Crue, so it's fair to say that he was no stranger to the odd tipple, and as they say in Ireland, 'When you're out, you're out!' And we went 'out' taking the show on the road regularly after an almost monastic first year. Our first big show on the road was in Northern Ireland.

In order to promote 6 Music, the powers that be sent several of the shows over to Belfast to participate in the BBC's Music Live project. As part of this, the station would be broadcasting on a spare local FM frequency, so regular punters in Northern Ireland would be able to listen to those exotic new sounds hitherto restricted to the digital airwaves. We had been told that we'd be broadcasting the breakfast show for three mornings, which I imagined would be quite a laugh.

The first time I went to Belfast as a stand-up in the early nineties, I was quite simply terrified at the prospect. Northern Ireland was a community torn apart by centuries of religious strife and accompanying violence. It was the first place where I ever saw soldiers carrying loaded automatic weapons at an airport, which to me was a bit of a mindfuck. But to see blokes ten years younger than me carrying machine guns and walking along a high street past little old ladies and shops sent me into a complete tailspin. But, as it turned out, Belfast was one of the most brilliant places I ever visited. The people were a laugh, the shows were always great fun and nobody let you away from their company without buying you a pint. On my first ever night out in Belfast I ended up in a raucous bar called Lavery's. At the end of the evening as they rang last orders I was swaying gently, a queue of six pints of Guinness awaiting my attention.

Four weeks before our Belfast adventure the bubbly and effusive John Sugar bounced up to us in the offices.

'Hello, chaps! Good show this morning!'

Wilding and I looked up at John and set our faces to 'petulant'.

'Listen, the Beeb are having their Music Live week in Belfast this year and have given us an FM frequency to use in town ...'

Wilding and I exchanged a glance.

'... so we're going to be doing three breakfast shows from Belfast!'

The Belfast request hung in the air for the briefest of moments before Phil and I started trying to shoot it down. I was the first one to piss in the cornflakes.

'Sorry, John, I don't know mate, you'll have to speak to Addison.'

John looked a little crestfallen, and rightly so. John was more than aware that 'Speak to Addison' was code for 'No'.

Phil was next. 'Who can we take? We aren't doing it if it means driving the show from here!'

Quite often with outside broadcasts, it is just the presenter who is actually 'outside' while the rest of the show is still broadcast from the home studio. Not only does this cut costs, but it guarantees that the quality of the music broadcasting doesn't suffer. As a presenter it's a pain in the arse because you're not driving the show yourself. You have to end every sentence with a pre-arranged verbal cue for whichever engineer they have drafted in to 'drive' the show back in London. And with it being a breakfast show, engineers are always delighted to have to get up at sparrow fart because some idiot's out on the road again.

'Not at all, lads. We're going to have our own studio …' John trilled.

I had been in to the studios at BBC Northern Ireland in Belfast before. They were quite swish. I didn't fully glean what Sugar meant when he used the words 'our own studio'. But I would find out soon enough.

* * *

As always with outside broadcasts, or OBs as we called them, we would be obsessed with where the BBC would be putting us up for the duration. It seemed that we would always be put up in the cheapest hotel they could find.

The staff at the reception desk were quite simply excellent. A warm smile of recognition from the young lady at the counter was crisply followed by a friendly 'Hello, Mr Jupitus, and welcome.' Or to give you that the way I heard it on the day, 'Hulloo Muster Juppidduss ond whale come.' (Man you have *got* to love a Belfast accent.)

I filled in the registration slip and took the key card to my room, which was located on the sixth floor. We'd been travelling since leaving Broadcasting House just after ten and it was now coming up to four o'clock. I was gagging for a shower and a cup of tea. Years of touring experience meant that I had developed quite a tolerance for hotel room tea made with those tiny plastic thimbles of what we will call for the sake of argument 'milk'. I was looking forward to getting into my room and the customary thrill of the five-minute hunt for the 'tea-making facilities'. In the past I had located them variously in a drawer, in the wardrobe, under the television and, perhaps my favourite place of all, on top of the toilet cistern. I was holding out for this one being on the outside window ledge.

It is therefore sad to relate that I never even got as far as locating the kettle. My room had a view out the back of the hotel which put me in a grim mood right out of the traps. Then I looked at the uninspiring bed. It was low. Too low. I put my foot on the mattress. It was soft. Too soft. Then I looked closer at the bedspread which covered the bed. You know that bit in *Fatal Attraction* where the bloke gets a UV torch out to show where all the fluids had been spread over the bed that Sharon Stone had been romping on with that bloke? Well, I didn't need a UV torch. I thought I might have inadvertently wandered into some Persil field-testing room and any moment now the bloke was going to come in and throw a bucket of motor oil over it for good measure.

I began to quietly seethe. I'm not exactly fucking J-Lo when it comes to hotels, and I will gladly go wherever I am being put. But I draw the line at setting my luggage down on a bedspread covered with more DNA than the Home Office database.

I took my Nokia out and called Wilding. He picked up almost straight away.

'Alright fella!'

'Dude …' My voice was cracking with emotion. He sensed that I was traumatised.

'What's wrong?'

'Mate …' I could barely get the words out.

'Phill, what's wrong?'

I felt like I was in a police interview room describing a hideous assault. 'There …' I faltered before going on, my voice a hoarse whisper, shaking with horror. 'There's come up the walls.'

'Oh fucking hell, *no!*' It was Wilding's turn to be appalled.

Then I asked him. 'What's your room like?'

'Not that bad, but still –'

'Don't unpack. Give me five minutes.' I disconnected the call and immediately rang the offices of my agents, Off the Kerb.

The call was answered in a split second by dependable South-East Londoner Danny Julian with a snappy, 'Kerb!'

'Dan, it's Phill. Where do you put Jack and Lee when they're staying in Belfast?'

'There's a place about fifteen minutes outside town called the Culloden … It's a bit pricey though, mate –'

'Fuck the price, Danny! I need three rooms now!' I almost wailed with distress.

'I'm on it …' and he hung up.

I then called Phil and our Broadcast Assistant, Mark 'The Shed' Sheldon.

'Right, we're not staying here, boys. I'll meet you in reception in ten minutes.'

Phil was immediately panicked. 'The BBC aren't going to pay for us to move hotels. Me and The Shed will stay here –'

I cut him off. 'Oh fuck that, Phil. I'll pay. We all need to be in the same hotel.'

Wilding wasn't about to disagree, so he summoned The Shed and we all met downstairs in the lobby. As I handed my key card back over the counter, the young lady looked puzzled. 'Is there a problem, sir?'

I bowed my head and mumbled, 'Errr … we won't be staying here after all, um … you can have the rooms … after all.'

As is customary for the British when in a justified position to actually complain about something, somehow the whole situation had become my fault and I felt my face getting hotter as I stood in front of her.

Of course what I wanted to do was say, 'PROBLEM? FUCKING PROBLEM? WELL, IF YOU CALL SOME OTHER BLOKE'S TROUSER BATTER ALL OVER THE FUCKING WALLS, BED AND FURNITURE A PROBLEM, THEN YES, SWEETHEART, I HAVE GOT A FUCKING PROBLEM! I WANT THE MANAGER OF THIS SHITHOLE FRONT AND CENTRE NOW. AND WHILE YOU'RE AT IT, I WANT THE BELFAST ENVIRONMENTAL HEALTH PEOPLE HERE TOO. AND CAN YOU GET ME A NUMBER FOR THE LAST SALES REP TO STAY IN THE FUCKING SPARSELY CARPETED PETRI DISH THAT YOU THINK PASSES

FOR HUMAN ACCOMMODATION BECAUSE I TOOK A QUICK LOOK AT THE PORN CHANNEL WHICH TECHNICALLY SPEAKING DOESN'T HAVE ANY ACTUAL PORNOGRAPHY ON IT AND I WOULD LIKE TO KNOW EXACTLY HOW HE MANAGED TO GET HIS MAN JUICE ON THE FUCKING CEILING WITH SUCH LOW-QUALITY SEXUAL IMAGERY TO INSPIRE HIM?'

But what I actually said was, 'Could you book a taxi for us please … Sorry.'

When we walked open-mouthed into the front of the Culloden, it was like one of the children stepping into Narnia after the grim reality of the Second World War. There was a spa, a gym, a swimming pool and the lush green surroundings of the Belfast countryside. The Shed took one look at his room and immediately phoned his wife Donna and told her to get on a plane and come over as quickly as she could. My room was about four times the size of the first flat I had in London. I did what I always do when I arrive in a new hotel room. I get naked and get a beer out of the minibar and pad around while channel surfing for ten minutes. Then I usually sit on the lav while reading the hotel guide folder and try to establish whether or not they have 24-hour room service. I have been known to crave Crème Brûlée at 4.00 a.m. and always sleep a little easier knowing it's a potential option.

It was only once we had arrived in Belfast that I was corrected on one massive misapprehension I had about the trip. We would not, in point of fact, be broadcasting from the BBC studios. Our workspace was what could charitably be described as 'a hut' smack in the middle of Belfast town centre. The BBC set up this delightful little

cultural igloo over the weekend, and by Tuesday afternoon when we arrived it had been given a swift makeover
by some local enthusiasts. Every window in the place had
been stoved in, so the BBC in its customary 20/20 hindsight wisely shelled out for some security to stand around
it. I'm sure the good people of Belfast were puzzled to
observe somebody guarding such a dump.

As usual with outside broadcasts the equipment was
unfamiliar and there were all sorts of new quirks to deal
with. As was customary, a surly engineer took me and
Phil through the peculiarities of our temporary home.

'Raight so, ye've only got the tee channels t'yeez
f'toggen ...'

My brain slowly computed that this meant that we only
had the two channels to use for talking. At the best of
times engineers had the kind of long-suffering attitude of
futility towards me that one might have if trying to teach
a spaniel to use a toaster. But in addition to this I was also
negotiating a heavy regional brogue.

'On doan pule opp yer fee-ader unloss ye've mon-yuley
stoaped yer seedy pleer forst ...'

The thing is that on a woman the loops and swirls of the
Northern Irish accent always made me feel rather horny.
But this bloke was just scaring me. I blame Ian Paisley
and Gerry Adams.

That night we would be dining at the hotel and would
be in the company of one of the 6 Music breakfast
show's first and most loyal listeners, Belfast resident
Paul Milligan. Paul is a bright and enthusiastic music fan
whose eclectic tastes dovetailed much more with Wilding's music collection than mine. The pair of them would
shuttle emails back and forth about the relative merits of

each long player by The Replacements for days on end. Paul almost immediately endeared himself to both of us by hating the playlist at 6 Music even more than we did. His attitude to the station was that it was at best a slightly better option than anything else out there but at worst was just XFM without the adverts. He was simultaneously our biggest fan and harshest critic, and we loved him for his spiky candour.

Also breaking bread with us that night was John 'The Badger' Pearson and Mike 'Mike Hanson' Hanson. John was the factotum for all things outside broadcast which 6 Music took part in. Whenever the BBC is involved with any kind of outside broadcast there's an incredible amount of liaising and organising to be done, and this was John's department. I think it was Spiderman's Uncle Ben who said, 'With great power comes great responsibility …' Well, in the case of the Badger it was more like, 'With great responsibility comes a massive intolerance for piss-taking …' and we constantly drove Badger to the very brink of his patience. For a start he didn't initially like the nickname, which was given to him by us. I'm not even sure why we called him Badger. Of course in the fullness of time he grew to absolutely love it and even picked up a small furry toy badger, which became his mascot.

The whole nickname thing I'm sure became quite wearing for those who had to work in close proximity to us. But we were snappy and impatient men, so why have the common courtesy of remembering someone's name when making one up was so much easier? It was a bit like naming pets. When Jaffa (she came with that one) left the show, she was replaced by Emma Hatcher. Emma is a bright, beautiful, slightly posh and statuesque blonde, at least six feet tall in flats, so Phil and I immediately started calling her Lily, short for Lilliput. She once stumbled over the name of her husband, who to this day Phil and I still call Steve-Pete. Mark Sheldon became The Shed because he once happened to mention to us that he had a garden shed. Kate Lloyd we called Kate the Hate because of her occasional lack of enthusiasm for some of our weaker ideas. Ruth Barnes we called Lucy because she looked a bit like Lucy Van Pelt from the Peanuts cartoons. Titian colouring and the slightest of overbites meant that senior producer James Stirling was forever 'The Hamster'. Chris Hawkins we called simply 'The Hawk', which he embraced so much that there is a rumour that he subsequently had a massive flying raptor tattooed on his back. The blonde and bubbly Lynsey Emery, because of a passing resemblance to Sarah Michelle Geller, became Buffy and simply because of her description of her soon-to-be-husband he became quite simply 'Little Ern'. Perforce these people must have fucking hated us, and, to be honest, who could blame them.

At our dinner we talked a bit of shop, told stories and quaffed and ate and had an all-round laugh. Afterwards we sat in the lounge of the hotel and all had nightcaps, each of us nursing golden warming glasses of Middleton Irish Whisky. As we cast our eye around the wood-panelled lounge we noticed a large oil painting over the fireplace of about a dozen religiously clad bearded grandees from the seventeenth century. Milligan raised his glass towards them.

'They're a happy-looking bunch. Probably Protestants ...'

The Three Englishmen, the Welshman and the Canadian laughed their uncomfortable laughs, eyes darting around the room as they did so. As ever in a situation that seemed to be on the brink of discomfort I looked up at the stern faces on the canvas and leaped in with a tension breaker.

'Nah, they're The So Stolid Crew ...'

Cue laughter and the tourists could all breathe easy again. As much as the province is a changed place from the horrors of recent decades, the undercurrents are still there. And so one tries to mind one's Ps and Qs. As we all drifted off into the night, Mike, Badger and Paul all clambered into a cab for town. Just before he got into the car, Milligan looked round at me and said, 'So Stolid Crew ... very good ...' It was one of my favourite ever compliments.

The next morning we tried to get our slightly bleary heads around the new equipment, as the chill Belfast air blew through the jagged holes in the smashed windows. We were getting a bit more feedback than usual as we were broadcasting on an FM frequency as well as our usual digital one. As the show trundled along, we received an email from a Belfast milkman who had never heard of the show saying how much he was enjoying it on his rounds. Rather than relishing this news it caused us to reflect ruefully on the fact that audience awareness of BBC 6 Music was still somewhere between a pitiful 1 and 2 per cent. Here was this exciting new radio station which had been on for two years, and the people paying for it hadn't even heard of it. As the years went on this became a familiar refrain. Nearly every week for five years we'd get emails or texts from people saying, 'What is this fabulous new radio station?' We were doing everything we could and it quite simply wasn't enough.

Three days in Belfast means that you can in effect do enough drinking to last you for a month. Pubs are full and steeped in tradition, and boozy tales abound of rebel plots being hatched at the very table where you are trying to enjoy your pint and your cheese-and-onion crisps. Endlessly fascinating but slightly off-putting. I dare say if we'd wandered into the Star of Belfast Tandoori the waiter would have leaned over conspiratorially while we nibbled on our popadoms.

'Of course, sir, you do realise that several key elements of the Good Friday Agreement were drafted at the very table you're sitting!'

It's a great city, but everybody's got a bloody tale to tell.

On the Thursday evening we would be going to the Limelight to see The Zutons. At the time they had just burst out of the Liverpool scene and were taking the country by storm. They were touring in support of their début long player, *Who Killed the Zutons?* Frontman Dave and guitarist Russell would be our guests on the show that morning. Now getting people on a radio show at the best of times is tricky enough. Your show has a small window of time, and so organisation has to be top notch. You usually rely on whoever is punting the guest around hoping for the twenty minutes of free airtime to get them to you punctually. That is the quid pro quo of the business. PR people offer their clients, you say yes, then it's down to them to get them to you. But we were a breakfast show with a guest slot of 9.30–10.00 – *in the morning.* Most of our guests were musicians. Touring musicians. For touring musicians, every day is like Saturday. Everything is building up to a party in the evening. Therefore, for touring musicians, every morning after a gig is like a Sunday morning after a colossal piss-up. You want a lie-in and you want to get up at the last possible moment, dragging your sorry arse into the van before setting off for yet another theoretical Saturday evening. The night before their interview with us, The Zutons had been gigging some 85 miles south in Dublin. You know, quiet place. Not a lot of drinking …

There is a film called *Flatliners* where Julia Roberts and Kiefer Sutherland and Kevin Bacon and another bloke, possibly a Baldwin of some sort, force themselves into near-death experiences in order to establish if there is an afterlife. So they are woken from the dead after 'flatlining' for at least a minute or two. David and Russell looked like they had been revived two minutes before being brought into the studio. But as it was early in their career they weren't yet jaded by experience, so their youthful constitutions meant that they were quite happy to sit in a chilly portacabin drinking rubbish coffee and chatting about their album after less than an hour of sleep.

I always enjoyed the way that some guests reacted to the unusual demands of the early-morning interview over the years. Several people we had on the show had clearly just decided to continue partying until they had to come and see us, and so were in a rare old state. Not naming any names but Fishbone, The Dub Pistols and Marah spring immediately to mind. In a curious way the faint whiff of booze over the desk would always quite cheer me up. Rather than getting their publicists to cancel at the last minute (Buster Bloodvessel, Shane McGowan) these boozy pioneers would happily go on air half cut. I was really sad to miss the chance to talk to Shane, but was somehow gratified as I left the studio after the show to see him wandering towards me down the corridor clutching a vodka and tonic, or, to be more accurate, vodka and vodka.

Dave and Russell went back to their hotel to grab a few hours of kip before their soundcheck and we went back to our hotel. As I stood in the doorway of the portacabin signing a few autographs for the children of bemused shoppers, I got chatting with our security man, whose meaty arms I could see were covered with a blue and crimson tracery of tattoos.

'Nice work, mate. Where did you get them done?'

He looked up at me with a frisson of pride. 'Jost op th' rode thore. Tommy Gon's got a wee steedio.'

Then for no apparent reason at all, I looked round at Wilding who I knew had some 'ink' done. 'Phil, do tattoos hurt when you get them done?'

'Course they do, but you get used to it.'

I pondered for a moment.

'Fuck it, I'm getting a tattoo.' I was forty-one and therefore pretty much bang on schedule for doing something that stupid.

Back at the Culloden Phil and The Shed hit the gymnasium while I did gentle laps of the cool circular swimming pool in the spa area. There's something quite restful about swimming. It gave me a chance to process the show and think about what I'd have permanently inked onto my body. I pondered a few options. I thought a barcode on the back of my neck might be amusing. I also briefly toyed with having the words 'Eat Fast Die Young' somewhere on my person, but at the last minute realised that might be tempting fate.

Finally as I swam in the water, my 22 stone buoyed in its liquid embrace, it came to me. A mermaid! Traditional, iconic, mystical. Of course the word I was neglecting to add to this list was 'daft'.

As I walked out of the pool through the spa area I saw some of the various treatments available. As I stood reading the leaflet about aromatherapy massage, kelp body wraps and hot stone therapy, my eye was drawn to the tanning options. Now, I am very pale – an almost blue white – and that, coupled with my bulk, makes for quite the apparition. However, on holiday in the Mediterranean I was struck by how cool fat blokes looked with a bit of colour on them. Enormous fishermen sat on crates by their boats shirtless in the sun, their guts a russet bronze. I was obviously in some kind of new experience meltdown.

I wandered into the spa reception area. The girl behind the counter looked up at me, slightly puzzled. I steamed right in.

'Hello there. Could I book a tan treatment this afternoon, please?'

In her eyes there was the briefest flash of 'Do we have enough tanning solution in stock?' before she snapped, 'Certainly, sir. Is one o'clock OK?'

I nodded and went to sign the slip booking my appointment, and as I did so I noticed the parlous state of my nails. 'And a manicure as well, please!' I said, grinning like a loon.

After a manicure, a spray tan and a tattoo, I'd be a new man, I thought to myself, not realising that I would in actuality be the same old bloke with a couple of accessories tagged on. That's the thing with anything like that. We imagine the effect to be much more far reaching than it actually turns out to be. After my tan and manicure I was told not to shower for at least four hours. This meant that the blokes in the tattoo parlour would see my streaky arm. Bollocks, I'm having a tattoo, I thought, I might as well undergo embarrassment as well as a bit of pain.

Back in my hotel room I scoured the internet for potential mermaid designs and found what appeared to be a medieval brooch which had a kind of circular theme to it. I printed the image up and made my way into town, stopping off for a swift drink just to dull the pain and give me a bit of Dutch courage. In the tattoo parlour I met the tattoo artist Tommy Gunn himself, who would be working on my pasty skin. We fussed and fidgeted over the design and he made the various small adjustments I requested. Then he delicately traced a template in order to transfer the image to my shoulder, which had already had a pale patch rubbed clean of tanning product. I looked in the mirror at the dark blue outline, which was about to become part of my body on a permanent basis, and nodded to Tommy.

'OK, let's get cracking.'

The pain isn't really a pain as such, more a sort of sustained stinging sensation. Having said that, a year later when I had a tattoo done in Boston, *that* was complete fucking agony, but I am assuming that the chap who did my Red Sox tattoo was a New York Yankees fan. But at the hands of Tommy this constant sting started to become almost pleasant. The high drone of the needle was all I heard as I sipped on the can of cider they had thoughtfully provided me with. As I sat there, my body's adrenalin and endorphins were racing through my bloodstream, giving me a bit of a buzz, I thought I heard someone saying something about nipples. After a nudge I looked round and Tommy was gesticulating at my mermaid's perfect breasts.

'D'ye want me t'poot som nupples oan her tuts?'

I shook my head. I thought that 'nupples' would be somehow crude.

After he had finished his excellent work, Tommy spun me round so I could look in the mirror and took a few photos for his portfolio. She was quite beautiful, arms open and shoulder-length hair, but already the blood was starting to bead slightly on her scaly tail. Tommy handed my a tube of antiseptic gel and gave me my instructions.

'Don't scratch it, put this on it every day and no swimming for at least two weeks ...'

To say I was euphoric was an understatement. My mind was giddy with pain and pleasure, and I have to say I almost stunned myself with what I said next.

'Could you do me another one?'

Tommy looked up, nonplussed. 'Aye, no problem. What d'ye fancy?'

I looked on the lapel of my jacket and saw a badge of the logo for Trojan records. 'Can you do me one of them?' I grinned.

That night at The Limelight The Zutons played a completely brilliant set as I stood twenty feet in front of them in the seething crowd, clutching a very large rum and coke. They really were extraordinary. Dave McCabe's soulful howl was mesmeric, just as was Abi Harding on the saxophone. She flailed around the stage, her hair thrashing wildly, before she would play a short passage on the sax. She was contrastingly wild and abandoned and then suddenly all control and precision. It was visually spellbinding. A set of arms was suddenly flung around me, and I looked around.

Tom Robinson stood beaming. He screamed into my ear, trying to be heard over the music, *'Phill this is absolutely incredible! How good are this band!*

I smiled, nodded and mouthed a mute, 'I know.'

Everything at that exact moment was perfect in the world. I was still tingling from my visit to the tattoo parlour, I was nicely drunk and 500 kids of all faiths in a city most people in the world would associate with strife and murder were going wild at a new band who were at the top of their game, and the bloke who wrote 'Glad to be Gay' had just embraced me.

It was one of life's perfect and unforgettable moments. And truth be told, I don't think anything else in five years topped it.

Roadkillers

'It's Going to Happen!' – The Undertones
'Too Good to Be True' – Tom Robinson Band
'Valerie' – The Zutons
'Take This Job and Shove It' – Merle Haggard
'Next Year' – Foo Fighters
'Mary Skeffington' – Gerry Rafferty
'45' – Elvis Costello
'All Apologies' – Nirvana
'Los Paraguayos' – Rod Stewart
'The More That I See the Less I Believe' – Fun Boy
   Three

Odds and Sods

Outside broadcasts became a regular feature of the show with our trips around the country broadcasting from universities all over the UK. When we first enquired about going out on the road, the most costly aspect was the engineers and the equipment. A fully functioning radio show can be broadcast from any home which has a BT landline. All that needs to happen is the line has to be upgraded to ISDN quality and then you need microphones, CD players, mixers, and you're off. We used this technique to great effect when we launched a competition for listeners to win the show for a day. By 'win the show' we meant that we would come into their home and broadcast. This wheeze was fun but costly, and involved quite a bit of organisation. Our outside broadcast liaison, 'Badger', would case likely contestants for proximity to telephone exchanges and the likelihood of us having a good show.

Our first 'Home Invasion' was in Leicester and our winner was Julia. The drill was simple enough. We'd pitch up the night before, all go out for a meal and bond a bit, then we'd agree to get together the next morning at 6.00

a.m. During the curry it became apparent that Julia didn't like Phil and me that much. Oh, she liked us well enough, but whenever we spoke to each other she thought we were taking the piss. Admittedly we might do that a bit on air, but off air and at mealtimes we were quite quiet. I think this threw her a bit, but the show turned out to be a laugh and she made some very nice muffins. Next time out we were in Nottingham and in the company of the Medd family, Jenny and John with their tall son James who was fifteen and in a band and by now must be fending off the ladies with a shitty stick. They had cats, and we set up in their living room. Jenny made bacon sandwiches which really hit the spot. Their neighbours kept poking heads round the door to see the show.

A year later we were almost in the middle of nowhere at the home of professional baker and confectioner Heike Harding Reyland. A German expat, Heike lived about twenty miles from Bath in the Mendips, and did I already mention *professional baker*? Her house and its surroundings were quite simply exquisite. This was the first time that we were able to start the show in the garden. I vividly remember standing in the grass on a brisk summer morning with Heike beside me and a BBC engineer looking at his watch, waiting to give me the signal that the show had started and we were on air. Halfway through the show when she brought out a fresh tray of piping-hot chocolate brownies and her husband produced a demijohn of homemade cider I almost wept.

The show seemed to really come into its own whenever we did outside broadcasts. The prohibitive expense of doing a show from somebody's home every month meant thinking more laterally. One week we did a 'Tour of Essex', which involved our broadcasting from five different locations in the county. On Monday we were in Colchester, in a BBC studio with an interview from Graham Coxon. On Tuesday we broadcast from the press room at Dagenham and Redbridge FC. Our engineer for this show was an old friend from GLR, Paul Strudwick, who was never one to knock back a gig.

As we sat there in the lounge at Dagenham we looked out of the window at the pitch underneath a dull grey sky. I idly muttered, 'It's a shame we can't broadcast from the centre spot. That would be a laugh.'

Without even looking up from his sudoku, Strudwick went, 'You can broadcast from the centre spot.'

Within ten minutes he had produced a new microphone, headphones and 60 metres of high-quality cable and I was standing in the middle of the pitch at Dagenham and Redbridge. I always loved an engineer who rose to a challenge. The tour continued to Chelmsford and the headquarters of BBC Essex, where we were quite obviously in the way of their usual breakfast team. In fact at one point in the show a bloke came and stood at the glass in front of me and stared at me during a link. It was like a baboon in an Attenborough documentary. I suppose that in the run of things we were lucky that he didn't burst into the studio and shit in the corner to mark his territory. Thursday was a tad more uneventful as we were put into the ISDN room at the offices of Basildon Council. When we opened the door there was a small console and two microphones. But more importantly there was a hoover, some buckets and a broom. The 'studio' was a utility cupboard. Our last show was from the part-time BBC studios in London Road, Southend.

Overall the week was declared a success. We generated a bit of local media interest and did a gig on the Friday night at Chinnery's on Southend seafront with Billy Bragg and The Blockheads. But the thing that became glaringly obvious was that using BBC local radio facilities was not ideal as they were all doing their own breakfast shows and we were just getting in their way. Then the Badger hit us with an idea that became a staple of the breakfast show for three years. We could do the shows from university radio stations. They had the kit, the facilities and truckloads of eager young helpers. From then onwards, the breakfast show would do at least one show a month from a university or college radio station.

Oh, those university shows turned out to be quite the thing: the near fight in an Oxford discotheque, only curtailed at the moment I realised that the young man trying to steal my hat was a mere child and I was holding him by the throat; getting a song dedicated to us by The Manic Street Preachers in Swansea and me and Phil embracing and giggling; hobbling my way on crutches around the campus at Bradford with Billy Bragg; me singing The Specials' 'Little Bitch' at the Rescue Rooms in Nottingham with The Ordinary Boys after announcing by saying, *'This is an old Mötley Crüe number called "Girls, Girls, Girls"'*; watching The View bouncing all over the stage in Belfast before finding a blue plaque outside the theatre saying that it was where Ruby Murray used to perform; the college station where the two student engineers were so determined to be up and ready for our arrival that they stayed up all night doing amphetamines; meeting Fay and Eugene from The Rezillos in Glasgow and walking past a hall full of kids doing their exams; dancing all night at the Waterfront in Norwich to The Go! Team; the tingle of excitement I felt when Lene Lovich's daughter came up to me to say, 'My mum says hello,' after a gig in Cambridge; Paul from Maximo Park explaining how he used to be a teacher before he joined the band; being given my first ever shot of Jaegermeister by Joel from Athlete; watching Brakes playing 'Cheney' twice at the Academy in Birmingham because it's only eight seconds long; Belle and Sebastian offering us some of their backstage catering; LCD Soundsystem hammering into 'Daft Punk Is Playing at My House' at the end of the evening.

These kinds of disjointed fragments of memory are the cherished moments of my time at 6 Music. Whenever we went out and met the audience we were aiming for it gave us the impression that we could genuinely reach people. Sadly we were operating in a bubble of delusion. In 1987 I was involved with the Labour Party's campaign to get Neil Kinnock into Number Ten and Thatcher out. So for the month leading up to the election I was doing gigs in front of nothing but Labour Party supporters. Everywhere. Thousands of them. When I got home after the tour I was utterly convinced that Labour would sweep into power. That night as they announced that Basildon had gone to the Conservatives I cried slowly into the duvet and pulled it over my head. Living in a bubble can convince you of all sorts of things. And Phil and I mistakenly thought the show was a lot more popular than it actually was.

But despite its niche appeal, it was still a good show. We were polite to guests and gave good interviews, and soon got a reputation with those few PR people who had digital radios as a place for guests to come when promoting anything. Stars from comedy, TV, film and music found their way to the 6 Music breakfast show. Meeting some of the people who had made music that had partially helped to shape my personality was both exciting and inspiring. While working in the music business had previously put me off buying records and CDs, meeting the artists who created it now had the opposite effect.

By and large we would get people in who were promoting new albums or tours. Quite often they were in the middle of gigs so there was always a sense of 'Will they arrive?' until the call came up from reception. Basically our booking policy for talking to bands was that we were up for talking to anybody interesting who was willing to come in, especially in the first year. Not being a trained journalist meant that my interviewing style was at best conversational and at worst all over the place. This was never a problem when one was talking to a new band, but when the old pros were in I would start to get a bit nervous.

Another gimmick we used was that all guests would be invited to suggest a piece of music to play in the middle of their interview. This had the benefit of giving them a chance to show their interests or introduce an artist, and it also gave us something else to chat about. Scottish singer-songwriter Malcolm Middleton brought in a copy of an album by an artist called Jackson C Frank, which was astonishing. At the end of the interview he handed it over to with a low-key, 'Y'can keep that, Phill. You should have a copy.'

When Mitchell and Webb came in to the studio to promote the new series of *That Mitchell and Webb Sound* on Radio 4, there was a certain amount of quid pro quo about the choice of music. Yes, as per usual they could pick a song, but only on the proviso that the three of us could play 'Numberwang'. Robert Webb sparked into action. 'OK now it's time to play Numberwang! The quiz sensation that's sweeping the nation. Our contestants today are Phill and David. OK lets play Numberwang! Phill goes first ...'

'Seven!'

'David?'

'Sixty-three.'

'Fourteen.'

'Fifty two.'

'Twenty-eight.'

'That's Numberwang! Round two!'

Oh, I was over the moon.

Robert recently remembered his visit to 6 Music with some unease. 'I remember coming in to the show and you asking us to pick a song. David wasn't going to pick anything so I thought I'd go for "Ghost Town". And it was only once it was on that I realised it was six minutes long. And we were all just sat there while this thing went on and on while we were supposed to be doing an interview ...'

Over the five years there were a few high-profile interviews, but one in the first year which took everyone by surprise was the creator of *The Simpsons*, Matt Groening. Jo Tyler had developed a good solid relationship with the organisers of the Animated Encounters Festival in Bristol. I had appeared at one of their first events in a show somewhat shamelessly called 'Desert Island Cartoons' where I was invited to spend an hour and a half showing some of my favourite cartoons. This year it was to be Matt Groening marooned on the island, and the Encounters people asked me to interview him.

Jo contacted them and suggested that Matt come in to 6 Music and do my show before we all travelled together to Bristol. They went for this idea and it was all set up. Meanwhile back at 6 Music nobody believed that we really would get the creator of *The Simpsons* in the place. We didn't have any audience figures yet, and we'd only been on air for a few months, so why would he come onto a niche radio show when any producer in the UK would bend over backwards to give him airtime? As it turned out, he not only came in, but also signed endless toys and books for listeners and turned out to be a massive music fan and an expert on Frank Zappa. It's a good day at work when you're listening to 'Peaches in Regalia' while the bloke who created *The Simpsons* is drawing a Homer for you with a speech bubble that says, 'Y'elllo Phill!'

Filmmaker Kevin Smith was in London doing one of his live Q&A sessions. I had been to his first at the Prince Charles cinema the year before where my question for him was the punchy and pertinent 'Where did you get those shoes?' We managed to get him to come in to the show on the Wednesday ahead of his getting an Empire Award the following Sunday. Phil was nervous about him coming in.

'Listen, fella, at some point he's probably going to swear.' I gave him an askance look.

'Oh surely not.'

'No, he won't mean to, I just don't think he can help himself sometimes.'

'Look, mate, don't worry. When I was in the States last year I heard Terry Gross interviewing him on NPR and he was good as gold. It'll be alright.'

'Look, if he does, you have to apologise properly straight away and play a tune.'

'He is not going to swear, Phil!'

And indeed, he didn't.

On the day Kevin was lovely. He took questions from listeners and was funny and smart. It was a sheer joy having him on the show. At the end of the interview it's fair to say that I was just a bit giddy.

'Well, that's it for the show today. All that remains is for us to thank our guest, the marvellous Mister Kevin Smith.'

Smith nodded graciously. 'Thank you, sir.'

'No, thank *you* mate. It's been a fucking pleasure!'

I will remember the look on Phil Wilding's face at that moment until the day I die.

As we said our goodbyes and Kevin made his way out he turned to us and casually said, 'That was cool. Can I come in again?'

'You'd be very welcome, mate,' I said as he ambled down the corridor, his trademark huge overcoat and back-to-front baseball cap rounding the corner. I got a frisson of joy with the realisation that I had just interviewed 'Silent Bob'.

The next morning it was around ten past eight when Lucy the BA popped her head round the studio door to tell us that our guest was here. We had an author due in at 9.30, so they were absurdly early.

'Tell 'em to go and grab some breakfast and come back later,' I said.

She nodded and nipped out before coming back a moment later, looking half uneasy and half excited. 'It's not that guest. Kevin Smith is back again!'

Smith was staying a hundred yards away at the Langham Hotel and was all over the place with jet-lag, so had decided to come on to the show again just to sit in and shoot the shit. And Thursday went so well that he turned up on the Friday too and, as well as being absurdly generous with his time, was a sassy and smart contributor to the show. A couple of nights later I took Kevin and his wife Jen and Jason 'Jay' Mewes and his girlfriend to Pizza Express and we sat and talked about life in general and nothing in particular. It's as close as I ever got to Hollywood.

The guest conveyor belt was always moving and we were rarely given cause to complain about anybody aside from various no-shows and The Black Keys who in their defence were just in a pissy mood. Quite often we would be slightly scared of the people who were coming in. Some artists we knew would not be joining in cheeky banter, because they were serious people. Both Phil and I were terrified the day John Cale, formerly of The Velvet Underground, came in. He sat opposite us and was very polite and answered all our questions in a low Welsh-tinged growl. This never really dovetailed ideally with my scattergun style of interviewing, but we got to the end and he was out of the door. I always thought that he had not enjoyed the experience, but a year later I was travelling in the lift at Western House and the doors opened on the ground floor. I looked up to see John Cale was standing there again. As his eyes met mine, he broke into a broad smile. 'Hello fella! How's it all going?' and he grasped my hand in his.

'Lovely, thanks, John!' I smiled back.

'All the best, mate. It's nice to see you again.'

You are never really prepared for 'cheery' from one of The Velvet Underground.

* * *

Probably the biggest name we ever had as a guest was Brian Wilson of The Beach Boys. His career had been re-energised by his collaboration with a band called The Wondermints who had enabled him not only to perform in public again, but also to perform the incredibly complex arrangements of songs from albums like *Pet Sounds* and the never-completed *Smile*. He was over in London to perform the newly completed version of *Smile*. The man was a musical genius like Mozart or Beethoven and like all geniuses he was a bit special. We were told to keep our questions short and direct and not too convoluted. It's fair to say that Brian had lived a full life and it had left its mark.

We were going to be doing a pre-recorded interview with him just to be on the safe side. That way if it started to drift a bit or if there were *longueurs*, we could tighten them up in the edit. As it turned out, we needn't have bothered. He was lucid and fun to chat with. But we were all a bit nervous about the whole experience. At ten to ten Phil looked up at me, and said, 'He's here.'

I sat for a moment and weighed up my options. At this stage I could either read up on my Brian Wilson notes and be fully prepared, or I could nip up the corridor and say hello just to introduce myself. I opted for the latter, took a deep breath, and checked how long I had to run on the record I was playing. Three and a half minutes. I stood up and made my way briskly to the green room to find a clutch of PR folk, and there sat in the midst was the man who sang 'God Only Knows'.

Just before we spoke, my heart was doing star jumps in my chest. I thrust out a hand. 'Hello, Mr Wilson sir, my name's Phill and I'll be interviewing you this morning …'

He looked up at me with his cool grey-green eyes smiling and spoke. 'Hey Phill, it's nice to meet you too. You need to lose about … fifty pounds.' I suppose he wasn't wrong.

* * *

Our persistently dodgy relationship with management started to properly sour during the third year. John Sugar left the BBC shortly after being replaced by Ric Blaxill. Ric had come onboard from the commercial GCAP group, and was therefore someone steeped in a culture of targets and statistics. He had several strategies to facilitate this happening with a minimum of fuss. I first met Ric when he hired me to present *Top of the Pops* in 1995. I was stunned to receive the offer as he'd only ever seen me hosting the Music Week awards, but I wasn't about to turn it down. I'd grown up watching *TOTP*. This was the pre-*Buzzcocks* days so nobody had really heard of me. Indeed the introduction to the show featured new Australian chanteuse Tina Arena and me having an amusing little exchange, because neither of us had heard of each other.

As a radio controller Ric seemed a bit less free spirited than when I first met him. He had been involved in producing a successful breakfast show himself on Radio 1 with Simon Mayo for years. So it's fair to say that he had some fairly set ideas about how we might maximise the appeal of 6 Music. One day he called me into his office and handed me over a blue book which he had picked up at a radio conference in the 1990s entitled *Presenting Breakfast Radio*. Now I have no doubt that he meant this to be a helpful gesture and I tried my best to see it as such. But as I'd been in the job for three years it seemed to represent a deeper malaise. I thought we were doing OK.

'There's some good stuff in there, Phill. Take a look.' He smiled up at me. I looked at him and tried to establish if he wanted me to read between the lines. But if there was some hidden agenda to him handing me a manual on how to present a breakfast radio show, I was oblivious to it.

Another arrival with Ric was 'snoop tapes'. Simply put, these are recordings of everything that happens on the show when the microphones are on. It is therefore just a recording of all the chit-chat between songs, or as they call it today, 'a podcast'. Ric wanted to meet once a week and listen back to my shows. Then, after listening, I would have to justify what I was saying on air and why. But the thing is that my presenting 'style', such as it was, was an incredibly imprecise beast. I had no idea why I said half the things I did. The lack of conscious thought in broadcasters is why 'Colemanballs' in *Private Eye* has an uninterrupted stream of new material. The same goes for their DJ Babble feature. My bottom line was just to try and be lucid, and nine times out of ten I managed that with no problem. But somehow the thought of discussing it made me too self-conscious.

When you are speaking on air during a radio show there are three distinctly separate tasks taking place. One third of your conscious thought is trying to prepare the next thing that's happening in your head. Another is trying to keep the flow of language going, and the last third is focused on the physical process of operating the hardware. You are in effect a three-ball juggler. There was no way that I could ever explain to Ric why I said the things

I did. And to be honest, if I did listen to myself I would hate it, and whatever confidence I had would crumble. So, somewhat unprofessionally, I went to Lesley Douglas and explained that having a weekly semantic debate about my internal motivational processes might cause my brain to implode. She graciously covered for me, and I was removed from the 'snoop tape' duty. But I feel sure that Ric wasn't best pleased that I'd gone over his head.

While he went about slowly changing the direction of 6 Music around us with several schedule changes, we just tried to carry on doing what we had done from the outset: presenting our few hundred thousand listeners with some kind of alternative to the mainstream and the commercial sector. Bearing in mind that the BBC envisioned 6 Music's listenership to be over a million after three years of being on air, we quite simply weren't doing well enough.

By the time Ric had joined 6 Music there were regular audience listening figures from RAJAR. They had taken some time to get us into the system so we didn't have any listening figures for our first eighteen months of broadcasting, which is probably for the best when you consider that our first set of listening figures in September of 2003 was 154,000. That's not quite Wembley filled twice. This meant that both Blaxill and Douglas were almost certainly getting pressure from above to deliver better results. And the way you get better results is with hip new presenters.

One of our first big-name signings was rising comedy phenomenon Russell Brand. Russell was a charming if slightly scatty Essex bohemian with a past that wasn't so much chequered as a dayglo tartan and matted with bodily fluids. His bad-boy chic image and skinny jeans were not the kind of thing comedians of the day would usually try to get away with, but Russell could. His name started to creep into the showbiz gossip columns of the tabloids, and the legend began to grow. It was around this point in his career that Lesley brought Russell into the fold to present a Sunday morning show. He lasted at 6 Music for a few eventful months, before he was fast-tracked to a Saturday night slot on Radio 2. A couple of years later, Russell and his friend Jonathan inadvertently poked Middle England so hard in the ribs that it is now almost impossible to make radio or television at the BBC without half a dozen people looking over your shoulder telling you that you can't say that.

One of the self-imposed problems I had at 6 Music was a distorted sense of how important the show was to the network. I am aware that my value to the station was simply in having a known public profile as a regular panellist on *Never Mind the Buzzcocks*. My knowledge of music and eclectic taste were at best an irrelevance to management and at worst a pain in the arse. The station appeared to be principally engaged in editorially playing catch-up with XFM as well as digital-only stations like Classic Rock. The 6 Music playlist ended up being almost a carbon copy of XFM's every week. Here we were, in a unique position to do something that no other station in the country was doing, and we were taking our lead from the commercial sector. My petulance about this knew no bounds. When interviewed by *Broadcast* magazine I delighted in publicly bellowing about how 6 Music should have the balls to operate without a set playlist. I would also crow about how I would never work for a commercial station because more adverts meant less music. Please bear in mind that at the same time I was quite happily doing voiceovers for radio commercials for Duracel and HMV. Oh, I was all over the shop.

Phil and I would pretty much constantly piss and moan about how shabbily we thought we were being treated. In retrospect this served us right for how badly we treated John Sugar. What can I say? Karma works. The thing is that we were not being treated unreasonably. The show had a greater degree of autonomy than any other breakfast show in the country, we weren't overly taken to task over the amount of free choice, and we were allowed to take on interns as well as go on outside broadcasts on a monthly basis. The reason that Phil and I were slowly destroying what we had built together was because that was just the kind of guys we were. If something's going well, then to us that can't be right and so we're duty bound to fuck it up.

As much as we would occasionally rave to each other about how brilliant the job was, we were becoming more aware of the changing direction of the station. And while we didn't like it, we were still occasionally coerced into 'playing the game'. For three years we diligently submitted entries for the Sony Radio Awards, and, as you might expect, never got so much as a nomination. My fragile ego was always bruised by this perceived snub, but I myself had been snubbing the Sony Radio Awards for years. Lesley Douglas tried her best to get me to understand the process by putting me forward as a Sony judging panellist in the category 'Best Comedy Radio Show'. A box of sixty CDs and a Sony discman arrived at my house a few weeks later and I slowly worked my way through them all. Naturally enough, my shortlist ended up being comprised of shows I was already familiar with or ones made by mates.

It was only after taking part in this process that it dawned on me that I had quite regularly belittled the work of the majority of broadcasters in the country. Not to mention that I was ostensibly making a radio show for myself and Wilding with little regard for compromise or the taste of others. It was after being in the job for four years that I began to develop the suspicion that the show we were making was not entirely what Lesley, Ric and the BBC were looking for. Mind you, this was all happening in my head, so there's no logical reason to suggest that they were thinking anything of the sort. The only solid indication I had that we might be falling out of favour was that Lesley Douglas was no longer taking Phil and me out for breakfast once every four months.

It has to be said that Lesley was very, very good at 'handling the talent'. She had this way of telling you stuff that made you think that she was vouchsafing you the most secret information. It was only after I had been taking part in these breakfasts for a couple of years that I said to Phil one day, 'You know those breakfasts that Lesley takes us for?'

'Yeah, what about them?'

'I've just realised that she must take all of her present-ers for breakfast and tell them the same kind of thing she tells us.'

'Well done, Fucky. Took you long enough.' He rolled his eyes, shook his head and carried on diligently poking his mobile.

The listening figures for 6 Music rose steadily through-out our time there. This is not down to me, rather the increased take-up of DAB radios, which were not only becoming more common but they were also becoming much cheaper. The first sets I bought in 2003 were £99, but by the summer of 2006 you could get a good plug-in DAB radio set for as little as £40. In the June of 2006 we were being listened to by 354,000 people, which meant our audience had more than doubled over the previous three years. Which wasn't really good enough.

* * *

The decision to leave 6 Music came about because of an email sent to my agents in the early summer of 2006, coupled with the nagging suspicions Phil and I had that we were about to be reined in from our excessive early-morning shenanigans. The email was from a West End casting agent asking if I might be interested in auditioning for the role of Nathan Detroit in a new revival of *Guys and Dolls*. The show had opened the previous year with Ewan MacGregor playing Sky Masterson. *Guys and Dolls* is one of my favourite musicals of all time, so the thought of play-ing the conniving and fragile Nathan Detroit was a dream come true. When you work as a clown for hire, offers of this nature are peppered throughout the year. You go for them or not pretty much as the fancy takes you. West End casting supremo David Grindrod, who would go on to cast me as Edna Turnblad in *Hairspray*, was a fan, and already looking for a part for me to take on. He'd sent me to see *Woman in White* with a view to my playing Count Fosco. Mind you, as I was working as a breakfast deejay, that might prove to be a conflict of interests.

When I first sat in Jim Moir's office one thing I did bring up was the possibility of being offered other high-profile gigs. I didn't want to completely give up performing, indeed I hoped to do a bit more acting at some point. Jim and Lesley said that they both understood completely and once I'd been at the station for a while we could talk about taking a sabbatical to do other things as and when they came up. This was only a verbal agreement, but to be frank I have only ever remembered the verbal stuff. I'll be fucked if I ever understood one word I've read of a showbiz contract.

I was quite excited about the idea of taking six months out and treading the boards in a musical. As the lift rumbled down to the first floor of Western House I started humming the tune of 'Adelaide, Adelaide'. I'd look fucking ace in pinstripes and a black felt Homburg.

* * *

Lesley was sat in her glass-boxed office, tapping away at her computer. I looked at Lucy, her lovely PA, and made an inquisitive face without saying a word, as was my habit. This absurd little mime was my way of asking if I was allowed to go in and see her.

'Hello, Phill. How are you?'

'Very well thanks, Luce. Is it alright if I nip in?'

She looked over at her boss and took a quick glance at her diary before giving me a smile and a nod in.

I leaned into the office inquisitively before bothering Lesley. I was always mindful that she was quite a busy woman. As the door opened she looked up and smiled and I plaintively asked, 'Got a minute?'

'Yes, come in. I saw your agent last night.' Her eyes were widening as she said this and she put an odd stress on the words *'your agent'*.

I held up a hand. 'Don't tell me. I'll probably hear later.' Addison stories were common currency in London, and as he was a prominent *bon viveur*, pretty much everybody had at least one good one. 'Listen, I've had a call from a producer about *Guys and Dolls*, and they want me to audition for Nathan Detroit, so I was wondering if I could take a sabbatical so I could do it.'

'No.'

There was no pause before she said this, and no preamble. This medicine would apparently be taken *sans* sugar. My look of horror prompted her to go on.

'We can't spare you for that long, and you're working here now. So I'm sorry, you can't.'

At this point any normal person would have brought up the verbal agreement made four years previously. Not me, though, I'm special. Instead of entering into a mature discussion, I stood up and said brightly with no betrayal of sadness, 'Understood … just thought I'd ask first …' before giving her a peck on the cheek. Walking out of the office that day I knew that within the year I would be gone.

Once I had decided to leave, that was it. I would use the free time to write a play for the Edinburgh Festival and do more live gigs. I spoke to Shelley about the financial implications and straight away she reminded me that I had only intended to stay at 6 for two years, and had in fact ended up doing five. We were doing OK. I then phoned Joe at Addison's office. Joe was Addison's business partner. He and I had been at school together and shared a love of obtuse music, West Ham and full English breakfasts. I just wanted to run it by him before telling Addison. He was, as always, calming and understanding.

'Phill, it's down to you, mate, and if you're not enjoying it any more then you don't have to do it!'

'What do you think Ad will say?'

'He'll understand, of course he will. He might try to point out a few pitfalls but that's his job.'

Addison was his usual buoyant self.

'RIGHTMISTERJUPITUSWHAT'STHISABOUTYOU LEAVINGMUSICSIXTHEN?'

In all the time I was at 6 Music Addison had insisted on calling it Music Six. That was but one of the more left-field reasons that I liked him. Wilful malapropism. Rather than embroil him in the whole *Guys and Dolls* story, I kept it simple. 'I've just had enough, mate. I want to do other stuff. I know I'll take a big financial hit, but …' He cut in before I could finish my thought.

'BOOKDEALITSABOUTTIMEYOUWROTEABOOK LISTENIKNOWALLTHEPUBLISHERSANDWE'LL GETYOUDOWNINASITDOWNWITHAFEWOFEM ANDYOUCANWRITEABOOKWHATSITGONNABE ABOUT?'

'Well, I'd never really –'

'WELLSTARTTHINKINGABOUTITNOWITCANBE ANYTHINGAUTOBIOGRAPHYSHOWBIZSTUF THEYLOVEALLTHATIDUNNOABOUTFICTION YOUEVERWRITTENANYTHINGBEFORE?'

'Um … no, I –'

'LISTENTROOPERDONTTELLLESLEYANYTHING YETI'LLLETYOUKNOWWHENYOUCANGOINAND TELLHERDOYOUWANTMEINWITHYOU?'

'No, you …'

'GOODIDEASONSOUNDBETTERCOMINGFROM YOUBUTLEAVEITAFEWWEEKSCONTRACTUALLY

YOUONLYHAVETOGIVETHREEMONTHSBUTIFYOU
CANGIVEHERABITMORENOTICE.'

When I told Phil about my decision to leave it didn't really come as a surprise to him. He had seen the station slowly changing around us and did not like what he saw either. And he told management that he would be leaving the station on the same day as me. It was hardly the end of *Butch Cassidy and the Sundance Kid*, but there was an endearing symmetry to us both arriving and departing on the same day.

It seems odd now, but once I had made the decision to leave I just started to gradually fall out of love with working at 6 Music. Ric took me out for a breakfast, which at first I thought would be the usual casual catch-up. Oh no, not this one. I was halfway through a rather lovely Italian fry-up at Carluccios in Market Place round the corner from Western House when it happened.

'Listen, we thought it would be good if you had some help on the show.'

My fork clattered onto my plate fairly loudly and I stared mutely. I would not be finishing this breakfast, which was a damn shame as it was fucking delicious.

I growled in a fairly unfriendly manner, 'What do you mean, "help"?'

'James Stirling is going to come in and help you.'

'You're putting another producer on the show …'

'Yes, but he can help you make it a better show … I don't see why you don't see this as a good thing.'

'You don't trust us. What's the matter? Isn't the show good enough as it is?'

'Look Phill, I just think the show could be better if James was in there as well.'

I was furious. Partly because Wilding and I were about to be policed by somebody who was a BA when we were both making radio at GLR, but mostly because the eggs really were fucking lovely.

The last straw of the final months at 6 was when Lesley called me into her office after the show one morning. As ever it was all sweetness and light to begin with. Lesley's daughter Sarah was a big fan of They Might Be Giants and a few weeks previously I'd played her a song from their album *No* called 'Where Do They Make Balloons'. So I leaped right into the conversational breach.

'Did Sarah like her song?'

Lesley laughed. 'Yes, she did, but can you not play them after ten past eight, please. She wanted to hear the end of it and she was nearly late for school!' I shrugged in apology, as Lesley settled down in the chair opposite me. 'Listen, I've got something to say and you're not going to like it …'

I looked up and braced myself for whatever it might be. As it was I'd already decided to go, so it couldn't be that bad. As it turns out, it was worse.

'I don't want Phil on air any more.'

Something which had evolved naturally over the time of making radio at 6 Music was the on-air relationship between myself and Phil. This kind of thing was usually frowned upon – indeed Andrew Collins had been forbidden from talking on air to his producer Frank in the first year. I can only assume that we had not been included because ours was the breakfast show. One of my problems with this kind of thing is that it wouldn't have happened if they hadn't put Phil in the room with me. If there is someone in the room then I am going to converse with them. It just seems rude not to.

This final perceived managerial slight made leaving 6 Music a complete doddle. In my view Phil was fundamental to the success of the show. He wrote comedy, sourced guests, constructed features and was a funny and intelligent on-air companion all the time I was there. We had apparently had things our own way for too long, so now we were being reined in. The thing is that I don't know whose decision it ultimately was. Lesley liked Phil so I can't believe that it really was her call. But she went out of her way to make it appear so. I have no idea whether the show was played to a consultant or a focus group that didn't like it, or if Jenny Abramsky heard something that she didn't like, or the Director General was once in a bar fight in Newport. One of the sad things about working for the corporation is that you are rarely given a straight answer to anything. I'd been doing it for nearly five years and now management had started dicking about with it without even explaining why.

The sad thing is that James Stirling was and is a lovely bloke and has made some brilliant radio throughout his career. I first met him at GLR where he worked on several shows. He started out as a volunteer working there for months for nothing before slowly working his way up to BA then eventually producer. He was a big music fan and was himself formerly a guitarist with post-punk beat band The Godfathers. He was someone quite determined to make a long career in radio.

When you work for the BBC it's much easier to effect change from inside the fence rather than choosing to stand outside and piss in. I didn't object to James being in the studio, but I really didn't like the fact that we had never been given the opportunity to make any changes to the show ourselves. Our hard-fought autonomy was being eroded in front of our very eyes.

Phil and I, in our customary over-dramatic way, took the view that James was a management stooge, sent in to keep us in line. But the thing is, he just presented a different viewpoint, and made several excellent suggestions during his brief time in the studio. But just by being there he inadvertently cramped our style, which I suppose might have been the point. But there was never any malice on his part. He genuinely wanted the show to be a success. The truth of the matter was that over the years Wilding and I had inexorably become too insular, partly born of our previous careers, me as a stand-up and him as a writer. Our belligerent attitude to the show was, 'You can listen and enjoy it or you can fuck off if you don't like it. We don't need you and we don't want your kind.'

And that, while utterly charming to a select few, was not an ideal way to bring new listeners into the fold. We'd had a good innings but the writing was now on the wall for the grand breakfast experiment. I thought again about the ungracious overdue departure of Jimmy Young and all the idiots at Radio 1 who overstayed their welcome, as well as those continuing to do so. It was definitely time for me to call it a day on being a deejay while I was still just about enjoying it.

Nantwich Skyline

'Suzanne' – Weezer
'Stand at Ease' – The Housemartins
'Only Love Can Break Your Heart' – Saint Etienne
'Tender' (Cornelius remix) – Blur

'Dancin' Fool' – Frank Zappa
'Where Do They Make Balloons?' – They Might Be
  Giants
'Apply Some Pressure' – Maximo Park
'The Ocean' – Richard Hawley
'Heroes and Villains' – The Beach Boys
'I've Got the Horse Right Here' – Guys and Dolls
  (original Broadway cast)

Chapter 15
Closing Time

One of the last times I went into the office of Lesley Douglas was to ask her a favour. I had no reason to think that she wouldn't tell me to piss off, but as I was leaving I thought I'd ask anyway. When I told her that I wouldn't be renewing my contract she said, 'Are you sure?' but she was hardly on her knees begging me not to go. It seemed that I had, after all, timed it right. So while not exactly glad to see the back of me, my departure wasn't causing her to lose any sleep at night. We were cool.

'I've had an idea about my last show …'

'What's that then?'

'I'd like to do it from my house.'

I was expecting her to do a bit of 'umming' and 'ahhh-ing' before she gave me an answer, but not a bit of it.

'That is a brilliant idea. We must definitely do that.'

So it was that on Friday, 30 May 2007 I was able to set my alarm an hour and a half later than usual.

For whatever reason, Lesley didn't let me announce my departure from 6 Music until two weeks before I was leaving. This meant that the final fortnight was fairly fraught, what with one thing and another. I slowly began to disregard all but the cream of the playlist. I didn't ask to do this, I just told James, 'I'm playing my stuff for the last couple of weeks.' Again, there was no argument from anybody. From April they wouldn't have to deal with me ever again.

The final weeks of the show were some of the best we did. Old friends came in to say goodbye and the listeners said some lovely things in their texts and emails. On one particular morning Sarah Cracknell from Saint Etienne came in. It was her fourth time on the show and she was as always a complete angel. We'd been chatting to her for five minutes or so and were playing a track from the *Tales from Turnpike Lane* album when the studio door swung open. Stood in the half light was Lesley Douglas.

'I've brought someone up to see you.'

And in walked Sir Terry.

He sat in and was his usual charming and wonderful self, and from where I was sitting was doing a real number on Cracknell. She was subsequently somewhat disarmed and became rather giggly. Having him sat in that studio with me was just another of the great odd moments that I experienced while working at Broadcasting House: Greg Dyke giving you the nod in the lift; using the urinal next to John Peel; catching a glimpse of Michael Rosen in reception. All these moments were part of my past.

As I remember it, the last show was pretty much as usual: records and chat. The difference being that I was doing it from my home. Finally my philosophy of doing the kind of radio show that you'd do from your own house had reached an inevitable conclusion. I was doing what John had done in his shows from Peel Acres. My dining table was covered in thousands of pounds worth of BBC hardware. A couple of dozen friends and family came to see me to say goodbye, and for good measure we had a live session from Billy Bragg. Bill was a more than fitting addition to this final show because, without having met him, I doubt I'd have even been doing it.

A week or so after finishing at 6 Music, I received a package from Kate the Hate, our lovely and long-suffering BA. She had enclosed a set of CDs of all the celebrity idents that we had made for the show. Snippets of Elvis Costello and Sir Terry Wogan and Ronni Spector rubbed shoulders with those of Peter Serafinowicz, Pete Yorn and Nick Cave. There were hundreds of them. Also in the package with them were three BBC CDs labelled 'Phill Jupitus Breakfast Show 30/03/07'. A little after three years later and I finally felt ready to have a listen to the show for the first time.

RECORD   'Dick-a-dum-dum' – Des O'Connor

RECORD   'The Queen Is Dead' – The Smiths

After the Des O'Connor track, we hear the beginning of another record because the presenter hasn't selected the single-track-only option on his CD players. It is apparently going to be a long morning. After The Smiths' record finishes we have a funny and quite moving farewell message from Terry Wogan …

'Phill Jupitus! Two Ls, a silly hat and an overcoat he'd been wearing for the last hundred years. Phill Jupitus! "Ave atque vale." Five years! You call that a feat of endurance, you call that a radio show? What's the matter with

you? Bailing out after five minutes, who do you think you are, Bam Bam? You've got to stick with it, Phill, I mean, look at me! OK, don't look at me. Look at Chris Moyles – ooh no, God, don't look at Chris Moyles. Phill, we're gonna miss you. I know, I know, I've never listened to you, because I've been frying other fish here on the senior network. But I'm gonna miss you. Why are you going? Where are you going? What are you doing? Do you know what you're doing? Are you drunk? Now I know you're doing this programme from your very own radio studio at home. Maybe if the BBC had been prepared to break out and spend a few quid you could have done the whole series and you could still be doing it until hell freezes over from your own little bothy wherever you live. I know it's not much but it's home, isn't it, Phill. I've said it before, I'll say it again, I don't know where you're going, I think five years doing the breakfast show you've merely sort of broken yourself in, but you know what you're doing and I look forward to seeing you whatever you're doing. Whether you're on the television or listening to you on the radio in the years to come as we soldier on, we old geezers. Some say we're too old for it, but I know you've still got a bit of snap in your celery. Good luck, Phill, and I hope we'll see you soon ...'

Sir Terry's little message was the most inspirational thing I had ever heard, and I was hearing it on my last day. Go figure ...

Then for some reason we hear a sudden burst of ice cream van music before ...

RECORD   'Milkshake' – Richard Cheese

After this we hear the chirping of birds and the exterior noise of my back garden before I come on air and admit to no fewer than three technical fuck-ups *'and we're not even a quarter of an hour in!'* I describe a little of the scene around me while inviting the listeners to write their own 'Essex bird' jokes in the wake of the birdsong. I bid Phil a good morning and he spends the first twenty seconds off mic. I reveal that we have around twenty people in the kitchen with us. Phil says that having people behind him makes him nervous while I counter that 'It can't be the first time for you.' I spend a brief time belittling my mother for only liking Wogan, and invite our kitchen crowd to say hello. I say hello to Stacey in Oakland, one of our regulars, before saying, *'It seems quite absurd, but some people have taken the day off today to listen to this crap, and er, you know, um, I thank you for it if I question your judgement ...'*

I remind those present not to jog the table despite the fact that I have marble floors. I bring in Andre Vincent, a comedian and very old friend who I've known for many years. It seems that Andre will be acting as a kind of *de facto* record librarian, running up and down stairs and fetching records and CDs from my office. Once again Vinny is off mic and we reveal that Billy Bragg is still upstairs and in bed. I talk about the fact that I haven't decided which record to play last on the show. The choice is between something by Ian Dury, The Clash or The Specials. Could I be any more obviously a music saddo in my mid-forties? I invite listeners to email in with their suggestions for which tune they'd like to hear last and go on to invite them to call the house.

record   'Margerita' – Champion Doug Veitch

I have to say at this point that I do tend to mumble and go
'uuuurm' a lot. I can imagine that after a while that might
become quite wearing to some. We go over to Andre who
is upstairs on a remote mic in my loft office in front of
the CD wall and both realise that Andre doesn't know the
ramshackle order my music collection is kept in and I am
going to have to describe to him where he has to go.

JUPITUS:	I'm trying to remember where I want you to go … It's not that … right so if you look at the back wall where the stereo is … do you see to the left of the stereo there's those two racks … OK the top rack …
VINNY:	It's like Anneka Rice!
JUPITUS:	That's my Mambo section.
VINNY:	OK …
JUPITUS:	… and underneath there you'll find my Calypso section.
VINNY:	I see the Calypso section!
JUPITUS:	Now to the right of that there are four compilation albums that appear to be in red cardboard covers.
VINNY:	Ummm, in the Calypso section I've got 'Calypso at Midnight', no, that's not red cardboard …
JUPITUS:	At the right end, at the right-*hand* end, I do apologise …
VINNY:	Yes, 'London Is the Place for Me'.
JUPITUS:	Bring them all down … So there we go, that's Andre Vincent, Calypso monkey,

ladies and gentlemen … And Vinny, you're probably thinking that you're saying all these lovely and whimsical things up there and you're getting no reaction down here, it's because *you're not very funny*. (LAUGHTER) No, people can't hear you, love, so please feel free to wander back down with the Calypso post haste …

VINNY: I've got them all …

JUPITUS: And we can play some Lord Kitchener 'cos that's a very popular item …

This is one of those moments that for me describes both why the show worked, and also why it failed. That kind of idle chit-chat to some is absolute gold. They love to see behind the curtain, so to speak, and the workings of the show. As someone who has always maintained a quite reductive view of music radio, i.e. 'It's a bloke playing records,' I never strived to make the show anything more than that. I always saw the ramshackle nature of it as somehow endearing, and while it may have been to some, people who should have listened to it stayed away from 6 Music in their droves.

We read out a few farewell emails from the listeners, and in the course of chatting and getting a few requests for some Calypso I recall that recently Young Tiger, a stalwart of the scene, has died, which means I can play one of his tracks to remember him, which prompts the following exchange:

JUPITUS: Part of what I always loved about this show was the immediacy –

WILDING: Some say clunkiness … I'll miss that …

JUPITUS: (LAUGHTER) Hamfistedness I think is the word that we're looking for here …

We may have been arrogant on occasion, but at least we were more than aware of our own shortcomings as a radio show.

RECORD   'Calypso Be' – Young Tiger

James jumps in and reminds me that Young Tiger appeared at last year's Electric Proms at The Roundhouse. There's a few more emails to read out, including one from Rick in Ramsgate, who because of predictive text appears to have signed off as 'Rick go Ramsgate', and I have a bit of idle fun with that. Then two listeners admit to the fact that they are currently having sex in my honour, which leads to some fairly run-of-the-mill saucy banter between myself and Mr Wilding.

NEWS & WEATHER   (Jason Kay)

MUSIC NEWS   (Adrian Larkin)

RECORD   'I Love the Sound of Breaking Glass' – Pat Buchanan and Thundermug

After this jaunty toe-tapper I wrestle my two daughters on air for a bit of a chat. After declaring themselves as being 'tired', my youngest, Molly, does a fairly good job of ridiculing my taste in both 1960s Ska and 1950s Calypso, before saying that she's quite a fan of the new music we play at just after eight. I explain to the listeners that I had to write a letter to their school asking permission for them to stay and be part of my last show, but in the light of their savage assessment of my musical taste I shouldn't have bothered. Andre tells us that he's still in his pyjamas, which I observe look more like astronaut's underwear …

VINNY: How many astronauts have you slept with?
JUPITUS: Do I have to tell you on air?
VINNY: Here's a step for mankind …
JUPITUS: Oh Buzz, he was so insistent!
WILDING: They don't call him Buzz for nothing …

I remind people that our regular contributor, Ian Nathan of *Empire* magazine, will be reviewing my DVD collection and we'll be having some live music from Billy Bragg. I introduce the next record as follows:

JUPITUS: You know what, because my kids were
           banging on about Calypso and Ska and how
           much they hate it … screw them!
           RECORD   'Vitamin A' – The Baba Brooks Band
           FAREWELL MESSAGE (Richard Herring)
           RECORD   'My Wife's Nightie' – Lord
           Kitchener

A little chat now about how 'My Wife's Nightie' has been such a firm favourite with the listeners before reminding listeners that the new 6 Music breakfast show will be starting next week.

JUPITUS: Monday things all start off with Shaun
Keaveney. I hesitate to use the phrase
'new boy' – he's won Sony awards, which
is certainly more than I ever did, the radio
establishment viewing me as some sort of
tumour ...

Then somebody in the room's mobile beeps and we chat
about that for a bit before trying to establish whether
anybody in the room is wearing a pacemaker. Then we
send Vinny outside in his pyjamas to root around in my
car's CD player to try and locate a CD that my eldest
wants to play a track from. Then my sister arrives and
I realise that my brother is not present and immediately
take him off the Christmas list. Billy Bragg makes himself
present, Terry Edwards arrives and I struggle to operate
the equipment while talking, which was never my strong
point, before launching into:

RECORD   'Baseball Baseball' – Jane Morgan and
The George Barnes Quartet
RECORD   'If I Could Turn Back the Hands of
Time' – Vernon Garrett
RECORD   'They're Talking about Me' – Johnny
Bragg

Playing two records back to back was something that I
always did if I thought I was talking too much. Conse-
quently I quite often played two records back to back.
The fact that I was playing three in a row at this point
meant that either I thought I had really been going on
far too much, or I really desperately needed the lav. After

playing these I remind the listeners that I'd quite often play records fresh out of the envelope, as the last two soulful stompers were. Then Phil reminds those listening that I am not wearing any underpants, which seems a tad unnecessary. I go on to say that Wogan's been doing that for years.

Billy Bragg points out that he is no relation to Johnny and posits that he may possibly be related to Melvyn. I then read out a long list of punters saying goodbye, one of whom announces in her text message that she is pregnant. Then for some reason Phil Wilding suggests that we are leaving the show so we can make babies, which forces me to point out that I have *'been taken off the mains for the good of the race'*. We throw forward to Billy playing later, which he reacts to with feigned surprise. Then it's time for the eight o'clock news.

NEWS

RECORD 'Finally' – Ce Ce Penniston

After dedicating this record to Kate Lloyd our BA, myself and Phil and Vinny indulge in a smidge of light banter before Terry Edwards and I start chatting about Prince cancelling his UK *Sign 'O' the Times* dates and I start banging on about needing to go upstairs myself to fetch the CD in question as I couldn't possibly explain to Vinny where it's located on the shelves. Then I have a chat with my elder daughter Emily about an album that she was after a track from, called *Rogues Gallery*, a collection of pirate songs by various artists put together by Johnny Depp and Gore Verbinsky. This prompts me to start talking about the *Pirates of the Caribbean* films with Ian

Nathan, who has to microphone share with Emily. Once I start slagging off the films Emily starts to get a bit cross. Which does lead to one quite funny exchange.

DAD: You picked this one, Emily. Tell us why …
              and have a microphone, dear –
DAUGHTER: That *would* be a good idea.
WILDING: Ooh! Sass!
DAD: You know what, it's my last show on the
              wireless, I'd appreciate it if you didn't
              get pissy with me on air. The public *are*
              listening.

I did try to push what was acceptable language-wise on air, and while not advocating the wholesale dropping of the F-bomb I did think that a certain amount of adult language should be permissible. Recently on 6 Music Richard Herring was reprimanded for using the word 'piss' in the context of a news story he was talking about. It is my view that a network aimed at adults should be able to operate with the sensible use of adult language. That way, concerned parents are made aware that if they listen to certain stations the likelihood is that there will be some adult language. I don't see why a time watershed works any better than a channel one.

RECORD   'Blood Red Roses' – Sting
RECORD   'You'll See Glimpses' – Ian Dury and
         The Blockheads

As more people arrive at the house, I am obviously losing a bit of focus. Also I seem to be doing very long links between the songs. A normal breakfast show would have a lot more music in it. The sudden yapping of Chester, my dog, prompts me to request that somebody put a lead on him. Then we get a microphone up to his snout and I observe that he sounds like he's doing drugs, which probably explains why Staffies can be so moody. The general sound of this whole show is quite chaotic, but it's worth bearing in mind that I am a man with one foot out of the door. In the room aside from friends and family are Lesley Douglas and Anthony Bellkom representing management, Ian Nathan from *Empire* magazine, Terry Edwards, Billy Bragg, Andre Vincent, and Harry my driver for the past five years alongside his wife Joan.

RECORD 'Limbo Jazz' – Duke Ellington and
Coleman Hawkins
FAREWELL MESSAGE (Gideon Coe)
RECORD 'Soccer Mom' – The Vandals
NEWS
MUSIC NEWS
TRAIL
RECORD 'Your Love Alone Is Not Enough' –
The Manic Street Preachers (single of
the week)

It's only taken us just over an hour and a half, but finally we play something contemporary. Ian Nathan of *Empire* magazine is our regular Friday contributor and comes in armed with gifts for us, a pair of mocked-up *Empire* covers with us featured as stars. Ian goes on to give very short shrift to *Mister Bean's Holiday* and *The Hills Have Eyes 2*. Then I say hello to one of our regular listeners,

Dee Scott from Brighton, who sends us enamel badges which she has had made for us bearing the legend 'Music' and 'Five years' loyal service'. I almost get a bit overcome in introducing her record, which causes the following to transpire:

JUPITUS: This is Prince from *Sign 'O' the Times* ... (*massive pause*) Ooh no ... You know what, I've put the fader down instead of my microphone fader so I have to start that one again ... This is the kind of quality, ladies and gentlemen, that has kept me –

WILDING: Out of the Sony's every year ...

RECORD   'Forever in My Life' – Prince

After this I take the time to read out a farewell missive from Madness, before pressing on with Ian 'Zorro' Nathan's breakdown of my DVD collection. He sticks it fairly firmly up a few of my favourite films, *A Life Less Ordinary*, *The Fifth Element* and *French Kiss*. And we say a goodbye to him with a round of applause. Then in a moment of madness, both Phil and I hatch a plot to kill Peter Purves and get ourselves some kind of dog-based TV show.

RECORD   'One More Chance' – Candie Payne
          (*first UK airplay*)

NEWS

RECORD   'Phone-in Show' – The Members

FAREWELL MESSAGE (Dave Green)

RECORD   'Chelsea Nightclub' – The Members

Every day at 9.00 we had a regular feature playing two tracks from a début album. One of the standing jokes we had on the show over the years was that if I ever announced the début album was *At the Chelsea Nightclub* by The Members then I would be leaving the station. So it seemed appropriate to actually make it our final début. At this point I start to feel a bit sad, and it manifests itself on air. We also announce that Phil and I are on MySpace and going to form a band called Find Cake, Buy Cake, Eat. Then I have a quick chat with my friend and artist, Paul Karslake, who told us the story of how he painted a portrait of Keith Richards as a pirate, which inspired Johnny Depp to base his performance of Jack Sparrow on Keith. Then a quick chat with Terry Edwards about Department S, which led us towards the radio début of ...

RECORD 'My Coo-Ca-Choo' – Department S
RECORD 'The Sound of Silence' – The Gaylads
RECORD 'In the Ghetto' – The King in Kingston

Then with little or no introduction I start chatting with Billy Bragg about how we would sit up late at his house and work our way through his old boxes of seven-inch singles, a couple of which he has brought to play on the show. His first choice is The Gaylads' version of the Simon and Garfunkel classic, which he follows up with a record by Reparata. I consult a friend of mine in the room called Lisa to see if she can remember this artist as she is always citing obscure seventies pop to me. She can't, but we play them anyway ...

RECORD   'Shoes' – Reparata

NEWS

MUSIC NEWS

TRAIL

RECORD   'Headstart for Happiness' – The Style
Council

I play this song for Shelley, my wife, with the words, 'She's
put up with so much shit over the years.' It seems that my
other foot is on the way out of the door as well now. Billy
Bragg is now in position to play some music for us and he
launches into his de facto Essex anthem:

LIVE SONG 'A13' – Billy Bragg

The next song Billy plays is a new piece. But what I wasn't
aware of is just how new. As it turns out, Bill wrote it in my
front room between eight and nine. And this is its first-ever
public performance. As he sings, I feel a sudden surge
of emotion that my on-air bravado has been covering up
very nicely. We have tried to bring a new kind of radio to
the British public at breakfast time and the vast majority
simply aren't bothered. As the introductory chords play,
I feel a familiar tightening of my throat, as I suppress the
need to weep copiously.

On good days doing the breakfast show was a thrill like
no other. I was bringing music to a wider audience that
might not otherwise be aired, save on the most obscure
specialist shows, and I was doing it at breakfast time. My
favourite broadcaster, Charlie Gillett, had written in *Music
Week* about the open-minded attitude to music and the
show's enthusiasm when finding new sounds. Like many

things in my life, I had given it a good go, but this one just hadn't worked out. I loved deejaying, but hated being a deejay. That is to say, I loved doing the job, but at the end of the day I realised that I was nowhere near as good as I thought I was. I mistook an overwhelming love of music for an ability to bring it intelligently and concisely to others, which I still couldn't do. I took it all too personally and too seriously. I found playlist radio an anathema, and still do to this day.

The song Bill has written in my front room seems to capture this realisation perfectly.

live song: 'Goodbye' – Billy Bragg

Goodbye to all my friends
The time has come to leave again
Goodbye to all the souls
Who sailed with me so long

The dawn has broke at last
The sails strain on the mast
The years have quickly passed away

Goodbye to all my friends
The time has come for me to say
Goodbye to all the souls
Who sailed with me along the way

The bells have all been rung
The songs have all been sung
This long river has run its course

Goodbye to all my friends
The time has come to leave again
Goodbye to all the souls
Who sailed with me so long

The coffee pot is cold
The jokes have all been told
The last stone has been rolled away

Goodbye to all my friends
The time has come for me to say
Goodbye to all my friends
Who've sailed with me along the way

Goodbye

As the final chord chimes away, all I can think to say by way of thanks to Billy is, '*Oh you bastard, I promised myself I wasn't gonna go …*' as the tears start to cascade down my face and I withdraw to the tactical safety of playing another song to cover.

RECORD   'Enjoy Yourself' – The Specials

As the show draws to a close I can hear the sorrow increasing in my voice, and I started to launch myself into a convoluted and somewhat lengthy goodbye of my own …

JUPITUS: So you know it's not The Specials at the end of the show at least. Of course The Specials from the delightful *More Specials* and 'Enjoy Yourself' here on BBC 6 Music, ummm … for the last time it's the last ten minutes of the show. Can I just start by thanking everyone that came along this morning for this, er, final broadcast from the house which is probably the quickest three hours of my life. It doesn't seem ten seconds ago that I sat down here and played Des O'Connor, and now here we are …

WILDING: You missed that, Harry …

JUPITUS: Harry's gutted … Ahhh … So thank you all very much for coming along to the show this morning … er … (*applause*) It's been a hoot and a holler. Thanks to all of you who listen, I've had so many emails and texts and I've not been able to get through any of them because I'm just gonna start crying and I could do with … not doing that …

I go on to thank as many people as I can remember, with Phil prompting me as necessary. Listeners, BAs, James, Badger and Jamie Hart, the two Steves and Rob our BBC engineers for the morning, Lesley and Jim … Everybody.

I then thank Phil for coming along as well, and the pair of us start to get quite emotional, before I press a button and start playing a song for the last time on 6 Music Breakfast.

RECORD 'Broadway'/'The Guns of Brixton' –
The Clash/Maria Gallagher

I've chosen this record as the last, principally because of the quirky little coda at the end of the song, where Clash keyboard man Mickey Gallagher and his three-year-old daughter Maria give a jaunty truncated version of 'The Guns of Brixton' which finishes with her saying, 'That's enough now! I'm tired of singing!' then they let the rhythmic thump of the run-out groove run for a few seconds and the microphones are faded up in the garden for my final farewell.

I say a brisk 'Thank you very much indeed' and with both my legs propel my body upwards and assume a kind of airborne sitting position before gravity takes over and I fall into the pool in the back garden. And with that one final resounding splash, I'm gone.

* * *

One thing I never really did during my time at 6 Music was to pay all that much attention to the audience listening figures. Looking back, perhaps I could have done a bit more to make the show more popular. But as I hope I've pointed out over the course of this book, I have never really been that into making nor indeed listening to *popular* radio. I think there are already more than enough stations doing that, and they have more than enough listeners.

Dartford Bridge Burners

'Debbie and Joey' – Helen Love
'Get Out of Denver' – Eddie and The Hot Rods
'Paradise' – Dr Feelgood
'Damaged Goods' – Gang of Four
'Suzanne' – Nina Simone
'Cigarettes and Chocolate Milk' – Rufus Wainwright
'Bell, Book and Candle' – Boo Hewerdine
'Ae Fond Kiss' – Eddie Reader
'Broadway' – The Clash
'It's Over' – Roy Orbison

Maintaining Radio Silence

Since leaving 6 Music I have appeared on radio very little. An unfortunate episode one Saturday afternoon saw me accidentally burning my bridges at the station as I was asked to present a countdown of the greatest collaboration records of all time as voted for by the listeners. This happened because I didn't read the email asking me to do the show properly. Somewhere between playing thirty seconds of 'You're the One That I Want' by Olivia Newton John and John Travolta and 'Relight My Fire' by Lulu and Take That, I simply had had enough.

The mistake I made was to air my dissatisfaction with such a lamentable idea for a radio show to the listening public. The producer in the studio didn't try to stop me at all, rather she seemed to find it all terrific fun.

After a bit, Lesley Douglas phoned me on my mobile mid-show and said, 'If you want to destroy 6 Music, then just keep doing what you're doing …'

I lost my rag and told her in no uncertain terms that the show was 'Fucking nonsense and shouldn't even be on 6 Music and is not what the station was supposed to be about!'

That was the last time Lesley and I spoke.

The online chat room at 6 lit up briefly over the weekend with listeners talking about my on air 'meltdown'. As per usual with me, about half of them were saying, '*Good for him!*' and the other half that I should '... *shut up and do as he's told!*'

All I know is that was the very last time I presented a radio show on 6 Music and it was two years ago. My mistake, as it usually is with any job I do, is to take things too personally. Well, excuse me.

A few weeks ago the first set of RAJAR listening figures arrived for Chris Evans's Radio 2 breakfast show after taking over from Sir Terry. Naysayers were predicting a large dip, and even optimistic supporters were predicting a hold within acceptable margins. Nobody predicted what did happen. The listening figures for Radio 2 breakfast actually *increased*.

It was when I heard this news that I realised that I truly have no idea at all of what the British public wants. We are out of sync with each other. But paradoxically I am still a member of that very same British public, and I pay my TV licence fee, and why should a radio station which addresses my musical tastes be first for the chop when the frankly lamentable BBC fucking Three is still on?

At the very same RAJARs mentioned above, 6 Music's listening figures doubled to 1.2 million, which experts will doubtless put down to a statistical anomaly because of publicity surrounding its possible closure. I just think that it now has the figures it always should have had, because people have now actually heard of it and heard how good it is. The sad thing is, it has been doing pretty much the same job since 11 March 2002.

Epilogue: Maintaining Radio Silence

I was taking part in a seminar for radio students at Bournemouth University a few months back, talking about breakfast radio in general and 6 Music in particular. We overran a little and had to vacate the room for the next lecture.

As we were leaving a student shouted over at me, 'Phill! Would you do it again if they asked?'

I had to stop and think. Nobody had asked ever me that before. Had I even succeeded as a breakfast broadcaster? I was struck with the notion that rather than being a deejay I was just somebody with curiosity, passion and a record collection who had adequate presentation skills. I was just missing that certain unquantifiable *something*.

I gathered myself and said to the young man, 'Erm ... I shouldn't mind sitting in for Keaveney once in a while, but I definitely wouldn't do it full time, no ... To be honest, mate, I don't think they'd ask me now.'

So after all those years of wondering, it turned out that I wasn't a deejay after all. And the realisation of this, while sad, was a *relief.*

Do It Yourself

Once I'd finished writing *Good Morning, Nantwich*, I realised that I had only really communicated how I felt about my own experiences of making breakfast radio. I thought it might be an idea to tell you, dear reader, how you could, within 24 hours and a following wind, be making your own radio, albeit online. That way you too could experience the dizzying highs and the crushing lows of breakfast broadcasting. So I went to my radio gurus at the Media School at Bournemouth University, Jo Tyler and Andy Higginson, who provided this handy guide to making your own internet radio show.

The Good Morning Nantwich Guide to Making Your Own Breakfast Radio Show

Setting up a home studio for broadcasting on the internet is not difficult, or for that matter expensive. It just requires some careful planning to make sure that you buy suitable equipment for what you are looking to achieve. Can it be done in 24 hours – yes, if you have access to Tottenham Court Road and a little bit of savvy.

The first major thing to look at is whether you have a reliable internet connection. You need a connection that has a reasonable upload speed (at least 256k), and one that doesn't drop out every few minutes. Without this, you might as well stop here and not go any further with your plans. Also remember that some internet providers will limit the amount of data that you can use each month, and some include uploading in this limit. If you broadcast with a 128k stream, you are looking at using approx 60MB of your data cap in just one hour!

So, your internet connection passes the requirements. What next? Well, you will need to start getting your equipment together. At this point you should look at your budget and decide how much you are looking to spend. This will determine what kind of kit you will be buying. The average radio set-up will need the following:

- 1 audio mixer
- 2 microphones and stands
- 1 computer for playing music and jingles
- 1 computer for encoding the stream
- 1 pair of headphones
- 1 friendly geek to put everything together

This equipment needn't cost the earth. A small mixer for example could set you back as little as £75, and you can pick up a couple of very cheap microphones and stands for under £100. The computers don't need to be the latest and greatest models, and suitable second-hand machines can be found on eBay for as little as £50 per machine.

The software needed to run on both of the computers is released under a GPL Licence (that means it's free), though you will need to run at least a Windows XP or later operating system on one of the machines.

For your playout computer there is a great piece of software called Rivendell Radio (www.rivendellaudio.org) which is a complete professional radio playout package. It does, however, run on Linux, so at first the average Windows fan might have a problem. There are, however, very good step-by-step instructions on how to get it up and running with very little difficulty. Or if you are feeling rich, you can go with VCS, which cost the BBC £5.2 million to develop …

For the encoding machine, look no further than Edcast (www.oddsock.org/tools/edcast/) free MP3 streaming software.

The last item on your shopping list will be a stream hosting company. This is an internet web hosting company that offers web streams as one of their services. You should look for a company providing MP3 streams using either Icecast or Shoutcast servers. The company will have guides on how to set up your stream. Costings for this are difficult as it depends on whether you are charged by number of streams, bit rate or size of file, etc. It's a bit like the range of mobile phone tariffs you can have.

Suffice to say to say most ISPs (Internet Service Providers) charge a monthly fee but this differs depending on whether you are charged by number of streams from your station or the download capacity for your speech or music content. This could be anything from £5 upwards.

A Limited Online Exploitation Licence (LOEL) covers music copyright – check this through the PRS Alliance website at www.prsformusic.com, where they also explain the difference between **streaming** and **downloads** if you are unsure about the definition of your station. Good advice for anyone who is starting out with this terminology. It's best to stay within the law in music; we want to make sure that musicians get what they are due.

Well, once you have everything in place, all that is needed is a little creativity to provide your listeners with something different to make them want to listen to your offering on the net rather than someone else's.

Good luck, and good morning!

Phill Jupitus
Leigh-on-Sea, 2010

Acknowledgements

I have a considerable number of people to thank who were not only involved with the writing of this book but also throughout my time working in radio, especially at BBC 6 Music.

From my time at GLR – Jude Howells, Steve Panton, Suzanne Gilfillan, Ray Paul, Gavin Lawrence, Bernie Caffrey, Jackie Clune, Gary Crowley, Jarvis Cocker, Norman Jay MBE, Ross Allen, Johnny Walker, Bob Harris, Bob Mills, Mary Anne Hobbs, Charles Carroll, Laurence Arnold, Steve Harrison, Miles Mendoza, Imran Khan, Matthew Linfoot, Tom Fenner, John Myer, Jim Lahat, Olga Buckley, Gideon Coe, Fi Glover, Peter and Natalie Curran, Eddie Piller, Pete Sport, Simon Crosse, Paul Ging, David Hepworth, Jeremy Nicholas, Robert Elms, Mark Simpson, Simon Barnett, Angie Errigo, Max Hutchinson, James Stirling, Matty Mitford, Mike Moore, Matt Hall, Christopher and Jennifer Rooney, Paul Strudwick, Claire McDonnell, Sally Bozeman, Chris Hawkins, Nigel Barden, Olly, Dottun Adebayo, Ranking Miss P, John Mann, Ella Kenion, Paul Leaper, Scott Piering, Dylan

White, Tim Smith, Richard Murdoch, Brian Bogue, Zak, Brian from Broxbourne, and all the staff of the Prince Regent public house.

From my time at 6 Music – Jim Moir, Lesley Douglas, Anthony Bellekom, John Sugar, Terry Wogan, Pauly Walters, Alan Boyd, Paul Rodgers, Ric Blaxill, Nikki Cardwell, Claire Runacres, Katharine Cracknell, Rachel Matthews, Harvey Cook, Nicola Gibson, Jo Youle, Lucy O'Brien, Guy Delauney, Jim Simmons, Tracy McLeod, Julian Markham, Chris Carr, Michelle Mullane, Frank Wilson, College, Tom Robinson, Brinsley Forde, Bruce Dickinson, Stuart Maconie, Huey Morgan, Cerys Matthews, Gary Bales, Julie Cullen, Shaun Keaveney, Zoe Fletcher, Vic McGlynn, Lammo, Gary Burton, Liz Kershaw, Mark Sutherland, Jody Thompson, Leona McCambridge, Nemone, Jax Coombes, Adam Dineen, Joti Brar and Mike Hales.

From the 6 Music Breakfast Show – Jacqueline 'Jaffa' Wood, Emma 'Lily' Hatcher, Mark 'The Shed' Sheldon, Kate 'The Hate' Lloyd, Jennie 'Gelfling' Smith, Lynsey 'Buffy' Young, Ruth 'Lucy' Barnes, Mona Dehghan, John 'Badger' Pearson, Jenny 'Hitler', Sarah-Jo, Charlotte Guzzan, Jamie Hart, Julian 'Alderman Cadfael' Spear, Wolfie, Kevin McCabe, Hayley Codd, and everybody who ever brought a guest in. Glasses raised to all regular show contributors Stevie Chick, Manish Argwal, Jenny Bulley, Betty Clark, Alex Milas, Dave Green, Nick Gillett, Rob Manuel, Neil Sean, Patrick 'Magwitch' Humphries, Chris Marlowe, Andrew 'Angry' Purcell, Ian 'Zorro' Nathan and Ian 'Penfold' Freer. Thank you for your professionalism and for putting up with our ceaseless bullshit. Also to all the interns who came along in the hope of learning something about radio – I truly apologise.

Celebrity thanks for their invaluable feedback, occasional requests and being listeners as well as top-notch guests to: Nicky Wire, Simon Dine, Ben Schott, Terry Edwards, Kevin Smith, Nicky Tesco, Paul Weller, Mark Steel, Don Letts, Richard Hawley, Harry Hill, Peter Serafinowicz, Andre Vincent and Billy Bragg. Cheers to the Dalai Lamarr for all the airtime he gave me over the years and the continuing glory that is *God's Jukebox* on Radio 2. Special love, thanks and a big 'Henge' must go to my favourite ever TV partner, Lauren Laverne, and unbridled bromance to Stephen Fry.

Many, many thanks to everybody who listened, but I'd like to express personal thanks to Paul Milligan, Peter Lovegrove, Dee and Ann Scott, Ally and Gail Lyall, Ian and Maureen Foakes, along with The Fox and The Bear, Matt Whitby, Robin Dewson, Christine from Ely, Wheelz Wheeler, Pete 'Hands of Death' Burke, Stacey from Oakland, Miho from Osaka, Heike Harding Reyland and family, John, Jenny and James Medd, Matthew in Bavaria, Matt Whitby, and, to all those regulars I have forgotten, a big apology snog.

From Bournemouth University – thanks to Mog McIntyre, Guy Larsen and Jess Bracey, Jacqui Kane, James, Nicole and all the MA, BA and FdA Radio Production Students and all at NERVE and BIRSt. Thanks to Andrew Higginson for technical assistance, and special thanks to all-round radio guru Sean Street for his knowledge and support.

Thanks also to Steve Saville and Tom Eames at Forest FM, and Andy and Gill at Hospital Radio Bedside (Bournemouth and Poole)

I'd like to thank my agents Addison Cresswell and Joe Norris from Off the Kerb for making this book happen, and have to doff my cap towards the ones who make the office throb: Danny Julian, Fay Clayton, Grazio Abela, Damon, Flo, Rick, Ann, Verity, Judith and Anthony.

Special thanks to my editor Natalie Jerome for slapping me about when I needed it, which was just the once. Huge thanks to everybody at HarperCollins for all the help and support, and for not staring at me when I was sitting in your coffee lounge.

Love and thanks for assistance and laughs over two decades to Jo Tyler, who has provided invaluable support and research throughout this project, as well as demystifying the complex world of radio.

Gratitude and love as always to Phil Wilding for his talent, humour and forbearance, and for making five years seem like five really funny minutes.

Finally, thanks to all of my friends and family for their support, love and patience. I am not and never will be a religious man but I would like Shelley, Emily and Molly to know that it is *they* who give my life its meaning.

And can I just say 'hello' to everyone who knows me …